Hugh Wray McCann, correspondent for New reporter for the *Detroit News*. David C. Smith, ex-business editor of the *Detroit Free Press*, is editor of Ward's Auto World. David L. Matthews practises as an attorney in South Bend, Indiana. He served with the 7708th War Crimes Group in Germany after World War II.

The Search for Johnny Nicholas

**HUGH WRAY MCCANN
DAVID C. SMITH
DAVID L. MATTHEWS**

SPHERE BOOKS LIMITED
30-32 Gray's Inn Road, London WC1X 8JL

First published in Great Britain by
Sphere Books Ltd 1982

TRADE
MARK

Set in Linotron Times

Printed and bound in Great Britain by
Cox & Wyman Ltd, Reading

To our fathers;
and to the men
who lost their lives
in the Gardelegen Massacre

A human life is like a
single letter in the alphabet.
It can be meaningless; or it
can be part of a great meaning.

– from 'Who Takes Delight in
Life,' New York Herald
Tribune, Sept. 5, 1956

Contents

Acknowledgments

We wish to thank our three surrogates for their sterling efforts in accelerating the *Search*.

James Dunne, a reporter for *Popular Science* in Detroit, took time out from his responsibilities in Paris to do preliminary interviews with Vildebart Nicolas and his wife.

Wilfred McConkey, manager of employee information services at Michigan Bell Telephone Co., turned his first vacation in Haiti into an investigation of several days. He was ably assisted by William D. Heaney, then a U.S. embassy official in Haiti. Nicolas is an extremely common family name in Port-au-Prince, and it took an exhorbitant tolerance for the heat and a lot of pavement-pounding before they found the right family. Needless to say, McConkey's terse communique informing us of his success gave a tremendous boost to our morale which, at that juncture, was flagging considerably.

Peter Hoffman, then deputy chief of the McGraw-Hill World News bureau in Bonn, West Germany, spent a weekend in Gardelegen inspecting the Isenschnibbe barn, the adjoining cemetery, hunting for survivors and witnesses of the Gardelegen Massacre and shooting up a storm of pictures. He also made a valiant but unsuccessful attempt to negotiate the snowy Harz Mountain passes in winter to visit what remains of the infamous Kohnstein tunnels: East German guards turned him back at the border. Later he did the preliminary interview with one of the key sources in the project, the Englishman Cecil Jay, whom he found living in Springe, near Hanover. Likewise the arrival of his picture and report affected us as a glass of water does a dying man in a desert.

Thanks also to Theodore Szymke (deceased) and Gabriel Werba, our Polish and French translators respectively, for their ready assistance in interpreting documents and tape and letter correspondence.

Of the more than one hundred officials of various governments whom we contacted in the course of our research, we wish to recognize one for permitting his private and personal enthusiasm for *The Search* to show through his professional decorum. He is Brig. Gen. William H. Blakefield, commander of the U.S. Army Intelligence Command at Fort Holabird, Md. His enthusiasm was infectious and kept us at our typewriters when everything else seemed to indicate that we were drilling in a dry hole.

Also a special thanks to two men who died before the completion of this book, without whose assistance and advice it might never have reached fruition: Thomas G. Cassady, former head of secret intelligence for the OSS in France; and Lt. Col. William Berman, prosecutor of the Nordhausen War Crimes trials, who were as anxious as we to find out who Johnny Nicholas really was.

Also to be thanked are Carmen Nicolas (deceased), who turned over to us many family pictures and official documents relating to her brother Johnny; his uncle, Fotune Bogat (deceased), with his vast and valuable perspective of Haiti and Johnny's place in it; to Lesley Bogat, Johnny's nephew, who functioned patiently and uncomplainingly as interpreter, driver and general counsel during the Haiti phase of our research; and Romuald Bak, of Brampton, Ontario, Canada, whose uninterrupted six-hour monologue of his fight for life inside the burning barn at Gardelegen was astounding in its dispassion and detail.

The penultimate acknowledgment is reserved for our wives, Beverley and Isabelle; our families, who made sacrifices so that we could devote much of our time to the project; and our typists, Laurie and Vickie.

And lastly a special acknowledgment to former Corp. David L. Matthews of the 7708th War Crimes Group. He had hoped for more than twenty years to write this book but could never find the time for what turned into eight years of international travelling, research, writing and rewriting. When we met him fourteen years ago, he agreed to share the idea with us.

Without him *The Search For Johnny Nicholas* would never have been finished because it would never would have begun.

Hugh Wray McCann
David C. Smith
Detroit, Mich.
April 1, 1980

Prologue

On a muggy summer night in 1965 the telephone rang in the suburban Detroit home of Hugh McCann, then a Detroit correspondent for *Newsweek* Magazine.

It was an old friend from McCann's undergraduate days in Fort Wayne at the Indiana Institute of Technology, Father Daniel Piel, who at one time served as the Catholic chaplain on campus. Fr. Piel was calling from downtown Detroit and said he was in town for a weekend workshop and seminar. He and McCann hadn't seen each other in years. 'Let's get together for dinner', the priest suggested.

A few hours later McCann and his wife were ensconced in air conditioned comfort at the Top of the Flame, a first-class restaurant located atop the twenty-six-storey Michigan Consolidated Gas Company building in the centre of Detroit. The view was superb: the lights of Detroit and its Canadian neighbour, Windsor, split by the sparkling Detroit River. The food was excellent. Against the background of tinkling ice cubes and a little jazz trio, the conversation centred on the good old days.

With Fr. Piel that night was a South Bend, Indiana, attorney named David L. Matthews and his wife. As the evening progressed, the chit-chat innocently elicited the fact that Matthews had been in World War II. McCann, who grew up in Kilkeel, Northern Ireland, where the United States 8th Air Force maintained a base during the war and who had got to know American GIs, was idly curious about Matthew's wartime experiences.

Matthews said he actually had served after the war with the 7708th War Crimes Group in Germany and that the

1

unit's job had been to gather evidence against Nazi war criminals and bring them to trial. Matthews said he covered the outfit's trials as a public information officer, and that he had become intrigued by testimony from liberated prisoners about the 'spine-tingling' escapades of an American spy – a Negro physician they had known as a fellow POW in the dreaded Camp Dora. This was the slave labour complex where Hitler was producing V-1 and V-2 rockets in a desperate attempt to reverse the inexorable Allied tide.

McCann sensed the makings of a compelling story. An American Negro in a German concentration camp? And a doctor at that? What was he doing there? How did he wind up there? McCann pressed forward with questions and Matthews supplied some answers. It was obvious that Matthews possessed the skeleton of a most unusual story – one that could make an absorbing book if the outline could be solidly fleshed out.

Matthews was way ahead of McCann. He had, he said, a six-page manuscript about the black man which he'd written in 1947. He had hoped to sell the story to the *Reader's Digest* or some other publication, but hadn't got round to it. As the years passed, Matthews' manuscript lay untouched as he became involved in raising a family and attending to his burgeoning law practice. But he still intended to get back to the story and to develop it into a fully-fledged account, he said. He was now fired up again and would return to South Bend to get started. McCann left the Matthews' and Fr. Piel that night harbouring the envy a writer feels when he has been scooped. But deeply involved in his second book at that time, McCann allowed the story to slip to the back of his mind where it would pop out occasionally to stir his reporter's instincts.

One day in 1968 McCann phoned Matthews. How was the book coming along? 'Sorry', said the South Bend lawyer, 'but I haven't had a chance to get on with it.' McCann thought the worst, of course – that some other journalist by now had surely got wind of the story and had

2

a three-year lead on him. Scooped again? But Matthews assured the *Newsweek* reporter that as far as he knew nothing about the black American had surfaced.

By the time their conversation came to an end, Matthews and McCann had orally agreed that the journalist would proceed in developing the story and Matthews would provide his original manuscript and other materials he'd collected. That agreement was formalized in September 1968 and soon after Dave Smith, McCann's longtime friend and then an editor on the *Detroit Free Press*, was invited to join in the project.

As McCann and Smith became immersed in the story of Johnny Nicholas, his life proved so provocative that they feared some World-War-II-vintage writer must by now have been in the advanced stages of a manuscript.

Indeed, as they were subsequently to learn, a number of major news organizations had come close to the Nicholas story, among them the *Associated Press*, the *United Press* (now *UPI*), the *New York Herald-Tribune*, the *Washington Times-Herald* and *Life* magazine.

Even with their belated start, the Detroit newsmen weren't over-looking any prospects. The 'search' grew to mean not only Johnny Nicholas' search, but that of the authors themselves as they travelled throughout North America, Central America and Europe.

Chapter One

As an aspiring actress Florence didn't mind stories. But a girl did like to know fact from fiction in a love affair. And that was her problem with Johnny.

She had seen her career come to a halt when the Germans had goose-stepped into Paris. The only way she could get in front of a camera now was by warming up to some middle-aged propaganda officer on the staff of Paris Military Headquarters whose job was to produce films on how much Parisians loved their conquerors. Florence's yearning to act, however, was still being fulfilled. But not in front of a camera.

To any Gestapo or S.D. security man who might have been prying, she was a bespectacled and proper French school-marm type. But to her friends in the Resistance she was a link in a chain of thousands of French women whose cunning and courage were daily saving American and British pilots shot down over France. There were lethal risks in the work. If they caught you, it was your final curtain call. And there was another kind of risk. A girl couldn't allow herself to become emotionally involved with the men whose lives she saved. But it was hard not to.

Big, aggressive American kids who had been the romantic terrors of the little English towns where their airfields were: they just couldn't keep their hands to themselves. Or the shy Royal Air Force boys who looked so helpless. They were so grateful, so lonely.

Florence's acting ability helped her to maintain a pose of professional detachment. Until she met Johnny.

Who knows how these things start? Certainly she was

shocked to come across an American who spoke French like a native. Most of them had atrocious accents. She was terribly curious. But what did the group leader keep telling the girls? Don't get involved! Don't say too much! Don't ask too much! The less you knew about the others and the less they knew about you, the safer it was for both women and pilots. If the Gestapo nabbed a girl, they could do their exquisite worst – but the most she could reveal would be two or three names. And the security of the escape line would remain intact.

The line hid Allied pilots in all sorts of places, moving them at night from house to house, town to town, until weeks later they'd be close to the French border with Spain, which was a neutral country. You could drive from Paris to the frontier in about eleven hours. Yet sometimes the Germans hunted the downed airmen so relentlessly that it took the girls as much as six weeks to smuggle them that far.

The favourite hide-outs were the haylofts of remote farm houses. Or the basements of working-class homes.

But Johnny? He was in an elegant apartment located in a high-priced address near the Eiffel Tower.

She wondered about that.

And there was something else that didn't make sense: for all his insistence that he couldn't wait to get back to his squadron in England and start fighting the war again, he didn't seem too anxious to leave.

The heavy black-out curtains held the dingy illumination of approaching dawn out of the bedroom. They were in total darkness. She turned her head on the pillow. 'Johnny, take me to America when the war's over?'

Johnny was a black man. He'd been with white women before. Whiteness wasn't the novelty it used to be. A girl had to have something more. And Florence did. It was an understatement to say she was blonde, blue-eyed and beautiful. But maybe he'd let it drag on too long. As playthings and diversions women were essential vitamins for his ego. But no matter how hard you tried to prevent it, when you made love to a woman she inevitably got the crazy notion that somehow she had the inside track on your emotions. When they became possessive they became dangerous There was no telling what they might do.

His voice drifted across the pillow. 'When will this miserable war end?' he said testily.

She wondered again about his beautiful French. 'What's the matter? If making love to me causes you to feel so hopeless,' she huffed.

He slipped out of bed and shivered. The heat in the apartment building was turned off at night to save fuel. He padded across the floor, pulled back the curtains and began scratching a peephole in the frost on the window pane . . . He was uncomfortable. He couldn't put his finger on it. Maybe he'd talked too much. Told her too much. Beautiful women would be the ruin of him. His street instincts were stirring. He didn't really know why.

In the fuzzy, grey light she saw his magnificent body silhouetted. Six feet tall or more, she estimated, and the grace of a cat in the movements of his two hundred-pound frame.

He scratched the ice until he had a tiny window to peer through.

Paris was unchanged from the morning before. Spires and chimneypots and bluish haze rose from the cook-stoves of early risers. It was November 1943 and the City of Light, under Nazi occupation for three and a half years, was cold, hungry, miserable, afraid. Every day the Gestapo and the S.D. knocked down front doors and dragged off men and women to God knows where.

She listened to the sound of his nail on the window. She wondered again how it was that a young American – mid twenties, she thought – was hiding out in so elegant an apartment. Who owned it? With several million Parisians – herself and her family included – cramped in the most abrasive austerity, who in Paris had a luxurious, green carpet on his bedroom floor? Who had a living room big enough to hold a ball in? And a grand piano?

Her group leader had said that the pilots, in their escape-and-evasion lectures back in England, were instructed to reveal to their French rescuers only name, rank, serial number, date of birth and unit. This information would allow the escape organization to radio London to check out whether a man was genuine – or a German infiltrator in disguise. The escape line couldn't go beyond the five questions. Yet that didn't prevent her from wondering. Whoever was hiding him was rich and probably influential. In the shadow of the Eiffel Tower, the Avenue de Lamballe was a much-envied location – or had been until the war. And the elegant clothes in the wardrobe: black market, certainly. Were they Johnny's? He used them as if they were. When a woman was captivated by a man she longed to know all the little things. What about his father? His mother? Where he grew up? The things he did as a little boy? America?

He never talked of those things. When she asked, his answers were perfunctory, general. He'd manoeuvre the conversation along to something else.

'You're shivering. Come back to bed.'

He continued to peer through the peephole.

'*Cherie*!'

'Yeah!' he said irritatedly.

She hesitated, feeling the edge in his voice. 'It must be very hard . . . I mean, being away from your comrades in the squadron.'

He continued to squint through the peephole.

'Johnny, I'm very fond of you.'

No matter how beautiful they were, when it became routine the challenge of the chase was gone; after that they could have been any of the ladies who walked the Champs . . .

'John-nee!' It was the expression she always used when she was miffed with him.

The sudden harshness chiselled into his thoughts.

8

'Did you hear what I said?... Maybe you'll be back with them for Christmas.'

He turned abruptly from the window. The drapes swished back into place behind him, plunging the room into darkness. 'Huh?... Have you been talking to those Resistance people again?'

'Johnny,' she whispered. 'They don't know you as your Florence does. They're afraid you could be a *Bosche* trying to penetrate the group. Don't blame them for being careful, *cherie*... What's wrong with telling us the name of your unit and the type of aircraft you flew? Give it to us and we can radio London and complete the verification and you can be on your way to the Spanish frontier in a few days.'

They'd argued about it before.

He didn't say anything. He stood in the darkness, thinking.

'Come back to bed,' she coaxed.

He shuffled across the room and slipped under the covers. She snuggled up to him and warmed him.

He was absolutely sure now that it was time to break it off. She was prying. She already knew too much. But he'd have to do it so that she'd never know it was happening. If she had the slightest hint that he was dropping her, she'd become enraged and do something spiteful.

He was a master at letting them down easy.

When he no longer trembled she murmured: 'I'll never understand you Americans... I thought more than anything else you wanted to get back to England.'

'Forget it,' he said softly.

'If you told me so once, Johnny, you told me a hundred times – '

'Forget it, I said,' he whispered in her ear. 'Just forget it.' She wouldn't quit, he thought, his restless mind turning on his own personal 'escape and evasion' plan. Yeah, that was it. He'd engineer his exit by confiding in her just enough to make his imminent departure seem reasonable. He'd tell her that it was time to get on with his

9

mission. Sure, he'd be back one day and take her off with him to the good old U. S. of A.

She kissed him lightly on the neck. 'What are you thinking?'

God, she just wouldn't quit. 'Nothing. Just how nice and warm it is here with you. I don't want it to end ... Why do you think I've been keeping the name of my squadron and the plane I was in to myself?'

She kissed him tenderly. '*Cherie*, I don't want to lose you, either.'

He sighed deeply. 'But I've got to go. Orders.'

'John-nee! What do you mean?'

Well, he thought, here goes – and I'd better make it good. 'I'm not like the others you've been helping get back to England.'

'I do not understand, *cherie*.'

'Look ... I wasn't shot down. I jumped. I'm a ... I was ... I was sent here on special business.'

They lay still, listening to the crowing of the rooftop chickens kept by tens of thousands of Paris apartment-dwellers to eke out their meagre wartime rations. It was dawning...

'What is it like to jump out of an airplane, Johnny? ... I know I could never do it ...'

He grunted a kind of self-deprecating laugh. 'Cold, honey. Real cold.'

'Oh, Johnny! You never take me seriously.'

Well, he thought, she asked for it ...

You'll be the first Negro spy to parachute into Occupied France in World War II. As long as you don't dig your grave with your head if the chute doesn't open.

But to hell with that kind of thinking.

Above the clouds over the English Channel the gleaming moon is three days away from full. Shafts of silver light stab the yellow gloom of the aircraft's interior.

You slump in the crudely padded metal seat, rehearsing

what will be the most stupendous act of your twenty-five years ...

Forward in the fuselage squats the dispatcher. He's made dozens of flights before. It should be routine for him. But it isn't. More than one plane of the secret-operations squadron has been riddled by Luftwaffe night-fighters en route to the DZ (drop zone). Too often the pilot just can't pinpoint the recognition signals of the reception committee on the ground.

Standing orders are – no nonessential contact between the crew and the Joe: if the plane's shot down, the less crew and agent knew about each other, the better. Before take-off you notice the dispatcher at the top of the ladder when you're at the bottom getting last-minute instructions from your conducting officer. Even in the airfield's poor light you notice the dispatcher's odd expression: How crazy can they get – dropping a black agent into lily-white Europe!

The dispatcher looks at you in your shabby, French-style overcoat and parachute pack. He hands you a mug of scalding coffee, then vanishes down the dark tube of the aircraft.

Through the hard seat under you, you feel the aircraft lose height and speed. A chill flashes through your body: You're approaching the DZ!

For the tenth time you run through the instructions they'd drummed into you: the DZ will be lit up by a prearranged pattern of small fires whenever the sound of the aircraft reaches the reception committee. Recognition signals, by flashlight or Aldis lamp, will be exchanged between the ground and the plane. When the dispatcher and the radio operator positively identify the DZ, the pilot will drop to between 1,000 and 700 feet for the jump.

The mug of scalding coffee jiggles in your hand as the aircraft bumps through the rough air. You sip slowly, feeling the fluid burn through your body, knowing that in a few minutes you'll be falling through the frigid air over Orleans.

You touch the coarse straps of the parachute harness and run your finger tips over the smooth, cylindrical quick-release lock. You focus on the vibrations of the engines throbbing through your body...

A vision of the sun-flooded streets of your hometown.

You're a boy again, trading absurd yarns of adventure and intrigue with your buddies. Once again you're telling them to remember your name, for one day you'll be rich and famous. You remember the dragging pace of your home town. The resignation of your elders to submit meekly to the hand of cards life has dealt them. Your home, parents, friends, the town you grew up in – they've all grown too small for you. You fret and fume until the day you're old enough to leave it all behind and take off with your limitless vision of yourself to the far corners of the world...

The light is flashing red! You're approaching the DZ!

The dispatcher, moving sluggishly in his heavy flight suit, relieves you of the coffee mug, gets awkwardly to his knees and twists several large handscrews positioned around a circular plate in the fuselage floor. He pulls and the heavy metal trap hinges back grudgingly. He points to you.

You coax yourself out of your seat and lower yourself to the floor, burdened by your huge parachute pack. Slowly you slide across to the yawning hole. A circle of snow-covered France appears a thousand feet below, bathed in the sheen of the moon.

Fear pokes into your bowels. You remind yourself of what Nietzsche said: the world is divided into only two classes – slaves and masters. You'd sworn you'd never be slave to anyone or anything – fear included. Now isn't the time to start.

As you slide feet-first toward the trap, the frigid air blasts your face and sweeps under your heavily cushioned cloth helmet... Now your heels are across the hole. Now your feet hang down into the freezing air.

Cowardice pricks you. You repeat Nietzsche's warning, remembering how your high school teachers told you to stay away from the heretical writings of a German ex-Catholic priest.

The blinking red light suddenly turns green!

You pull the heavy goggles down over your eyes and run through your checklist – identity card, ration card, curfew pass, money, Colt automatic. Then you put your mind in neutral and wait for the dispatcher's fist to hammer your shoulder . . .

Just before dawn in the courtyard of 9 Rue des Saussaises, Gestapo headquarters in Paris, a black car with two men wearing civilian suits in the back seat races out through the gates. It cuts across the Rue St. Honoré, the Rue de Rivoli and then the Champs Élysées, heading south for the Pont de la Concorde across the Seine.

It is still very dark and there is little traffic. The car's blacked-out headlamps throw slits of light along the vacant streets. As it reaches the south end of the bridge the driver wheels right along the Quai d'Orsay, then drives down the Boulevard de la Tour Mauborg. As the bulk of the Écôle Militaire shows up in the headlamps' skimpy illumination the driver slows and comes to a halt by the curb. The Écôle, no longer an academy for French officer-cadets, is the most magnificent barracks that German Army troops have ever enjoyed. The car, its motor idling, parks behind an empty canvas-topped army truck. On the snow-covered lawns of the Écôle a dozen German soldiers stamp their feet and briskly rub their hands against the predawn cold. In the back of the car the tip of a cigarette glows as one of the civilians draws on a Gaulois. Occasionally he flips back his glove to check his luminous-dial watch. A few minutes later the cigarette smoker rolls down the car window, throws away his butt and calls to the officer in charge of the platoon: 'Into the trucks!'

The tailgates clank tonelessly. The soldiers, bulky in

their greatcoats, their rifles and equipment jangling and clicking, clamber into the truck. Their breath puffs clouds in the thin air.

The car, followed by the truck, rumbles away from the curb and heads down the Avenue de Lamballe. The vehicles barely change into high gear when the car swings over to the curb, dutifully followed by the truck.

They park on the avenue near some ancient but magnificent townhouse buildings. Rising from the clutter of their roofs is the steel skeleton of the Eiffel Tower like an apparition in the foggy dawn.

In the car the senior civilian leans forward. His eyes move back and forth between the entrance to a particular townhouse and his wrist watch . . .

In a few seconds the soldiers are deployed in and around the building . . . About fifteen minutes later the two civilians leave the car and walk into the building.

The dispatcher presses the earphones. Something is wrong. He can't hear the pilot's instruction. The wind howls. The engines drone. Poised to jump, your brain is a telephone switchboard with a single line left open. Every other thought is banished as you tense for the dispatcher's thump on your shoulder . . . But something is wrong! The dispatcher shakes his head. He makes little circles in the air with his finger: the pilot can't pinpoint the DZ. He's going around again.

The tension breaks in you like a burst water bag. You have no strength to slide back from the trap. Fear tries to rebel. You fight back, telling yourself that when you hit French soil you'll be the most intelligent, most resourceful agent the Allies will have in all France. You've lived there. Gone to school there. Speak the language better than most French natives. *Gott in Himmel*! You speak excellent German, too!

A mental picture tickles you: being captured by the race-conscious Germans. Their dumbstruck expressions

14

as their captive, a Negro, addresses them in faultless German!

But long before they put the cuffs on you they learn why no one ever tangles with Johnny Nicholas. In fist fights back home you've beaten many a man. Sometimes two and three at a time. The bigger the odds, the better you like it. You remember the brothel. How you hated to find the lovely black girls monopolized by the arrogant, free-spending white U. S. Marines. You'd taken them on many times and heaved them into the street.

You don't really like fighting. You're afraid of it. But you fear being afraid. Like the hurricane, the flood and the drowning people. You'd dived in and saved half a dozen of them . . .

The light is flashing red again.

You snap the blind down on your memories and slide cautiously to the open door. You grip the edge of the hole with your heavily gloved hands. Your feet again dangle in French air. You sweat through the second run. You think the entire Gestapo is looking up at the soles of your shoes.

It's bitter cold down below. If your chute catches on a high-tension pylon or in trees, you can freeze to death – if you don't have the reception committee to rescue, welcome and warm you.

Something slams your shoulder. A switch clicks in you. Your body is a machine . . . pistoning you forward . . . plummeting you into space.

Florence held onto him very tightly, then slowly released. 'You are terribly brave . . . I'm glad I'm not a man.'

'So am I, sweetheart.'

'I could never do it,' she said in a quiet, desperate tone – as if she wished she could.

'You do braver things every day,' he said. 'With the pilots, I mean. You hide them away when they come down. If they're injured you find a doctor. You cook for them. Go out into the market and buy clothes for them.

15

Buy their tickets at the railroad station. Get them on the train. Get them off. Do all the talking for them. Hell, I make one jump. Sure, there are risks. I could have landed on the roof of German headquarters. But you, Florence; you and the other girls: you do it day in and day out. That takes real courage.'

Outside more cocks joined in the crowing. Cars, trucks and buses were rumbling and the city was awakening. Behind the curtains there was a faint glow of grey as dawn filtered into the room.

He started to get out of bed.

She clung impulsively to him and smothered him with kisses.

He disentangled himself from her and threw the blankets off.

'John-nee!' she whispered, still clinging possessively to him.

Jesus Christ! How he despised possessive women. He gradually worked his way out of her embrace and got out of bed.

'*Cherie*?' she questioned softly, her tone thick with concern. 'Where are you going?'

He swept back the curtains and the grey light filled the room. He peered through the peephole again. 'I'll only be a minute.'

On the bed behind him she slid her hand under his pillow and felt the cold, hard corners of his pistol. She let him take his time at the window, then called him to come back to bed. 'We may not see each other for a long time. Let's make the most of the little time we have left together,' she whispered enticingly.

As always he found her overtures in this vein irresistable. He hurried back across the floor and slid under the covers. 'Do you think –'

She smothered his mouth with hers.

It was not the time for talk.

Afterwards he lay in her embrace, subdued and

16

wondering if perhaps his decision to discard her had been made too hastily.

An insistent knocking on the door shattered their solitude.

He jerked upright. He put his index finger to his lips and looked at her. He slipped his hand under the pillow and produced his Colt automatic. He set the gun on the bed and quickly slipped into his robe.

She marvelled at the speed and grace of his movements.

He picked up the weapon and tip-toed to the door. He positioned himself against the wall and stood poised on the balls of his feet like soccer players she'd seen about to take a free kick.

There was another knock, louder.

'Who is it?' he asked.

The male voice on the other side was soft and urgent. 'I have a message for Florence.'

His body relaxed. He glanced toward the bedroom door, where Florence was standing fully robed and watching intently. He motioned for her to open the door. As she glided across the room he noticed her sensual sway and the exquisite ankles that had first caught his attention.

She took the door knob in one hand and the night lock in the other. Before she turned the two knobs she looked at him, awaiting his signal.

He nodded.

She opened the door.

From his position behind the door all he could see was the expression on her face.

'Yes?' she queried. 'What can I do for you, gentlemen?'

'You are Florence?'

'*Oui, monsieur.*'

Behind the door Nicholas gripped his automatic tightly, waiting for her to invite them inside. When she did he'd be right behind them and have the drop on them.

'We apologize for disturbing you, *madamoiselle*, at such an hour,' said the older man in cultured French, 'but it is important. We have a message from François.'

'I am sorry, *monsieur*,' said Florence, 'but you must have the wrong apartment. I know several men by the name of François but none who would inconvenience me so early in the morning.' She began to close the door but the man stepped forward and blocked it with his foot. 'It is time for the rooster to crow,' he said slowly and deliberately.

Florence replied: 'The rooster is always crowing... Come in, my friends.'

When the two stepped inside, Nicholas quietly swung the door closed behind them. As the lock clicked shut they whipped around nervously and saw Nicholas, his gun pointed toward them.

'They are all right, Johnny,' Florence said reassuringly.

His gun hand didn't waver.

'Who is this?' growled the older man suspiciously. 'We were told you'd be alone.'

'Don't mind me,' said Nicholas nonchalantly. 'Just give her the message and get out of here.'

The men glared and the older one turned to Florence. 'Who is this man? We were not told about him? We cannot talk in front of him!'

'It's all right Johnny, I tell you,' she said, reaching out and touching his shoulder. 'Your pistol's making them nervous, *cherie*.'

He ignored her appeal and waved the weapon to indicate that he wanted them to raise their hands above their heads.

The men complied, boiling with anger and humiliation.

'Higher,' coaxed Nicholas. 'That's good. Now you first,' he said, pointing the pistol toward the older man, whose arms were ridiculously high.

'Is this high enough?' inquired the man sarcastically.

'Just keep your mouth shut, old man, and empty your pockets.'

'*Madamoiselle* Florence!' the man appealed. 'This is outrageous!'

'John-nee, please,' said Florence, as if she was being embarrassed. 'This is very humiliating for loyal members of our escape group.'

'If they're loyal,' Nicholas shot back laconically, 'they don't have a thing to worry about. Okay, let's see your wallets.'

'John-nee!'

'Be quiet, Florence!' Nicholas snapped, then he turned to the two men. 'C'mon, move!'

They stood motionless with their hands held high.

Nicholas squeezed the trigger.

The older man's hand was trembling as he slipped it inside his overcoat and tossed his wallet on the carpet.

'The oldest trick in the book,' snickered Nicholas. 'Pick it up and hand it to me.'

The man sullenly retrieved the wallet and gingerly handed it to Nicholas, who accepted it with his free hand and parted it open with his thumb. He looked down for an instant and glimpsed a red identification card bearing a thumbnail-sized head shot of the older man – and a swastika.

The sight of it stunned him momentarily, and when he looked up at the wallet's owner he was staring into the bore of a Luger.

The younger man then produced a gun and held it at Florence's head.

'We are agents of the Gestapo,' announced the older man, as if making a speech. 'You are both under arrest. Drop your gun!'

Nicholas stood absolutely motionless. 'Touch a hair on her head, you son-of-a-bitch,' he rasped, 'and I'll blow your brains out!' He saw the German's knuckles get whiter as the man squeezed harder on the trigger. His heart flipped queasily and he knew that if he didn't shoot, the German would drill him.

He snapped back the trigger – and nothing happened. Instead of a deafening boom there was nothing more lethal than a click. He stared at it and squeezed again, contracting his body like a plucked snail as he steeled himself for the German's bullet. His gun clicked again. He looked up stupidly at the two Germans like a poker player whose full house has just lost to a royal flush in a winner-take-all game.

The older man was smiling. 'You can be sure, Major Nicholas,' he said theatrically, 'that if you force me to use my pistol there will be no misfire. Drop your American toy and put your hands above your head.'

Dazed, Nicholas tossed his useless weapon aside. My God! What fantastic nerve the German had! he thought.

He was still puzzling over it as the young Gestapo man slipped a pair of handcuffs on him and took him to a far corner of the room.

From a distance Nicholas watched as Florence and the older German chatted.

Something didn't seem right: the German smiled smugly as he helped her on with her coat. She put her hand in her coat pocket and took something out. A small rectangular object. Blue-steel in colour. She gave it to the Gestapo man.

It was the magazine from Nicholas' pistol.

The blood of a colossal anger pumped into his cheeks . . .

She glanced toward him and blew him a kiss as the German opened the door for her. '*Au revoir, cherie*,' she called tenderly across the room.

It was the only line that hadn't been written into the script by her German employers.

Chapter Two

There was no need to ask where they were taking him. He knew: the Rue des Saussaises or Avenue Foch.

Both meant the absolute worst.

From the rear of the car, seated between the two Gestapo agents, the city he knew so well didn't look the same. Familiar yet strange – like something well known viewed through the wrong end of binoculars.

What the hell! They were just two stupid Germans. He'd handled their kind before. He had a distinct advantage over them because they took one look at his black skin and leaped to all their smug, Aryan conclusions. He always delighted in watching their stunned expressions when he opened up on them in his fastidious German – *Hochdeutsch* that was far superior to their peasant dialect. It incensed them and exhilarated him.

For an instant it made him forget about Florence's betrayal, but once again he vowed retribution under his breath.

He'd take care of her, don't worry. She would get her proper reward. Erasing her hated image from his mind, he visualized the expression on the face of whichever dull, Swabian woodcutter would interrogate him when he announced that he was on a first-name basis with a senior officer on the personal staff of the Paris military commandant.

When you sparred with the Germans it was a matter of exceeding them in arrogance. You name-dropped profusely, scattering ranks and titles around with abandon. They might have their doubts – but they were scared to risk offending some higher-up.

The Mercédès droned on through the brisk morning and he found himself thinking about the caper on the Metro several months earlier. He'd been standing at the station with his little friend Hans Pape, the medical student, waiting for a train. It was always the same for French civilians: if there were any Germans waiting, they got preference. A civilian would stand for more than an hour while train after train pulled in, filled up with Germans, and pulled out.

He'd waited for a long time that day. 'I don't give a damn,' he told Pape. 'I'm getting on the next train that pulls in.'

The next one was full – except for a single car in the middle. It was painted red, and everyone in wartime Paris knew that this meant the car was reserved for senior German officers.

'You're crazy!' he heard Pape call out as he headed toward the car, pulling his little friend into the car with him.

There were six Nazi officers inside.

One wore a monocle, a chestful of ribbons and a haughty expression. Sitting apart from the others, he obviously outranked them. As Nicholas entered, all six looked up inquisitively. The senior officer, seeing a pair of Negro civilians, screwed his monocle into his eye socket and impaled the intruder with an outraged stare.

Nicholas froze . . . Slowly, he slipped his hand into his jacket and withdrew an old-style pocket watch. Pretending it was a monocle, he raised it to his eye and stared right back at the German. Except for the clacking of the wheels and muffled gasping there was silence in the car.

Nicholas advanced toward the monocled Nazi and halted snappily in front of him. From his commanding height he looked down at the man's medal-bedecked tunic. He tapped the first medal with a probing finger. 'What's this?' he demanded in German. 'In which campaign did you win it?' He tapped a second medal, then a third, asking the same questions.

The German was flabbergasted by the effrontery of a civilian in a reserved *Wehrmacht* car. A black-skinned one at that. Totally at a loss for any other response, he invited Nicholas to sit down.

For the next fifteen minutes, as the subway train glided underneath Paris, the officer recited the circumstances of his battlefield citations while Nicholas gave him his undivided attention.

The other German officers sat in shocked silence.

When the train arrived at Nicholas' station he rose, clicked his heels smartly, bade the German *auf wiedersehen* and, towing the quaking Pape behind him, disembarked...

In the back of the Mercédès the two Gestapo men ignored him. Maybe they were handling him with kid gloves because he had claimed to be a close friend of Colonel Schmidt. Or it could be part of their psychology: let the black bastard sweat it out, not knowing what was ahead for him.

But he also could play that game, he told himself.

He crossed his legs nonchalantly and tried to create the impression that he was much more interested in the Paris street scenes flitting past the car windows than in where they were taking him.

The Germans hadn't fired a single artillery shell into Paris and had dropped only a few bombs, but even so, they'd desecrated the city with their ubiquitous presence. The swastika flew everywhere. There wasn't a public building without one. If you didn't trip over the flag, you stumbled into one of their thousands of black-and-yellow sentry boxes. It was impossible to stroll the arcades of the Rue de Rivoli as in the old days without bumping into them.

Funny, though. As much as the morning ceremonial march down the Champs d' Élysées by the First Sicherungeregiment, with its blaring brass band, raised his hackles, something else provoked him even more: asinine names a foot long that any civilized nation would long ago have

23

broken into manageable syllables. But not the Germans. *Der Militarbefehlshaber in Frankreich ... Hauptverkehrsdirecktion Paris.* The arrogant sons-of-bitches!

He glimpsed the flared muzzles of the 40 m.m. anti-aircraft cannon poking over the edge of the parapet atop the sacred Arc de Triomphe. The guns' presence there wasn't a military necessity; the Germans did it just to rub French faces in the dirt.

They'd done it in many other ways, too, like shutting down the magnificent Metro from eleven to three o'clock each day and completely on weekends. They'd cut off most of the gasoline supplies and driven nearly all civilian cars off the streets. If you wanted to go somewhere you could take a velo-taxi, an enclosed cab pulled by a bicyclist. Mostly you walked. If you did and were out after the eleven o'clock curfew, German patrols could hear you a mile away, clop-clopping home on your wooden-soled shoes. If they caught you, the least that could happen was a night spent in the local station of the field police. The worst: if the Resistance happened to have eliminated a few Nazis that night, you might wind up as one of the hostages shot the next morning in retaliation.

But it was beautiful to watch how hard the Parisians worked at ignoring the Germans. The pretended they didn't exist.

Even at rock bottom, when there was almost no food, little electricity and people were cooking on their Rechaud '44s – 10-gallon cans welded together and filled with balls of crushed newspaper sprinkled with water – they continued to put on their act. They'd sit in pavement spots like the Café de la Paix and sip an *ersatz* coffee brew called Café National, pretending the war had never happened. On weekends, they'd head for the paddocks at Auteuil and Longchamps and watch their ribby ponies race.

Perhaps his two Gestapo escorts wanted him to humiliate himself by bowing and scraping to them and initiating

24

be a way. He'd bide his time and wait, as so often he had, for Lady Luck. When his break came, he'd be ready . . .

He wondered how long it would take for his brother, Vildebart, to find out what had happened to him; 135 Rue de Charonne, a working-class residential section of the city, wasn't too far from the Eiffel Tower area, yet he and Vildebart didn't see much of each other. Two or three times a year at most. But in Johnny's line of work that was to be expected.

Vildebart was four years older and had a wife. As far back as high school he'd never approved of his younger brother's antics and friends. He knew they were too different in personality to be really close. They kept in touch mostly from a sense of family duty. So when Johnny would knock on his door at six in the morning with three days' growth of beard on his face, hungry, dirty and bedraggled, Vildebart wasn't especially happy to see him. But blood was thicker than Vildebart's fear of the Nazis and he and his wife were always good for a bite, a bunk and a few hundred francs to tide Johnny over.

They'd tried to pump him on his first few visits; when he didn't tell them anything they finally gave up. Other than saying that he was taking some medical courses at the University of Paris, he kept them in the dark. It annoyed Vildebart, but in wartime Paris the less you knew about a friend's or relative's activities, the better it was for everyone.

When Johnny left, Vildebart wouldn't have the faintest idea when he'd see him again.

So if Johnny waited for his brother to come looking for him, he knew he'd probably rot in jail. Vildebart never knew what to expect, and Johnny delighted in surprising his straight-laced brother. He'd show up dressed as a fashion plate, swaggering with the confidence born of a pocket full of cash, and spreading around bundles of five hundred-franc notes thick as cigars.

Maybe Pape would miss him when he failed to show up in the Latin Quarter bistros. Perhaps his other medical-student acquaintance Jacques Coicou would too. If he was missing for any length of time, would the two of them come hunting for him as they had once before? In terms of his present activities, he certainly hoped not.

Pape was loyal and had courage. He hadn't fled when Nicholas had brazenly encountered the Wehrmacht officer on the Metro.

Coicou was just as dependable. He'd let Nicholas hide in his apartment at 116 bis, Champs Elysées, for several months. Nicholas had shared an attic room with the U. S. Air Force lieutenant, Pete Edris, for all that time. He'd wound up knowing all about Edris' squadron in England and the lieutenant's life in the States.

Coicou worked for the Resistance as a doctor. Edris' plane was shot down, and Coicou had taken care of him.

Nicholas remembered the morning they'd picked up the lieutenant.

The phone rang in the apartment late the night before. Coicou answered. The voice said that his aunt had taken a turn for the worse. Could he come and see her? It was the Resistance code: an Allied pilot had been shot down and needed medical attention.

Coicou got out of bed, drove his little canvas-topped Citroën all the way across the city, deserted except for the German curfew patrols, and took care of Lt. Edris. As a senior medical student at the University of Paris, Coicou was permitted to practice medicine – up to a point – by the German administration because there was a shortage of French civilian doctors. This meant Coicou qualified for a ration of gas for his car and an *Ausweis*, the all-important little piece of paper from German headquarters permitting him to be out after curfew.

Coicou made the trip as usual – with his heart in his mouth. While the *Ausweis* kept him from being arrested, it didn't stop the patrols from flagging him down and questioning him. On the way across the city he tried to keep off the big, empty boulevards and stay with the narrow, twisting back streets. But the snore of his little car ripped through the Paris night, leaving a trail of decibels.

Amazingly, he arrived at the 'safe' house where Edris was hidden without being intercepted. But they learned on arrival that the Germans had the house under surveillance: they were in great danger. Everyone would have to scramble – and fast. Because nobody had a place to take the injured lieutenant where he could be treated, the task fell to Coicou.

He couldn't refuse. First, though, he had to let his wife know. He couldn't phone: the Germans probably had the lines tapped. He'd have to drive all the way across the city again.

Knowing that the Gestapo was closing in, Coicou was emotionally exhausted when he got back to the Champs Élysées. Again, no patrols. That in itself doubled his fears: the Gestapo was definitely on to him. They were going to zero in on him in their own good time and had arranged that the army patrols wouldn't blunder into him and foil some exquisitely contrived capture plan.

His wife agreed without hesitation to take Edris; he could share the attic room with Nicholas. But could Coicou once again make the trip across town and bring the injured American back without being caught?

Nicholas didn't have to look twice at Coicou to know that he was exhausted. He volunteered to go along.

This time, however, they'd take *his* car and he would do the driving.

Good old Gardemann. Through him Nicholas had obtained a car, gasoline coupons and his own personal *Ausweis*. By God, there *were* a few good Nazis at that, he thought.

When Coicou got into the car, he was astonished. Not just that in car-famished Paris it was a large Citroën. But big French tri-colours fluttered at both front fenders!

'*Mon Dieu*, Johnny,' he sputtered. 'We don't want to let them know we're coming!'

'Take it easy, Jacques. They expect us to sneak around. They're not expecting three high-ranking Vichy government officials at this time of night on a top-priority mission,' Nicholas said, grinning.

'Three?' queried Coicou.

'Relax,' teased Nicholas. 'It's all taken care of.'

He let out the clutch and the car jerked down the Champs. In the Passy area he pulled on the wheel and guided the car into a darkened street lined with elegant apartment houses. He leaned back and opened the door to the rear seat.

A young man slipped out of the shadows and entered.

'Our insurance,' said Nicholas.

The stranger was the son of the Prefect of Police under the German administration.

'Don't worry,' said Nicholas, obviously enjoying Coicou's nervous hesitation. 'He's a good friend of mine.'

At the 'safe' house they bundled the injured Edris into the back of the car and threw a travelling rug over him. Nicholas gunned the Citroën back to the Champs.

Coicou was sweating in the back with Edris. It seemed to him as if Nicholas was deliberately looking for German curfew patrols. And he got them. Each time they were flagged down all three produced their *Ausweis*. If it looked as if some Wehrmacht N.C.O., with nothing to do but kill time, was going to give them the third-degree, Nicholas addressed him haughtily in German, heavily laced with military protocol and studded with references to the fact that he was a personal associate of Colonel Schmidt and that his back-seat passenger was the Police Prefect's son.

About a month later, when Lt. Edris was fully recovered, there was an imperious knock on the front door of Coicou's apartment. When he answered, a squad of troops in S.S. uniform followed by some German civilians swarmed in. Everyone in the house – except Nicholas, who was not there at the time – was arrested and taken to Gestapo headquarters.

Nicholas, returning a couple of days later, also was picked up.

Germans in general – and the Gestapo in particular – had a special hatred for anyone caught helping Allied airmen. The more fliers who returned to their bases in England, the worse it was for the German cities they were bombing. So Coicou, his wife and Nicholas could expect harsh treatment.

Miraculously, they were released!

Why? Coicou, a medical student, almost fully trained as a doctor, was too valuable to be shot or sent to a concentration camp, said the Gestapo. He would therefore consider himself under a suspended sentence. He would have to work in a German military hospital in the Paris region. Like all parolees, he would have to sign the register at Gestapo headquarters each day.

Waiting in line there one morning, Coicou happened to be gazing out through the front door. His curiosity was drawn to a Citroën. It had a pair of French flags fluttering from the fenders. The driver was a uniformed German. Inexplicably, the two passengers in the back were Nicholas and Edris! The young flier was not in the khaki shirt and olive-green pants Coicou remembered. He was in the *bleu de travail* of the typical French working man . . .

After several days the toilet in Nicholas' cell at Gestapo headquarters was overflowing and the stink was revolting. He couldn't eat. The agonizing screams all day and all night from the floor above didn't help either. Maybe the bastards had a recording they played all the time, he thought.

All feeling had gone from his buttocks and legs. The chain and the low wall-ring prevented him from exercising much, but he did what he could to keep the circulation flowing. For a few days he'd ignored the dry bread and the pannikins of mangel-wurzel soup. But it occurred to him that by not eating he was weakening himself and aiding them in their psychological softening-up. So he forced the slop down his gullet.

He wondered how long it would be before they started interrogating him.

He wondered when Vildebart, Pape and Coicou would miss him and start looking for him. If they did they'd become innocently involved; he didn't want that.

He wondered who Florence was sleeping with now, who she was setting up . . .

The two medical students, Pape and Coicou, had gotten used to meeting their gregarious black friend in the cafés and student haunts of the Latin Quarter and in Montparnasse. Almost always surrounded by a party of theatre or motion-picture people, and never without an exotic-looking girl on his arm, Nicholas had a magnetism that attracted them and their friends and classmates.

He flattered them with his hungry interest in medicine. Some thought he might be a former medical student himself who'd succumbed to the glamour of show business – but whose first love was really medicine. He'd hinted that he was taking some courses, but neither Pape nor Coicou had ever seen him in class. He'd visit Pape's very modest apartment in the Quarter and they'd talk about medicine for hours. They never discussed the war, and they studiously avoided any discussion of Resistance activities.

Nicholas turned up one night at a party that the senior medical students were throwing for their faculty. Early in the evening he drew Pape aside and asked him the best procedure for doing an abortion. Pape told him. A few hours later Pape found himself on the periphery of a clutch of students circled around Nicholas: he was authoritatively describing modern abortion techniques.

Pape and Coicou, like most of those who were drawn

to Nicholas, had heard the rumours and were hesitant about getting too close to him or being seen too often with him. They knew he was a frequent visitor at German Army headquarters; that he associated with German officers and had been seen riding around with them in their staff cars.

Yet Nicholas was not only fascinating, sophisticated and at home in glamorous circles; he was also very generous with money, always good for a loan. To perennially destitute university students on austerity budgets it was a quality sufficient to allay their most profound doubts about him.

Pape and Coicou hadn't seen him for a long time prior to his arrest. When the weeks lengthened into months, they decided they'd better check and see if anything was wrong. They'd never been to his apartment before; he had always come to theirs. But they had his address.

When they went there they found he'd left – without leaving a forwarding address.

As senior medical students, they were busy with their studies and had patients to attend to in their capacity as doctors in limited practice. So it took a while until they could arrange for time off to hunt for him.

Their search took them a long way from the Latin Quarter. They worked their way through a succession of landladies and concierges, bartenders, waiters and hat-check girls. They crossed the Seine to the Right Bank and into the clubs and cabarets of Pigalle and Montmartre. Their questions led them through the working-class districts of La Chapelle and La Villette west to the middle-class area north of the Arc de Triomphe known as Les Batnigolles.

They found him there in a small office in a fairly modern building. It was adequately but not extravagantly furn-ished, and on the wall above his desk hung an impressive, framed document bearing a red-wax seal.

Behind his enthusiastic greeting they sensed that he was not entirely happy to see them. He adroitly side-stepped any explanation for his mysterious movements or his long absence by bombarding them with questions about their medical studies.

Under the circumstances Pape and Coicou felt a little ill at ease, but they didn't let that inhibit their curiosity about the document. They got close enough to read it. Setting aside all the ornate language, it said that 'John Guy Nicholas' was licensed to practise medicine and that his specialty was gynaecology. On their way out they picked up one of his calling cards. It stated that he'd obtained his M.D. at the University of Heidelberg...

The cell door squealed open. 'Nicholas, you're next!' a guard grunted.

He squinted in the glare of the flashlight. They unlocked the chain and slid it out of the ring. He got to his feet unsteadily, running his hands over his rump and thighs to restore circulation. He didn't want to move until he was sure he wouldn't fall; it would be too humiliating. He had lost track of the days. He didn't know what time it was, but he'd be damned if he'd ask them.

The guards escorted him down a long, dark corridor. They hadn't removed the manacles on his ankles and he was forced to hobble. A rectangle of light flashed in the gloom as one of the guards opened a door and pushed him inside.

He was in a small office with a bare-topped, heavily scarred desk and several decrepit chairs. Cigarette butts littered the floor and newspapers and magazines were scattered around, giving the place the cheap, worn look of a small-town police station.

He straightened himself and squared his shoulders as he entered, hoping that his physique would intimidate the nondescript little N.C.O. with the *Sicherheitsdienst* patches on the sleeves of his S.S. uniform.

The German muttered to the guards not to leave. He took a long, printed form from his desk, rummaged around

34

for a pencil stub, then poised himself like an officious railroad clerk.

A typical Bavarian peasant, easily cowed by the German tongue spoken as it should be spoken, thought Nicholas. He was sure he could browbeat the little S.S. pencil-pusher into calling Army headquarters and asking for Col. Schmidt.

The S.D. man posed his questions in atrocious French. Nicholas giggled inside. Like an accountant preparing for the annual audit, he was ready.

'Your name?' asked the S.D. man behind the desk.

'Jean Marcel Nicolas,' Nicholas replied evenly, spelling out his last name and carefully Gallicizing it by omitting the 'h.'

'Your date of birth and birthplace?'

'20 October 1918. Port-au-Prince, Republic of Haiti.'

'Nationality?'

'French.'

'We aren't playing games here,' snapped the S.D. man. 'If you are from Haiti, how can you claim French citizenship?' He smirked triumphantly like a prosecutor who has just trapped an elusive witness.

'My mother and father were French. Anyone born of French citizens outside France is also a French citizen,' Nicholas replied, squelching the other man's momentary exultation.

'All right, you smart bastard. When did you come to France?'

'The first time was in 1929.'

Searching for the correct line on his form, the S.D. man looked up quizically. 'What do you mean – the first time?'

'I left in 1935 and returned to Haiti, then came back to France in 1938.'

'Every time I ask a question you come back with a riddle. We can make it miserable for you if you don't end the riddles. Why did you come to France in 1929?'

'To begin my education.'

'And why did you come back in 1938?'

'To join the French navy.'

The questions went on and on. The S.D. non-commissioned officer seemed to be in no hurry. He wrote slowly, like a tired desk sergeant in a busy precinct house.

So far Nicholas had satisfied his interrogator. He quickly sensed, however, that this was merely the first stop. If there were any serious questions to be asked, it wouldn't be the pudding-head in front of him who'd be doing the asking.

After forty-five minutes it was over and the guards took him and the lengthy form to another room.

It was a much more impressive office and the man behind the desk was a blond, alert-looking young Gestapo man in civilian clothes. He scrutinized the form even before Nicholas was seated. He looked up briefly, told the guards to remove the handcuffs and manacles, then resumed his study of the form.

Nicholas smiled inwardly. How he could read the Germans: next he'd be offered a cigarette, told that they were both civilized men, that he already knew all about Johnny Nicholas, and that a great deal of inconvenience could be avoided if he were to confess everything.

The Gestapo man did just about that. His French was good.

Nicholas replied that the S.D. N.C.O. had been very thorough and that just about everything was already on the form. The Gestapo man asked for his Navy discharge papers and for more detail on his naval career.

He had been discharged in March, 1939, six months before the German invasion of France, he pointed out, handing over his discharge card. Why, the German asked, had he been mustered out. A medical discharge, Nicholas told him. What kind of medical problem had it been? A head injury. What kind of a head injury? He had fallen while climbing the mast of a training ship. The name of the training ship, please? *Le Courbet*.

36

'Does your head ever give you any problems these days?' he asked, as though genuinely concerned.

'Once in awhile,' Nicholas replied.

Now the Gestapo man wanted details of his education. Which schools had he attended in France? The Aristide Briand School at St. Nazaire and the College de Garçon at Grasse. He asked him about the subjects he studied. About his teachers. How had he liked the bleak St. Nazaire winters of the north and the glorious weather of Grasse in the south?

Suddenly his conversational tone ended. 'What are your parents' names?' he snapped.

'Hilderic and Lucie Nicolas,' Nicholas quickly replied.

'Your mother's maiden name?'

'Dalicy.'

The Gestapo man was becoming annoyed by his prisoner's unrelenting self-assurance. 'You're not French. You can't be. Haiti is a republic. Your parents could not be French. If you know what's good for you, you'll give us the truth!'

'My parents were born in Guadeloupe, a French possession. They moved to Haiti later, but they remained French citizens. Therefore I am a French citizen.'

Whether he believed it or not, the interrogator seemed to accept his explanation. Lighting a long thin cigar, he moved close to Nicholas and blew a smoke ring in his direction.

'When did your father go to Haiti?'

'I once knew but no longer can recall,' said Nicholas, softly blowing back the smoke.

The German tapped ashes from his cigar into an ashtray, inhaled deeply and blew more smoke in Nicholas' direction. 'What does your father do?'

'He's dead.'

'When did he die?'

'In 1937.'

'Before that?'

'He was a secretary in the British Embassy in Port-au-Prince.'

The Gestapo man demanded details. Nicholas told him that he was very young at the time and that he didn't really know much about his father's activities – except that it was a very important job his father had held.

The Gestapo officer shifted the questioning. What did Nicholas do after his discharge from the French Navy? He had gone to medical school at the University of Paris, Nicholas told him. Where was he when the war broke out? In Paris. Where was he when the German Army entered Paris? He had left with hundreds of thousands of other refugees for Chartres. And then? To Marseilles in the Unoccupied Zone. Why did he return to the Occupied Zone? Germany and France had agreed on an armistice and he wanted to continue his medical education. How was he supporting himself? His family in Haiti had been sending him money to a bank in Marseilles; but when the German Army took over the Unoccupied Zone they could no longer do so.

Nicholas knew the German would soon ask the question he couldn't risk answering until he'd been able to make contact with Gardemann: How had he been supporting himself since then? There are three possibilities, he thought. As soon as Col. Gardemann knows where his trusted black friend is, his predicament is over because the colonel will come to Gestapo headquarters and personally vouch for him. Or relations between the Gestapo and the *Abwehr* have become so bad that the Gestapo won't even bother to 'phone Gardemann. Or worst of all, the Gestapo has grown so powerful that even if they do phone Gardemann and he comes over, they won't release him.

So Nicholas realized that he would have to answer in such a way that if Gardemann could not be counted on, his cover would still be intact without him.

'You're an educated man,' the Gestapo officer continued. 'What *lycée* did you attend?

38

'The Harry Tippenhauer Academy in Port-au-Prince. Baccalauréat Part I and Part II.'

'What was the name of the ship you took across the Atlantic?'

'The first or second time?'

'Both.'

'The first time? I can't remember. The second time, a French naval vessel.'

'Have you ever been outside France since your discharge from the navy in March, 1939?'

It was a key question. After the fall of France in 1940, tens of thousands of Frenchmen had fled their homeland for the safety of England or North Africa and joined the Free French fighting forces of the exiled General de Gaulle. Many of them had been recruited by the Allies, trained in intelligence-gathering, sabotage and subversion and parachuted back into France.

'No,' said Nicholas.

'What about your old teachers at the Aristide Briand School, *Monsieur* Nicholas? Do you ever visit them?'

As Nicholas had already revealed, the school was in St. Nazaire – which was also a major German submarine base whose mammoth, reinforced-concrete U-boat pens had defied scores of British and American bombing raids.

'No. Boarding school was not a pleasant experience,' said Nicholas with an elegant, Gallic shrug.

'And the College de Garçon. That is in Grasse, is it not?' said the German.

Grasse was barely twenty miles southwest of Nice, in the south of France on the Mediterranean. The Germans knew that in the Nice area the Allies, with the aid of scores of French civilians, were operating an 'underground railroad' for rescuing shot-down airmen and smuggling them back to England. Nicholas's thoughts shifted briefly to Lt. Edris. By now Pete should be crossing the Spanish border on the way back to London.

'Have you been back in Grasse since the war began to renew acquaintances?'

39

'No.'

The German asked numerous questions about the school and the town. Nicholas knew he was trying to see if he really had gone to school there. It was also obvious that he was fishing for anything his hook might snag.

Why wasn't his interrogator more aggressive? Was it just his technique? Was the rough stuff to come later? Or had the German already checked with Gardemann and was playing it safe with so close an associate of an important member of the Paris *Abwehr*?

He offered Nicholas another cigarette, then lapsed into silence as he re-studied the long, detailed preliminary interrogation form. 'The arresting officers say you speak fluent German,' he said, suddenly switching to German, not bothering to look up.

'*Ja*,' acknowledged Nicholas in German. 'Many Frenchmen speak German.'

'Indeed,' continued the Gestapo man, 'but why would a Haitian Frenchman study German?'

'If he were an avid student of Nietzsche and wished to read him in his mother tongue.'

The German looked up. He smiled as if genuinely pleased. 'What better reason! You liked Nietzsche?'

'*Ja*.'

'What did you like about him? That he was a renegade Catholic priest'

'*Nein*. To me Nietzsche is saying: "The world is divided into two classes – the masters – and the slaves." And he impressed upon me that I must be among the masters.'

The Gestapo man looked amused.

Nicholas knew exactly what he was thinking: What arrogance for a nigger!

'That's not only Nietzsche's philosophy,' observed his interrogator, 'It's the philosophy of Adolph Hitler and the Third Reich, which will last for a thousand years.' He went back to his study of the prepared form, then added in a quiet, distinct voice: 'Is that why you have associated your fortunes with those of Col. Schmidt?'

Tricky bastard, thought Nicholas. Well, he'd sat long enough with his cap in his hand. The Kraut had brought up Schmidt's name, which meant he was aware of the connection. So now he could use heavier artillery on him. He sat up straighter, squared his shoulders and adopted an authoritarian tone. '*Herr Hauptsturmfuehrer*! I have patiently answered your questions for approximately forty-five minutes, and I have not attempted to embarrass you by informing *Oberst* Schmidt of your preposterous mistake. If I am released immediately, I will drop the matter. I now demand to know why I have been arrested!'

'You're in no position to demand anything,' the Gestapo man told him tartly. 'And it means little to me or the Gestapo if Col. Schmidt knows that we've arrested you. The colonel's organization has had considerable doubt cast on its loyalty in recent months. And he is not in Paris at this time. For the moment, *Mein Herr*, you are our business exclusively.'

Nicholas felt a nauseous spasm as if he were in an elevator and the cable had snapped.

He looked down and remembered that the handcuffs were gone. No shackles on his feet either. The guards weren't in the room. Probably standing outside in the corridor. The Gestapo man had a gun on his belt. But he could reach across and snap his neck in a wink and then. . . No. It wouldn't work. There were too many of them in the building, and sooner or later they'd nail him before he got to the street.

'I'd have thought a man like you would have been more careful . . . French women are notoriously jealous. Even we Germans have learned that in a very short time in Paris. The *madamoiselle* got suspicious. She waited outside your apartment on several occasions and saw your other ladies. Naturally I recognized that she came to us not out of loyalty to France's new rulers but out of spite. Love and hate – two sides of the same coin. The one who loves you the most is also capable of the deepest hate . . .'

41

While the German rambled on, Nicholas struggled to conceal his anger. Spiteful little bitch! After all he'd done for her. If it was the last thing he'd ever do, he'd wring her little neck. If she'd told them all she knew, they'd beat him to a pulp, then tie him to a post and blow his goddam brains out.

If he could only work his way closer to the bastard at the desk. Snatch the gun from him. Threaten to blow his head off if he didn't escort him out of the building without giving the alarm. How far away could he make it from Rue des Saussaies? He'd just take the German with him until they were well out of sight, find a 'phone, call Coicou or Pape, then dump his hostage.

'Then we both know, *Herr Haupsturmfuehrer*, that you can't place too much on the words in anger of a spiteful lover?'

'Of course,' the German readily agreed. 'But there are a few things that are not difficult to check. She says you speak fluent English.'

He responded in German that he spoke some English, not knowing if the German spoke English, too. If he did, would he speak it well enough to notice that Nicholas' English had an American accent – not the British-accented English of most English-speaking Frenchmen? He scrutinized the German's face. The man, about his own age, looked too intelligent to let his prisoner slide closer on any pretext. If Nicholas tried it and the German caught him, it would be a neon sign flashing the message that he had something big to hide. Then they'd put him through the wringer.

'*Madamoiselle* Florence insists there is something suspicious about you.'

Nicholas felt the hairs prickle on the back of his neck. He affected genuine surprise. 'But haven't I answered all your questions?'

'*Ja*,' nodded the German, watching his prisoner very closely. 'Unfortunately that's part of the trouble. Perhaps your answers have been too complete. You remember too

42

well. You remember too much and too well. And another thing, she has the notion that you are an American air force officer posing as a French civilian. Why would she possibly say something like that?'

In his imagination Nicholas already had the gun in the man's back and his other hand at his throat, using him as a shield. He was jamming the barrel in his back and telling him to order the guards to hand over their pistols. He was racing along the dark corridor, holding the German officer by the scruff of the neck, using him as a shield. But further than that his wild imagination couldn't see. Another spasm of hate for Florence rippled through him as he sensed what was coming next: the Gestapo man would ask him to converse in English and there'd be no way to hide his accent. They'd interrogated enough American airmen and they knew an American voice when they heard it.

It was make a break for it or . . .

Certainly not stick around for the routine in which they pulled out your fingernails and toenails. Stuck gasoline-soaked cotton batten between your toes and set fire to it. Handcuffed your hands behind your back, tied a rope to the handcuffs, flipped the rope over a beam and hauled you up off the ground. While your shoulders slowly dislocated, they went to work all over you with a two-by-four. The most brutal was the bathtub treatment; they held you under ice-cold water until you almost drowned, then revived you. Then started all over again. Some poor bastards had suffered it six times a day, seven days a week . . .

The German pressed a button on a console at his desk and the two huge, barrel-chested guards instantly entered the room and flanked Nicholas.

He ignored them.

'Nicholas, I've heard enough. You've been lying ever since you came in here. I have tried to be tolerant, but you have not co-operated in the least. All of that talk about Haiti . . . lies! Admittedly clever, but lies! You're not French at all. You are an American! You are an American

43

officer and you are in France to commit sabotage and espionage against the Third Reich...'

'That is not true. I am a French citizen and...'

On signal from the officer the guards simultaneously pumped the butts of their rifles into Nicholas's ribs. He grimaced, but still stood erect.

'I will do all the talking. You will keep your filthy *schwartze* mouth shut unless asked a question,' screamed the Gestapo officer, dropping his mask of urbanity. 'We have it all here.' He held up a manila folder.

Nicholas couldn't read all the printing on the folder's cover, but it looked like similar folders he'd seen in Gardemann's office. Almost certainly it was a dossier they had prepared on him.

His interrogator flicked a speck of dust from his suit, turned to him and continued. 'I will say this: you've memorized your story well. Too well. Even I can't recall the details of my life in Germany as minutely as you have recounted yours. When I add that fact to the girl's information, it is obvious that you are an American agent with an excellent cover story. You are an enemy agent in our midst. I detest and despise you – but I'm forced to commend you for your effort.' He paused, took a long, contemplative draw on his cigar and said: 'Now you will tell me the real story – in English.'

Nicholas laughed heartily. By Christ, he thought, I've got the Gestapo as confused as Vildebart, Pape, Coicou and the others.

'You black pig! We'll teach you to laugh at a German officer,' snarled the German, signalling the two guards.

In arced the rifle butts as they thudded him between the legs.

The piercing pain dilated his pupils. He felt his knees turn to sponge as he fell forward on the desk – but his mind continued to whirr as he tried desperately to calculate his next move. 'Okay,' he groaned in American English. 'Okay ... so I'm an American. You win.' The pain robbed him of his breath. 'But I'm a pilot. Not a spy. I was only trying to get back to my unit. Same as you'd do if you were in my spot.'

When he had completed the 'American' version of his story, the young German seemed pleased. '*Ja*, that fits with the other pieces,' he announced triumphantly, waving the folder. 'Even *Oberst* Schmidt would appreciate your honesty. It's too bad he won't hear about it. The Gestapo and the *Abwehr* don't write each other much any more. Besides, the *Herr Oberst* was transferred recently. Didn't he tell you? And the mail service to the Russian front is not too dependable these days.' The Gestapo man smirked victoriously.

Nicholas gritted his teeth to hide his shock and despair. 'When he does hear about it,' he muttered, 'it'll be your rotten hide.'

The Gestapo man nodded to the guards again. The rifle butts clubbed him unmercifully and the house lights went out . . .

When he came to he found himself being hustled into the back of a big French police 'Black Maria' van with a crush of other prisoners. The vehicle groaned under its heavy load as it accelerated out of the Rue des Saussaises courtyard.

There wasn't much light inside. The long, narrow slits were barred and the most he could see when he peered out were the sides of buildings and people on the sidewalks. He scanned the faces of his companions. They looked like typical Parisians arrested for activities with the Resistance, pummelled for information, then rushed off to a dungeon or a firing squad. A few others were obviously pimps.

Some looked extremely well-dressed. Probably black-market operators. And some didn't look at all French. From their features they could've been British, and they looked as if they'd been through hell, too. Fat lips. Broken noses. Smashed, bloody heads – just like his.

He held on to a strap from the ceiling and tried to edge his way closer to one of the slits. They were on the Avenue

Marigny, then the Champs, now the Boulevard St. Germain, now the Boulevard Raspail.

They were going south, he guessed. Then sometime afterwards, when the sounds of traffic had waned, the vehicle bucked and lurched over cobblestones.

When the van doors opened, they faced a platoon of German soldiers staring up at them. '*Heraus! Schnell!*' bellowed an N.C.O.

When they climbed out of the truck they were ordered to line up in a large courtyard for a roll call. The whispered word went around that they were in the notorious German Army prison of Fresnes.

When the roll call was over they were marched down an underground passage into a mammoth hall with a ceiling many stories high. Gallery upon gallery of cells rose to the ceiling, and all Nicholas could hear was the clang of cell doors and the rattle of armed guards' boots along the miles of catwalks.

Chapter Three

In the prison at Fresnes he lived in a tiny, dark cell which had an iron bed with a filthy mattress. There was a flush toilet without a lid. Above it was a single faucet. A small table. The walls were filmed in grime and scraped with initials, names, dates and slogans.

Each morning a huge German Army sergeant burst into his cell and announced: 'American air force officer! You are a black pig and a dirty spy and we will kill you slowly.' With that he would punch Nicholas in the face and kick him in the groin, then depart.

Several times a week soldiers crowded him and other prisoners into trucks and took them to downtown Paris for additional interrogations by the Gestapo. There he was kicked, beaten, cajoled, flattered and beaten again. Back in his cell in the evening, however, he would continue with his unflinching regimen of daily calisthenics: he planned to be in top physical condition when the opportunity came up for him to make his break.

It never came. One day he was pushed into the back of a truck and taken to a place which, to hundreds of thousands of former prisoners, marked their entry into the German concentration-camp pipeline. It was the Royal Lieu transit camp near Compiegne, about forty-five miles north of Paris.

The former French Army barracks was enclosed by barbed wire and tall guard towers – but the library was still in operation! The Germans held roll call every morning and evening in the big parade ground. During the day, prisoner work details marched out of camp after breakfast and returned well before the seven o'clock curfew.

Nicholas[1] was never among them and his main problems were boredom and uncertainty. There was the daily sweeping of the dormitory, with its double rows of twin-tiered bunks on both sides and the long table down the middle. There also was an occasional potato-peeling detail in the camp kitchen.

But his overriding pre-occupation remained escape.

Compiegne was the last stop on the way to the Third Reich. It was absolutely imperative: he had to get out of here. It was on his mind every waking hour. Everything he did, everything he saw, everything he heard was sifted and evaluated and categorized in terms of how it could help him get through the barbed wire and out.

He guessed that the Germans knew how every prisoner was afflicted with escape mania. So you could bet that all the obvious ways out of Royal Lieu barracks – over the fence, under it, via a tunnel – had long ago been sewn up. It would have to be something different.

[1]His Prisoner Number was 24644.

There had to be a way! Hell, after all, it was only his first day in the barracks. He'd give himself a few days to look around, then devise something.

The other men in his quarters were from every province in France, every page in the social register: resistance leaders, government officials, doctors, priests, writers, policemen, pimps, fairies, whorehouse operators and black-market racketeers.

He'd watch them at the open-air washing trough in the morning. Snow on the ground. Cold as the devil. It made the bruises look blacker, the weals look purpler, on their pallid, goose-pimply flesh. The men who shuffled along slowly with an odd way of walking – almost as if they'd been riding a horse for a week straight – they were the ones who had been kicked in the balls so often and so long they'd never walk or make love right again in their lives. If you watched them long enough, you could soon separate the phoneys from the genuine articles.

He learned from the old hands that there was no way of telling how long they'd keep you at Royal Lieu. Some were there only a week when they were shipped out. Others had been there for months. He concluded that it was a pipeline operation between the French prisons and the German concentration camps. When the camps were full, everything else along the line was jammed up. When they emptied out, they were restocked with shipments from places like Royal Lieu.

Of course, whispered the old timers, there were always ways of slowing things down – if you knew the right people. Like arranging with someone in the camp office to 'lose' your records. Or when it came to the physical that you had to pass before going on a shipment, a healthy prisoner with some savvy could arrange to flunk it.

Once you found out who the right people were, then it cost you plenty to buy their services.

The long roll calls gave him time to look around and case the set-up.

Each guard tower had two S.S. soldiers and a big, ugly Spandau machine gun with an ominous-looking perforated barrel. The guards acted nervous. At night the big searchlights in the towers crisscrossed the entire area with their beams. On top of that, special squads of S.S. patrolled the camp streets and alleys after curfew. They had machine pistols and dogs. The old-timers said they were just thugs in S.S. uniform who notched their belts for every prisoner they killed and were so bored on a long, cold snowy winter's night that if a face appeared at a barracks window a second after seven o'clock, they blasted it.

A fenced-in section at the camp's main entrance intrigued him. New prisoners were held there while they were processed. Sometimes, when an incoming group arrived late at night, the Germans would wait until the next day to start the paperwork and leave the prisoners overnight in the fenced area.

It didn't look heavily guarded.

If you could make the fenced-in area before the curfew and hide there until night, it might be easier to sneak behind the main, barbed-wire fence where there were several small buildings. One was a hut where they stored straw for the mattresses. You could stay under the straw until you were ready to make a break. Because the fenced-in section was located almost directly under one of the guard towers, you'd be in the tower's blind spot.

He couldn't sleep. It wasn't just the bed bugs and the stink of the overflowing barrels. He was enraged with himself: he'd been in Royal Lieu for almost a week and he hadn't come up with a single, solid scheme for getting out.

In his mind he again ran through the escape possibilities of the fenced-in area. Yes, it could work. It could – as long as he was able to cover up his tracks in the snow. They'd lead from his block directly to the straw-storage hut.

But maybe there was another angle – the sewer. The manhole which was located in an alley between the long blocks of huts and out of the line-of-sight of the guard towers.

As the days of December 1943 dwindled, Royal Lieu's barracks became more crowded with new arrivals. A hundred one day. A hundred-and-fifty the next. Two hundred-and-fifty the day after.

The roll calls took longer and longer. The tension grew; who'd be on the next shipment out? When would it be called?

In the dormitories the prisoners huddled in little cliques and conspiracies. It was more to keep up morale than to escape, because the Germans had thought of everything.

Nicholas saw only one prisoner who looked as if he might be of some use. He was a big, fleshy Frenchman who had run a whore-house in Paris for German officers. The velvet-tongued brothelkeeper moved easily among the French prisoners. He had befriended a pimp named Michel, whom the Germans had put in charge of Nicholas's block. Through Michel the whoremaster was able to have food parcels smuggled in past the gate guards. Men sought his delectable goods on the outside; now they likewise yearned for his delicacies on the inside.

For some reason he took a liking to the black American and invited him and other select prisoners to share his cold lobster, smoked salmon, sausages, hams, chocolates, cigarettes, coffee, brandy, and wine.

Nicholas eagerly accepted. So did Michel.

The set-up was perfect for cultivating the man, who had good contacts among Paris's German officer corps, and the pimp, who knew how to persuade the German guards to look the other way. Nicholas was betting that the pimp could get a letter through the barbed wire; the brothelkeeper could certainly arrange for it to be delivered to some officer who, in turn, could get it to Gardemann.

It was a long shot, but ... meantime he'd continue to brainstorm for other possibilities ...

If Colonel Gardemann knew the mess his black friend

was in, Nicholas assured himself, he'd spring him in twenty-four hours, even if it was just to keep him from talking: Gardemann knew Nicholas had incriminating information on him. He'd known for years, which was why the colonel had been so responsive to Nicholas' steady stream of requests in the past: to keep his mouth shut.

Nicholas knew that the colonel lived in fear that his superiors would one day find out he'd been sleeping with an exotic black woman while on the other side of the Atlantic, and that he had fathered her several children. What would the race-conscious, Aryan-worshipping German Army have to say about that? If Nazi ideology held that Jews were subhumans, what about blacks? Gardemann's career would be finished. He'd be drummed out of the *Abwehr* or banished to a concentration camp for the sin of race-defilement, as Hitler called it.

Gardemann had thought that by abandoning the woman and children he'd solved his problem. He had – until the day that Nicholas had shown up in Paris on the doorstep of the Hotel Majestic.

The Germans and their honour, thought Nicholas. To protect it, Gardemann had given him almost anything he'd ever asked for. A car and gasoline. An *Ausweis*. Money.

Gardemann wasn't just any German officer. He'd been serving ostensibly as the military attaché to the German embassy in Haiti when he met the black woman. In reality he'd been a secret agent of the *Abwehr's* North American desk. And being with the *Abwehr*, it was highly doubtful that Gardemann was his real name. All such agents used cover names and identities.

But in appearance Colonel Schmidt or Gardemann hadn't changed: Nicholas had recognized him right away when he'd visited him in Paris Military Headquarters.

Nicholas was confident that the message – with the help of the whorehouse operator and the pimp – must have gone through the barbed wire. When Gardemann received it, he'd run all the way across Europe to rescue his black nemesis.

The dawn of the New Year 1944 slanted in over Royal Lieu. The water supply was down to a dribble. The prisoners held tin cans under eavestroughs to collect melting snow.

It was a sure sign that the camp's facilities had been stretched to the limit. It could take no more bodies. A shipment out was only a matter of hours away. It would be a mammoth one.

Morale was depleted. Hopelessness infected them all like an energy-draining disease.

Damn the Germans! thought Nicholas. The letter to Gardemann was on its way. Soon he'd hear them call his name over the public-address system, summoning him to the gatehouse.

There would be his good friend Gardemann.

But mid-January came and no word from the colonel. The shipments started. At roll call the numbers were fired off, striking the men in front of him, behind him, those on the left and right.

It was unbearable watching them pack. Their comrades would slip them a can of food and a few words of encouragement. They'd shuffle out of the barracks like kicked dogs, their little rucksacks on their backs and wisecracks on their lips that fooled nobody.

For Nicholas it was now really hitting close to home. In the barracks at night he'd see the empty bunks. He stole down the dormitory aisle to the brothelkeeper's bunk and huddled there with him a long time. The next day he reported to the camp infirmary with a toothache, as the whoremaster had told him to do, and received from the camp dentist an injection that boosted his temperature for about ten days.

It was strange: the Germans would beat you to death if they felt like it. But they'd never break the rule which said that a prisoner couldn't be put on a shipment if he had a fever!

Just as Nicholas was due to return for some booster shots, his fat French benefactor himself vanished on a shipment.

It was long past curfew.

From his bunk he watched the searchlight beams flit across the dormitory wall. Periodically he heard the crunch of heavy boots on snow as the S.S. patrol tramped by with their whining dogs.

The smell wasn't too bad; half the men were gone: the buckets no longer slopped over. There wasn't as much snoring and screaming as before.

Still he couldn't sleep.

Still nothing from Gardemann.

Why hadn't his name been called for shipment? Maybe Gardemann had received the letter and pulled some strings. No, he was forced to concede. Gardemann hadn't received the letter.

He was sweating heavily despite the cold, burning with a slow rage because the S.S. had succeeded in breaking through his bravado.

Nietzsche mocked him: slaves and masters! He was trembling. He had sworn that he wouldn't let them do it to him! But they'd done it, by God.

He eased back the evil-smelling blanket, raised himself on one elbow and peered through the dormitory darkness. Slowly he got up, quietly placed his feet on the floor and began to pull on his clothes.

The carpet of fresh snow muffled his footfalls as he stole into the shadow-filled alleys between the long lines of barracks. His ego gleamed with the prospect of defying the S.S. *and* the predatory searchlight beams.

He pressed himself flat against the sides of the buildings as he slid past barracks after barracks.

The frigid air seared his nostrils and stung the tissues of his throat. He stopped frequently to listen and look, breathing deeply, exhilarated by a sense of freedom and the clouds of his own vapour freezing on his forehead. At the corner of one block he waited for the searchlight's silver shaft to glide elsewhere before he flitted across the street ahead. No sounds of patrols. Or dogs. He pressed his ear to the barracks wall. Silent as a morgue.

It was too easy, he told himself, reflecting on all the tales he'd heard about how alert the guards and their beasts were and the notches on the belts.

He dashed across the street – less cautiously.

Fifteen minutes after leaving his dormitory he had reached the corner of the alley by the sewer. He squatted, unable to believe he'd not been detected. Stealthily he began moving down the alley, crouching low, staying close to the barracks. Two-thirds of the way along he stopped, slid into the centre of the alley and began combing the snow for the manhole cover, gradually expanding his radius of exploration.

After several minutes his fingers were numbing, his anger rising.

He couldn't find the cover!

He stopped. Maybe his fingers were too dead to feel it. Or was it two-thirds of the way from the other end of the alley? Jesus! Could he be in the wrong alley?

No! He couldn't be wrong. He had rehearsed it so carefully in his mind.

He was clawing away again at the snow, panting so hard with frustration and exertion that he almost didn't hear the crunching footsteps.

He froze. His ego swore at him, cursing him for being afraid and commanding him to go right on scratching. But his instincts screamed at him to get out of there . . .

With agonizing reluctance he grudgingly surrendered to his pragmatic side. Slithering off down the alley, he was flooded with shame; it was an emotion that he loathed.

Blocks away he skulked in the shadows, leaning against a barracks, afire with humiliation. He tried to persuade himself that he hadn't really intended to escape; that he'd just been curious. If indeed the manhole *were* wide enough to fit a man's body, the Germans would have sealed it long ago. But the cans of food and the rolls of smoked sausage in his pockets, courtesy of his rotund French friend, made a liar of him: he'd bungled it!

He slumped in the snow banked up against the barracks and gazed absent-mindedly at the searchlight elipses gliding across the white-mantled roofs, the exhilaration of the past half-hour leaking out of him. Gradually he became aware that he was in an unfamiliar section of the camp. Ahead was a street. Not the usual street. This one was about twice or three times as wide as the streets he'd been travelling. It was the no-man's land between two sections of the camp that all the prisoners talked about.

His sullen features began to crinkle in amusement as he realized where he was! But where were the guards? The two pairs of them said to patrol that top-security sector twenty-four hours a day?

He didn't have to wait very long. Two soldiers, heavily muffled against the cold, trudged past his hiding place. Their machine pistols dangled from their shoulders and their gloved hands were jammed into their pockets.

As he waited for them to pass, he felt his disgust over the manhole debacle softening. He was about to redeem himself.

He zipped across the wide street and disappeared down the dark alleys between the barracks. Cold but tingling with uncontainable excitement, he stopped, checked the food in his pockets and rapped softly on a door.

He rapped again, this time whispering a French greeting.

The door opened a fraction and the fragrance of perfume, the essence of female, assailed his nostrils.

It had been two months since he'd roused to a woman's primal odours.

They'd never believe it back at the dormitory – but he'd made it!

The women prisoners of Royal Lieu hadn't seen a non-German male – let alone a black Adonis with a velvet tongue – in months. They smuggled him inside, giggling

55

nervously, hugging him and relieving him of his gifts. Smothered by their welcome, he slowly thawed his frigid body against theirs . . . For a fleeting instant he longed for Florence.

When he left, it was nearly time for the reveille whistle. If his block leader discovered him absent, he'd be reported to the N.C.O. holding the roll call.

He didn't give a damn. His big body was one great smile. And besides, his luck was coming through once again: the snow was falling heavily, mercifully covering over his tracks.

It was 25 January 1944. As the first names and numbers were bellowed, terror shrank each man's belly. An hour later, when more than a thousand names had been called, the terrible tension became bearable: no longer did they have to wonder when. They knew and could resign themselves to quiet desperation.

Few could eat. The latrines were overcrowded. In the dormitories they tied string around their cheap, battered suitcases and stuffed precious personal items into pilfered mattress covers.

The great phalanx of doomed men emptied out of the parade ground. Some of the prosperous ones wore skiing outfits and heavy fur boots reminiscent of campers on a hike. But it was the last time that clothes would separate the privileged from the poor.

The line curved sinuously through the fenced-off enclosure and past a shack where tired, irritable guards checked identities and records.

At the Gare de l'Est station in Paris the train was already at the platform when they clambered out of the trucks. German soldiers slid back the doors of boxcars bearing stencilled notices of their carrying capacity – 'Forty Men, Eight Horses' – and ordered them to climb aboard until each was crammed with 120 men. Into their midst they slid a large, metal tub along the floor. Then they slammed the doors shut and locked them on the outside with a lead seal.

Light slanted through slatted windows latticed with barbed wire. Bodies were packed tightly. Even before the train moved they were cursing and elbowing each other as the bigger, tougher ones fought to corner the space. There was a sudden, stabbing scream of terror in the packed gloom as one bully planted a knee in the crotch of a frail, grey-haired university professor who'd been urging that the human mass go about allocating space in an orderly, intelligent manner. The younger man then flung the doubled-up old professor into the crowd and took his spot on the floor, daring anyone else to come close to him. In the back of the car, another man moaned in claustraphobic agony but he was quickly muffled by a fist that shot out from somewhere like the tongue of a startled snake.

Nicholas bulked large and unassailable in the crush of bodies. He felt oddly elated: for the first time since being snapped up by the Gestapo in Florence's apartment he was no longer directly under the heel of the Nazis. He tingled with anticipation at the opportunity to regain control over his own circumstances. True, he and the others were caged animals who'd be instantly shot if they tried to escape. But inside the intolerable boxcar he knew he could be master of his own situation. He even experienced a pang of forgiveness for his traitorous blonde girlfriend who'd put him there.

But now, as he listened to the bickering and battering among his fellow passengers grow in intensity, for once he wasn't thinking only of his own hide. Sure, he could whip anyone in the car. Maybe two or three of them at the same time. He knew how to handle himself. Once he'd seriously thought about a professional boxing career. Joe Louis was his great hero, and he also had the Brown Bomber's physique. People had even told him he had a strong facial resemblance to the famous American heavyweight. His calisthenics had kept him in shape. He was a full head taller than most of the Europeans hunched around him in the mobile pigpen.

His size commanded attention. But there was more to it than that. He had been the only American at Compiegne. All of the prisoners knew him and the stories about him had become the talk of the camp. His escapades that snowy night in the women's compound had made him a big hero – especially among those who'd led lives of forced abstinence for months. The prisoners had relished his accomplishment vicariously. They had recounted his 'evening abroad' many times as a way of killing the boredom, adding all kinds of embellishments and garnishments that would amaze him when he heard them. Still, he denied nothing.

When quizzed about the episode, Nicholas would grin enigmatically, then deflect the queries in provocative generalities calculated to whet their appetite for additional details. It was great theatre, and he revelled in once again being the centre of attention, at having the adulation of an audience. Usually he'd spin them a yarn or two – sometimes partly true, sometimes completely conjured out of his full-colour imagination – just for the occasion. Hell, it didn't matter. There was nothing else to fight the misery of Compiegne. Let them have their fun, he thought.

The story of his arrest had got around the camp, too. They wanted to know more about how the Gestapo had dragged him out of the blonde's bed at six in the morning. Tell us, Johnny.

It was my bed, not hers, he'd tease.

Hey, Johnny. Was she really *that* good? Was she really worth it?

A gentleman never, never tells. You guys ought to know that.

And he'd get a loud guffaw out of them.

They kept quizzing him about the United States. About the long-awaited invasion of Europe. About everything and anything. And if he didn't know the answer, it didn't inhibit him from inventing one.

Hey, Johnny, when did you drop into France? What was your mission?

C'mon now. If I told you, the Gestapo would feel bad: I wouldn't want to hurt their precious feelings.

He talked and talked but said very little. This provoked his admirers to a blizzard of wild, high-flying speculation about him – which he wouldn't confirm or deny. 'You know how it is,' he'd say, which explained nothing but flattered them by implying that they had a worldliness matching his. And after the bull sessions, his audience would hustle back to their blocks to re-tell the latest anecdote about 'Johnny' – embellishing it with their own hyperbole.

'Johnny,' pleaded a young French student in the boxcar, 'if we don't get some order in here they're going to kill themselves.'

The bickering, the pushing and shoving was growing worse. A fist rammed out over Nicholas' shoulder and crunched against the student's mouth. Nicholas reached up, grabbed the wrist and yanked the arm down, almost snapping it over his shoulder. Its owner squealed with pain. 'Everyone shut up!' Nicholas roared.

The snarling and snapping partly subsided.

'I said shut up, goddammit!'

It became very quiet.

'Okay,' he continued loudly, 'Calm down, for Christ's sake, before we have a panic on our hands!... We're going to take turns sitting and standing!'

'Go flog yourself nigger!' rasped a voice from the back of the boxcar. 'Who made you the boss?'

'Come a little closer and you'll find out!' Nicholas spat back at his challenger.

'Give 'em hell, Johnny!' a Nicholas supporter called out.

A small crowd roared approval. One of them scoffed at

the man who had challenged Nicholas's growing authority. 'Yes, big man. Why don't you come over here and tell Johnny who's going to run things?'

'Okay, as I said,' continued Nicholas, his authority now confirmed, 'we'll take turns sitting and standing. Let's get on with it. Each of you take a number. Sound off with a number and remember it. Even numbers'll sit for a half hour. Then odd numbers'll take their place.'

They picked up the idea loudly and enthusiastically, calling out their numbers in order. It was difficult in the boxcar's half-light. Sometimes two or three yelled a number simultaneously, so Nicholas had to referee. It finally came to an end when the count reached 120.

No one had a watch: the guards had seen to that. Nicholas told them to count the clacks of the wheels on the track as a rough guide to the length of the half-hour periods. Until the train started moving, however, he tagged two prisoners to monitor the time by counting aloud.

The hum of conversation, the shuffling of feet and the rustling of bodies gradually waned, and each man was soon alone with his fears.

They heard the Gare de l'Est's familiar sounds through the boxcar's wooden walls. The impatient whistling of trains ... the clatter of thousands of footfalls in the great amphitheatre of the station ... the rapid-fire French of harried railway conductors.

Outside, life was going on. Inside, it was the beginning of the end.

At 1 p.m. the boxcar jerked. Buffers clanked and they glided out of the station.

Nicholas's foghorn voice boomed the opening strains of the *Marseillaise*. Instantly a chorus of hoarse voices exploded in support.

They sang until Paris was far behind and silence pulled on their vocal chords like a heavy pack after a long journey. From time to time some of them, catching sight

60

of railwaymen at the little rural stations along the way, tossed notes out through the slats.

It was the desperate hope of sailors lost at sea for rescue.

By the time the freezing European night had shrouded the long train, Paris was more than a hundred miles away. In the crammed boxcar the stacatto clack-clack resonated painfully through their skulls. The tub was close to overflowing. In the airless space the stench thickened. They vomited, unavoidably splashing their neighbors. Tempers flared, but Nicholas kept order.

Suddenly the train jerked to a halt. A babble of nervous conversation rattled like rain on a tin roof. Then silence as they heard the clicking sounds of someone outside turning a key in the locks on the boxcar. The doors scraped back and a blast of frigid air swept through the rectangular opening.

'Out of the way! Out of the way!' shouted two helmeted German shadows.

The prisoners were paralyzed.

Nicholas called out in German: 'Where are we?'

'You'll soon find out!' said one of the soldiers. He pointed to the urine tub and ordered two prisoners to lift the brimming vessel onto the platform and replace it with an empty tub.

A flashlight beam stabbed the boxcar's dark interior. An officious voice ordered all to crowd into the back half of the boxcar. An S.S. officer, in gloves and topcoat, vaulted inside. 'On your feet!' he snarled to the weaker ones who were slow to comply. 'To the back of the boxcar!'

Nicholas thought: they wouldn't give us a new tub if they were going to kill us. He tried to look behind the flashlight glare to see the officer's face. He could only distinguish the typical arrogant, high-crowned, peaked-cap silhouette he knew so well.

When they were crammed back as far as possible, the

officer pointed to them with a riding crop. '*Ein!*' he shouted.

The prisoners didn't understand.

'*Ein!*' he shouted impatiently. '*Zwei!*' He gestured angrily. '*Drei!*'

'He's trying to count us!' Nicholas called out in French. 'Follow me!'

He moved directly into the glare of the German's flashlight. The others, who had been cowering like frightened deer, scampered after him.

When the head count was completed, the officer jumped down onto the platform. Nicholas heard him report to a senior officer that all *Stucke* were present and accounted for.

Stucke meant head of cattle. From now on they were no longer regarded as human beings.

The train rattled eastward into the German heartland. The air in the boxcar once again was thick and the vile tub splattered its loathsome contents each time the train lurched.

To set an example for the others, Nicholas had refused to take his sit-down time during the half-hour intervals. It wasn't easy. His feet were numb. The muscles in his legs and back were paralyzed by cramps. He braced himself against the wall and tried to fight queasiness. He chastised himself for not attempting to break through the fence at Royal Lieu. Intermittently he lapsed into a standing sleep. Then he'd awaken and force himself to play mental games to stay alert: if given another chance to escape, by God, he'd be ready and he'd take it . . .

In the early hours of the morning the screeching of the train's brakes jolted him awake. He was angry for having dozed off.

The train halted, releasing puffs of steam that wafted by Nicholas's boxcar. Then silence. He heard footfalls on the cement platform. The click of bolts. The sliding of the door. He felt the rush of icy air.

'My friends,' said a throaty female voice. 'We are the

Swiss Red Cross. We have coffee and food for you. You may get out on the platform and stretch your legs.'

Nicholas was sure it was some evil German trick. After the miseries of Fresnes and Compiegne he knew there was nothing a German wouldn't stoop to. Yet the aroma of hot coffee and soup couldn't be denied. He cautioned his fellow passengers to remain inside while he poked his head through the doorway. By the dim, coloured station lights he saw the platform crowded with prisoners from the other boxcars. They were holding cups and cramming sandwiches into their mouths. Weak with relief the men in Nicholas' boxcar followed him down onto the platform.

'What's the name of this town, *madamoiselle*?' Nicholas asked a girl who handed him a mug of steaming coffee.

'Trêves,' she said pleasantly.

'That would put us close to Luxembourg,' said Nicholas.

'Yes, *monsieur*.'

He picked at his sandwich; his stomach couldn't make the transition. 'How far, *madamoiselle*?'

'Please, *monsieur*,' she whispered. 'The German commandant has instructed us not to discuss such things. He permits us here as a courtesy. If there were any incidents, he would not allow us to do it again. It would spoil it for those coming after you.'

'I understand, *madamoiselle*... Perfectly. How far?'

She casually glanced up and down the platform, checking on the location of the surprisingly few uniformed Germans in evidence. 'About ten kilometres,' she said softly.

'You're very kind,' he whispered back.

'Please,' she pleaded. 'Don't do anything that will make it impossible for us to do for others what we've done for you.'

'Don't let them fool you. They're doing it for propaganda purposes – and you and your friends will go back

63

to Switzerland and tell the world the Germans are humanitarians.'

'Please, I must not be seen spending too much time with you. I must go.'

'About ten kilometres?'

'Don't let the absence of uniforms deceive you. The station is ringed with soldiers – only you can't see them. You would never get away.'

'*Merci beaucoup, madamoiselle.*'

'I'm very sorry,' said the girl sadly.

'Tell me one more thing: where's this train headed?'

The girl lowered her eyes.

'Where? Where?'

'I beg you, *monsieur*,' she said in a soft, anguished voice. She pulled her coffee cart back and rushed off to serve another group of prisoners.

Nicholas was left standing alone, sipping his coffee. He watched his bearded companions in their splotched and wrinkled clothes self-consciously stretch in the freezing pre-dawn air. With their shoulders hunched, wolfing down the black bread, sausage and cheese pressed on them by their Swiss hosts, they were rumpled beggars with no resemblance to the defiant Frenchmen who had roared out the *Marseillaise* twelve hours earlier.

Ten kilometres or one hundred, thought Nicholas. What difference would it make to a black man trying to escape in Europe? He mingled with the little groups of prisoners, quietly telling them what he had learned about their location and the small chances of escape.

Deeper into the Fatherland rattled the train, puffing more strenuously now as it snaked into the foothills of the Harz Mountains.

Those standing and those sitting had traded positions many times since leaving Paris. By the end of the first day, however, many had collapsed from nervous exhaustion and fatigue despite the half-hour rest periods that Nicholas and the other, stronger prisoners had fought successively to maintain.

Whenever there was a fight or a problem they called to 'Johnny.' He had become their leader. He liked it. In his own exhaustion he still found the strength of will to enjoy it. He continued to keep them stilled and hushed with his tales and stories of better days... the U.S. Eighth Air Force in England bombing Berlin to cinders ... the Free French, a crack fighting machine in England, poised for the crossing of the Channel and the liberation of their homeland ...

The body heat lost at Trêves gradually built up again. The air, breathed and re-breathed, stifled him. He was afraid he would throw up and lose face. To him it would be the most humiliating thing imaginable after the power play he'd engineered. He fought the nausea, wave after wave. He struggled against the overpowering urge to drop off to sleep standing up. That would also be embarrassing. The babbling of the sick and the dying had worn down his powers of concentration and his mind began drifting.

He could see the sun disappear behind the mountains of his home on the other side of the ocean. In the silence he could hear a *burro* braying, a dog barking. Up in the hills the poor were cooking their pathetic little suppers over charcoal fires, and he'd soon be going home to an elegant meal in his elegant home. But the beach was broad and white, and the girl on the blanket slender and black ...

Johnny! Why are you home so late? Where have you been? Oh, Johnny! What are we going to do with you? We've told you again and again: we don't want you associating with that girl! She is not from a good family. You will never be the man your father is, Johnny, if you don't spend more time at your school work ...

He could feel again the clawing boredom. The urge to stampede ...

He thought of Paris in peacetime. The *gendarme* with his white baton always at Rue du Harve and Boulevard Haussman. The parapet at the Pont des Arts as the barges floated by. The writers, the politicians, the musicians and movie people populating the Deux Magots, the Café de

Flore and the Brasserie Lipp. Sipping a wine outdoors with a newly found painter friend. Across the street the girls of the Grande Chaumière waiting for an offer to paint them in the nude . . .

How pale Florence's skin had looked beside his brownness. What a body! He wondered whose sheets she'd slipped between that morning – the poor unsuspecting bastard!

And then there was Gardemann. Did he ever get the message? Jesus! What if he'd received it but wasn't going to lift a finger, figuring his troubles were over at last, now that Nicholas – the only one who could squeal on him – was on a one-way trip to Germany?

For three anguished days they travelled. Nicholas's stories had worn thin. He'd maintained his monologue of optimism, but it hadn't been enough to sustain a dozen of his fellow prisoners now stacked like a bundle of wood in the back of the car. Their faces were frozen in the furrows of despair, their bodies stiff as boards.

Strange that they had to die, Nicholas thought. At Compiegne the Germans wouldn't put a man on a shipment if he had a fever. These men all had been passably healthy three days previously.

Was it possible, he wondered, that three days of vomiting and diarrhoea could have fatally dehydrated them? In biology they'd impressed on them how vital it was for a cell to have water to survive. Other than their own urine, they had no water aboard. Maybe the cause of death *had* been dehydration, he thought. But as he inventoried his medical knowledge, it seemed that shock was a more likely explanation. At the hospital where he'd worked they said that any trauma to the body – physical or emotional – could produce a dangerous drop in blood pressure and a pulse that was feeble and rapid. Three days of being compressed like subway riders at rush hour: for a man with claustrophobia it was like being buried alive in a mass grave. If you weren't terrified by closed spaces, it was still an unimaginable mental trauma.

He wondered why they all hadn't gone crazy: when the oxygen content of air dropped below twenty percent, he'd been taught, the brain stopped performing at peak efficiency. When it got down to sixteen percent, the mind started playing tricks, sending and receiving false sensory signals. One hundred and twenty men in a boxcar made to hold forty men and eight animals. That meant roughly half the normal air supply. Yes, he told himself, that would do it.

The physiology of it all piqued his insatiable curiosity about medical things and provided him with something to take his mind off his aching head and churning stomach. He had a sudden wild fear that the twelve men weren't really dead. But he went over his procedures in his mind again and assured himself that he'd done correctly everything he'd been taught: there'd been no pulse in the wrist, so he'd pressed his fingers into the neck, feeling for a beat in the carotid artery. In the dark, where no one had a match, he knew it would have been pointless to thumb back the eyelids and look for pupil response. So he'd done the only other thing possible; he'd put his ear against the chest and listened, hoping that in the incessant hammering of the wheels he wasn't missing a heart sound or the rise and fall of a rib cage.

Yes, he told himself, they were dead. Quite dead.

From what he'd been able to judge by feel, they were all fleshy, overweight corpses. If they were middle-aged or older, he reflected, that would make them probable candidates for cardiovascular complications – particularly under severe emotional stress. So, he concluded, the unlucky dozen had most likely suffered cardiac arrest or cerebral haemorrage.

He wondered if an autopsy would confirm his diagnosis. But, then, he'd never done a postmortem . . .

The frustrating thing about it was that he could do nothing to help; he didn't even have an aspirin!

The train hissed and screeched to a stop. The boxcar doors scraped back again. Guards poked rifle butts into the soft, numb and stuporous mass of prisoners, trying to pry them out onto the station platform. '*Aufstehen! Aufstehen!* On your feet! On your feet! *Heraus! Heraus!* Get moving! Get moving!'

Nicholas stood defiantly at the door and slowly looked around. He breathed in the sweet air gratefully and stretched to ease the terrible cramps and pains shooting through his body. It was dark. The station was dimly lit. He stared at the cordon of sullen guards, obviously enraged because they'd been rousted from warm bunks for another shipment of *stucke*. Their fierce-looking police dogs yapped peevishly and bucked on leashes. In the background S.S. officers clumped in twos and threes, chatted casually.

Nicholas jumped down off the boxcar and turned to face his friends. He read the terror etched on their faces. Awful as the boxcar had been, it represented the known and they seemed reluctant to leave it. Ahead was unknown. 'Gentlemen!' he said to them, gesturing expansively toward the receiving line of guards, 'welcome to the Riviera! Taxis will be along shortly to take you to your hotels!' Incredibly, after three days of hell, his effort produced a few snickers.

'Okay,' said Nicholas. 'Let's get the bodies.'

By now it was automatic: when 'Johnny' said something, they moved and asked no questions. They formed a chain and passed the bodies from the boxcar to the platform's freezing concrete.

Eventually ninety-five corpses from the entire train were laid neatly side by side at the station of Weimar.

Weimar! How sadistically ironical, thought Nicholas. The birthplace of Nietzsche, whose philosophies he had so admired: the world is divided into slaves and masters...

It was early morning of 28 January 1944, and Nicholas was standing on the station platform, one of a thousand slaves waiting meekly for their German masters to herd them off.

But first the roll call.

It was noon when the S.S. was finally satisfied that all *stucke* were present and accounted for. Then they were marched off in a column-of-fives to waiting trucks. They stumbled docilely toward the vehicles and jerked spastically when the burly stormtroopers barked at them.

Nicholas had been separated from his boxcar companions. The men in his truck were strangers. He noticed that while the other trucks were packed, with some bodies teetering on the tailgates, his truck was half empty. When the tailgate clanked shut, two S.S. men with machine-pistols rode in the back with them.

They were driven through Weimar's narrow, winding streets hemmed in by steep-gabled houses whose roofs were layered with snow. In other circumstances, thought Nicholas, the beautiful setting would have captivated him.

The town receded behind them and they were soon rolling smoothly through country clumped with majestic snow-laden trees.

Had Nicholas and the others in his truck known that the initials 'NN-RU' were penciled behind their names on the S.S. roll-call list, they would have understood why they were being accorded a special reception.

The impending arrival of Christmas in 1943 reminded Vildebart Nicolas that he hadn't seen or heard from his brother in months. Vildebart was ill and in hospital, so he sent his wife André across Paris to the apartment in the Eiffel Tower area to see if Johnny was all right.

On a cold, dreary December day she arrived there to discover that a new tenant occupied the luxurious quarters on the fifth floor.

The family there was sorry: they knew nothing about a *Monsieur* Nicholas. They had never heard of him.

She took the elevator down to the first floor again and inquired at the office of the concierge. He told her that her brother-in-law had been arrested about a month previously. Many, knowing the significance of a Gestapo arrest, would have gone home, content to leave well enough alone. Yet André, a small but determined white woman, went personally to Gestapo headquarters in the Rue des Saussaises. She was told that they had never heard of any Johnny Nicholas; that the name meant nothing to them. She told the German on the desk that her brother-in-law was a tall, light-coloured Negro and that it was impossible for them not to have noticed him. They repeated that they had no record of him. They admitted that there had been arrests on November 23 in the Eiffel Tower area but denied that any of them had involved a Negro.

André and Vildebart were shocked and mystified. They didn't know then of the infamous *Nact und Nebel* arrests being made all over France at the time. If they had, they would have understood the conflicting information they had received.

Nacht und Nebel (Night and Fog) are the opening words of an incantation in the *Nibelungenlied*, a 13th-century German epic poem. The words were adopted by Hitler, and thus by the Gestapo, for an executive order authorizing the deportation of persons in Occupied Europe considered lethal enemies of the German state. When people were arrested as NNs, they automatically became non-persons as far as official records were concerned. All trace of them was erased. They disappeared into the 'night and fog,' and administratively had never been born. Yet they lived on in the limbo of concentration camps, with the letters NN-RU behind their names on a roll-call list.

Every S.S. camp guard knew that this notation licensed him to submit such prisoners to the utmost in brutality and deprivation. The complete phrase *Nacht und Nebel – Rukkehr Ungewunscht* translates into 'Night and Fog – Return Not Desired.' In effect it meant 'Dangerous Terrorist – To be Eliminated.'

Chapter Four

The snow was falling when the truck pulled into the earthly hell of Buchenwald concentration camp.

The scene was deceptively peaceful – almost picturesque with the thick, white mantle clinging to the roofs of the barracks and swept up in luxurious drifts around their walls, erasing their harsh, forbidding lines. Outside the electrified fence the tall branches of the stately pine trees drooped under their heavy load of snow, reminding Nicholas of a Christmas card. The naked light bulbs outside each building seemed to form a decorative string of stars against the night sky. From the top of the tower a searchlight's narrow beam probed the night, sweeping back and forth across the camp, lingering here and there in the shadows between the buildings, exploring them momentarily, then circling on.

He noticed a building that looked like a chapel. It had a tall steeple. In the dark it was hard to be sure.

The truck skidded to a halt in the thick snow and a guard barked at them to get out. Nicholas and his companions from Compiegne were glad for the chance to stretch their stiff limbs; they'd ridden from the railway station at Weimar in the open truck and were shivering. The truck whined off, leaving them standing there, stamping the ground to start the heat flowing once again in their frigid bodies.

An S.S. noncommissioned officer told them in broken French to form into a column, then marched them off.

The snow muffled their steps, and their battered suitcases – the last remaining links with home and the familiar – swung by their sides.

71

The building blazed with light. They squinted and had to cover their eyes as they entered. Suddenly the pungent odour of disinfectant burned their nostrils and throats. The floor was brick and scrupulously clean. Along one wall was a row of gleaming, white wash basins. The only other furnishings were several long, wooden tables.

The S.S. guard told them they would spend the rest of the night there.

At four o'clock in the morning the lights suddenly flooded the room. The guard told them they must be ready to go in thirty minutes.

In half an hour he came for them and lined them up outside the building in which Nicholas had thought was a chapel. Atop the huge curved archway of the main gate a battery of searchlights blazed on. Nicholas followed their thin, pencil beams down to a vast, bare area carpeted with fresh snow. Beyond that he could see endless rows of barracks separated by broad, symmetrical walkways. From the first rows of barracks, men in bizarre costumes began to emerge. They would have looked more at home in a circus in their crimson trousers and green vests. They hurried double-time, beating on drums and blowing horns. Then they formed a perfect formation in the vast assembly area facing the huge main gate.

Looking beyond the costumed musicians to the barracks Nicholas now saw figures flood onto the assembly area; waves and waves of them, until the snow was black with bodies packed tightly in perfect squares.

The walkways between the squares were blocked here and there with motionless figures lying on the frozen ground.

The morning roll call at Buchenwald concentration camp had begun.

The prisoner hordes were skeletons in rags that stank like dead rats. Their blue-striped uniforms were vulcanized into a rubbery grime. Beneath their stubbly faces their skin pulled taut against their cheekbones. They wore

72

their shapeless caps pulled low over their faces and ears as if they were drowned in shame.

Although the snow muted their movements, the freezing air carried the hum of their whispering, moaning, coughing and wheezing. The gatehouse searchlight beams flitted capriciously over their tortured ranks, pausing occasionally to satisfy the curiosity of the operator, warm in the gatehouse tower. In brilliant cones the light bathed an old man with feet swathed in paper and tied with string, a young man with his head wrapped in pus-soaked bandages so bulky that they almost covered his face. Intermittently, the beam would fall on better-clothed men with clean prisoner uniforms and armed with clubs. They roamed the walkways, snarling and cursing, beating the rapidly freezing men into tighter, more perfect formations.

Nicholas watched incredulously.

The command '*Mutzen Ab*!' crashing across the public-address system and amplified a thousand times, shattered his eardrums.

Instantly 35,000 men removed their caps. Incredibly, they did it like puppets on a string.

'*Mutzen Auf*!'

With the same impeccable precision the puppets snappily replaced their caps.

The roll call began. It would not end until every single name had been accounted for. Regardless of time, weather, life or death, the roll call ground on and on as the prisoners shivered and died in the cold.

Dozens of times the S.S. roll-call leaders mispronounced names. A prisoner could be present, but if he didn't hear his name correctly, he didn't answer; he was therefore listed as missing and assured of a brutal beating when the guards eventually located him. Sometimes a prisoner couldn't answer: he had died during the ordeal, which often lasted three hours. It wasn't unusual for the S.S. records office to fall behind in its massive paperwork. As a result names of men who were dead or who

73

had been transferred to other camps would be screamed meaninglessly and endlessly over the loudspeakers. To fill the blanks on their clipboards the tenacious roll-call leaders would launch a second roll-call, using prisoner numbers instead of names.

Time meant nothing to them: a roll-call such as this could take six hours.

Nicholas saw a figure topple over and hit the granite-like ledge of compacted snow with a brittle snap. Like a movement in a carefully rehearsed military drill, those around him picked up his body and passed it hand-to-hand until it was finally laid on a sidewalk by the barracks.

Immediately the men with the clubs, the *Lagerschutz* – prisoners appointed as security police – milled into the formation with clubs swinging, hammering the living into the spaces left by the dead.

Nicholas, mesmerized by the spectacle, had lost all track of time. He didn't know if it was one hour later or two or three when the public-address system again boomed '*Mutzen Ab!*' Once again he saw the caps come off in amazing unison. '*Mutzen Auf!*' They were replaced with equal precision. But this was not good enough to satisfy the chief roll-call leader. Standing on a raised platform, his greatcoat buttoned up to the neck and his hands heavily gloved against the brutal cold, he screamed the pair of commands a half-dozen times before he finally dismissed the formation.

Immediately the mass of humanity disintegrated as the pitiful prisoners hobbled stiffly back to their quarters, driven by the flailing clubs of the *Lagerschutz*. '*Aufstehen! Aufstehen!* On your feet! Get in there,' they snarled.

Nicholas heard an S.S. NCO shout an order at him and his comrades to march back to the washroom where they had spent the night. On the way he felt his stomach churn with the memory of the prisoners' skins stretched across their cheekbones like parchment, their gaping mouths, their sunken, staring eyes. When the morning's dead trundled past him in handcarts toward the building with the steeple, he knew the structure was no chapel.

Back in the washroom, prisoner attendants ordered him to strip. He was told to put his clothes on the hanger they gave him, place his valuables in the bag they handed him, pack everything into his suitcase which he had to tie with the length of string provided him. Finally he had to write his name and address on a label and stick it on his suitcase.

He was ordered into an adjoining room where a dozen electric clippers were hanging from the ceiling. One of the attendants grabbed a pair and began shearing Nicholas's head, face, armpits, crotch. It made no difference to the attendant that the clippers were blunt and nicked and cut his skin repeatedly.

The cuts burned fiercely when they ordered him to jump into a huge creosote bath. Once Nicholas was in, the attendant pushed his head beneath the slimy surface, then told him to get out and motioned him towards a shower where he was deluged first with ice-cold water, then scalding water.

Fighting to suppress an expression of pain, he searched for a towel. There weren't any. He had to stand while his own body heat evaporated the scummy liquid.

By this time the burning was not as painful. But the attendants moved in with hand pumps and sprayed him all over with another chemical. It stung as if they had rubbed salt in his cuts and it left him coated with a chalky dust. Eyeing himself in the stainless steel mirror, he couldn't suppress a cynical snicker at his new-found whiteness.

The washing and delousing completed, Nicholas and his comrades, still naked, were herded out of the washroom, through a subterranean passage, up a flight of stairs and into a long room with several rows of counters. At each counter he picked up a different item of clothing – a shirt, a pair of blue-and-white-striped trousers and matching jacket, a cap, a pair of socks and a pair of wooden clogs. There was no time to get a proper fit: the prisoners behind the counters flung the clothes as the inmates double-timed through the line.

At the last counter an S.S. guard ordered them in German and bad French to line up by fives. As he yelled Nicholas's name, he handed him two triangles of red cloth and two rectangles of white cloth; also a needle and thread to sew them to his uniform.

The colours differentiated one class of prisoner from another. Green was for convicted criminals, yellow for Jews, pink for homosexuals, black for gypsies, and red for political prisoners and prisoners of war. Politicals wore the red triangle with the point down. POWs wore it with the point up.

The rectangle of cloth, bearing a stencilled prisoner number, was worn on the left breast below the coloured triangle. The triangle-rectangle combination was repeated on the right trouser leg.

Nicholas, still completely nude, hastily sewed on his identification.

His prisoner number was 44451.

'Skilled workers front and centre!' shouted the S.S. labour-service officer.

Nicholas stood absolutely still. In the world of the concentration camp he was an infant. A veteran prisoner could have told him to step forward whether he had a skill or not and try to bluff it: the men with the skills got the indoors jobs. The unskilled were detailed to the outdoors jobs. Inside the chances of survival were poor; outside they were remote.

The reward for his ignorance was assignment to the dreaded rock quarry.

On 29 January 1944, when Nicholas marched out through the huge main gate of Buchenwald, nature gripped the magnificent, pine-covered country-side of Thuringia in snow and frost. The near-zero temperature ignored his thin, cotton uniform and invaded the marrow of his bones. As his clogs clopped and clacked and slipped beneath him, he reminded himself that it was a dream. It could not be reality. What he had witnessed in the few hours was part of a corroding, horrific nightmare that leaves the dreamer soaked in sweat when he awakes. Yet there they were, a long, winding line of marchers, five abreast, their picks and shovels over their shoulders, armed S.S. guards riding herd on them, all sinuously winding out into the white, blanketed nowhere, each man hiding with his thoughts, hoarding his memories of home and family to sustain his will to stay alive.

Gradually the column ascended the slopes of the Ettersburg. They stood for a moment, their breath clouding in the pre-dawn air, the older, weaker men near exhaustion, the younger men panting vigorously, awaiting the order to start digging.

'*Aufstehen*!' shouted the detail leader, an S.S. NCO.

The great prisoner army began swinging picks and sliding shovels, attacking the cavernous bite which it and others over the years had gnawed into the stubborn Thuringian granite. They swung their tools greedily because it rushed their anaemic blood through their bodies and kept the cold at bay – except at the hands, the feet, the tips of the nose and the earlobes.

It was dig or die, for Thuringia in winter was the Siberia of the Third Reich. Even if nature had not innocently been their policeman, there were S.S. guards all around, with rifles and vicious Alsatian wolfhounds. There were the prisoners who, like trustees in a civilian prison, had been given some authority. These prisoner foremen, or *kapos*, rivalled and could surpass the S.S. guards in brutality; that was how they earned and perpetuated better food and less bestial treatment for themselves. Often, merely to justify their presence and authority, they walked around haranguing the labourers, occasionally kicking, hammering and beating them into working faster.

Only when a prisoner foreman had strutted further on down the mountain slope or had had his predatory curiosity aroused by something further up, could the quarry workers risk conversation. Nicholas heard someone curse the Russian and Polish prisoners for monopolizing the top level. He asked why? They can see a long distance from their vantage point, he was told. When the S.S. detail leader or the prisoner foreman wander off, the workers can take it easy.

'How do you get up there?' he whispered.

'Forget it,' muttered his neighbour, a Frenchman who had been in the camp a long time. 'I've known a few who made it, but they don't last long.'

'Why?'

'The Russians and Poles kill 'em,' muttered his companion, swinging his pick mechanically.

A small group of prisoners didn't swing picks and shovels. Their job was picking up broken rock and loading it into large, wooden carts. They pushed the carts up and down the slope from one level to another, making pick-ups. Nicholas watched with fascination as the emaciated men, who had no more breakfast in their bellies than a slice of bread and a pint of watery soup, struggled with the heavily loaded carts. When they had to push uphill, the cart threatened to roll back and crush them. When they went downhill, they braced themselves to keep it from careening down the slope.

'You haven't seen it all yet,' his companion muttered. Between pick swings he told Nicholas how some of the S.S. sadists amused themselves. Instead of doing the merciful thing and shooting prisoners through the head, sometimes the guards killed them slowly by making them push a tremendously overloaded cart uphill. Under a hail of kicks, blows and threats the doomed men would try the impossible, only to have the cart roll over them. 'Make sure you're never assigned to the cart detail,' the Frenchman advised.

Nicholas attacked the quarry granite with sudden vigour.

'Of course,' continued his new-found friend, 'the cart routine isn't always fun. It's surprising how strong a man becomes when he's trying not to die. He can push and push for a long time. But that makes the S.S. impatient. They want their fun immediately, so often they'll get fed up waiting and just push the man off the top level. Look for yourself; it's a long way to drop.'

Nicholas worked on, listening and learning.

He learned that the greatest danger was the boredom of the German guards. It was impossible for these black-uniformed sadists to languish in the freezing wind and icy blizzard and not long to be back in their warm barracks: they were obsessed with the belief that they could be there if it weren't for the filthy, lice-infested *stucke* from every country in Occupied Europe who were prepared to escape at the slightest invitation.

Some S.S., the Frenchman told him, broke the monotony by standing on the top level, picking up rocks as big as they could lift and dropping them on innocent prisoners on the first level. If they missed their targets other S.S. laughed them to ridicule. Then the frustrated, embarrassed guards would draw their pistols and maniacally pick off some poor devils three levels below just to prove their marksmanship.

He was told that old prisoners afforded the jaded S.S. their greatest diversion. They'd order a tottering grandfather to climb one of the young, slender pines that dotted the mountain slope. '*Mach schnell!*' they'd command. When they got him up there, three or four of them would shake the tree violently until he toppled out of it to his death.

'But don't worry,' the Frenchman added, 'there are worse places in this hell-hole than the quarry – the gardening detail.'

The S.S. had a vegetable garden tended by prisoners on punishment detail. The garden was constantly being expanded. Tons of plowed-up rocks had to be carted away, and it was continuously being fertilized. Tons of human waste had to be hauled from the prisoners' gigantic sewage ditch. Prisoners, two at a time with a wooden carrying rack, were pressed into service as the beasts of burden for two weeks of punishment. It was deadly to move too slowly; but if they moved too fast under the threats and curses of the guards, foremen and detail leaders, the human ordure slopped over the edge of the rack onto their uniforms. Since washing facilities were almost non-existent, they stank like a dungheap. When their two weeks ended, they were shunned by all other prisoners.

Fourteen hours later, it was pitch black and time to march back to camp.

Half an hour before the end of work Nicholas's friend warned him to be on the look-out for a suitable rock.

'What for?' queried Nicholas.

'An old German custom,' said the Frenchman cynically. 'Everyone has to carry a rock back to camp. It has to weigh as least ten pounds. If you can't find one, you'll discover the S.S. are very understanding: they'll accept five bricks. Start looking as early as you can. When the rush comes, the only rock left may be thirty pounds. If it's all you can lay your hands on, you'll have to take it – if you want to live to see tomorrow morning.'

Illuminated only by the glow of the snow, the procession of exhausted men wound its way back to camp. Nicholas clutched his rock close to his chest. He still believed he'd wake up out of it all and find himself in his plush Paris apartment with the luxurious green carpet.

He noticed some prisoners *did not* carry rocks; they pushed wheeled carts piled with bodies that would never again have to endure the agony of the rock quarry.

'What now?' Nicholas whispered to his friend.

'Roll call.'

Nicholas's memory flooded with the Kafkaesque scene of the early morning. 'My God, *twice* a day? I watched it this morning.'

'Twice a day at *least*. They're afraid they may lose some

of us. Like an anxious parent, they want to know where we are twenty-four hours a day.'

Nicholas shuddered.

'Let me give you a piece of advice,' confided his friend. 'Stand perfectly still in whatever square you're assigned to. Don't talk, of course; and don't cough or even sneeze, otherwise the damned *Lagerschutz* will work you over with their clubs.'

'I've already seen them at work.'

'Yes, and make sure you sound off when your name's called. Be alert: the bastard won't pronounce it right. If you don't answer, you're listed as missing. If you're missing, the goddamn roll call goes on and on, until they've accounted for you – dead or alive.

'Don't put your hands in your pockets or turn up your collar against the wind. Keep your back straight. Do you smoke? If you do, don't pick up the rare cigarette butt you'll see lying around. If you've stashed away any extra food, don't have it on you at roll call.'

'What do they do to you?'

'Could be the *Bock*. It's a wooden rack. They set it up right by the roll call leader. They stretch you over it so your backside sticks up, and they usually give you five to twenty-five lashes. They use a horse whip, sometimes a cane. Then they'll have one of the medics from the prisoner hospital paint you with iodine. And after that about fifty to 150 deep-knee bends to "strengthen the muscles," he'll tell you.

'Then maybe he's not in the *Bock* mood, so he might tie your hands behind your back and toss the end of the rope over a tree limb. When they hoist you up about six feet, your shoulder blades pop out of joint. They'll beat you in the face or kick you in the balls, while you're strung up there. It might last half-an-hour. Then again it could be four.

'That's what they'll do to *you* – if they catch *you*. That's not even talking about what they'll do to the rest of us. If you cause trouble and you live in my block, everybody

81

pays. No food for an entire day, maybe. Perhaps double-timing it all over the assembly area – it's full of holes and gullies – for an hour with every man lugging a huge boulder. The first to stagger or slow down, well, it's a one-way ride to the ovens – the building you thought was a chapel.'

The column was approaching the sprawl of barracks buildings behind the high, barbed-wire fence with the 600 volts of electricity running through it and the twenty-foot-high guard towers every 250 feet. 'Straighten up there!' yelled the S.S. detail leader, starting to count in cadence. '*Ein-zwei-drei-vier!*'

'Anyone ever get out of here?' muttered Nicholas.

'Not as long as I've been here,' said the Frenchman. 'The old-timers say a couple got away back in 1938. They turned up missing at roll call, so the bastards made every single man stand there for nineteen hours. The temperature that night was five degrees above zero. By morning twenty-five had frozen to death. By noon it was seventy.'

They did not speak for several minutes. Finally Nicholas asked: 'Why tell me all this?'

'Listen,' whispered the Frenchman hoarsely. 'The only thing you can depend on here – and you can't always depend on it – is nationality. You know what the Russians and Poles did with those guys who tried to make it up to the top level! Don't think because we all hate the Germans that we all love one another. The politicals despise the criminals. The criminals hate the politicals because they're intellectuals. There's a power struggle going on all the time for control.'

'Then the politicals themselves are divided into Communists and non-Communists. Naturally they hate each other's guts. And each is constantly trying to win converts.'

'And what about people like me – the POWs?' queried Nicholas.

'Nationality is stronger. The English POWs keep to

themselves, the Dutch POWs to themselves. The Russian POWs to themselves. It's impossible for a man to remain alone here. He must join some organized group if he's to survive. It's the only strength he has against the rest of the prisoners, against the Germans.

'If you intend to survive here, you'll have to stick with me and the other Frenchmen. It won't be easy. Some of them don't like our black Colonials. But I'll do what I can...'

'But I'm not a Frenchman,' Nicholas interjected. 'I'm an American. A major in the United States Army Air Corps. Are there other Americans here?'

Startled, the Frenchman nearly dropped his rock. 'American? Other Americans? There have been a few. They're all dead. The S.S. branded them "*Nach und Nebel*."'

The torment of the evening roll call was over and Nicholas, frozen and in agony, hobbled to the barracks. On crude, trestle tables illuminated by a single electric-light bulb glaring harshly down at them, each man ate his single piece of bread thinly spread with margarine and his tiny piece of sausage. 'Eat fast,' the Frenchman had warned him, 'otherwise you may not get to eat at all. Some drunken S.S. sergeant – maybe even your own barracks leader – is liable to stagger in and there'll be hell to pay. For no reason at all. Maybe there's a button missing from your uniform. It could be your uniform's dirty, he'll say. If they want to get you, there's a rule or regulation that lets them get you – legally. If there isn't, they'll make one up on the spot.

'Maybe it's some imagined grievance. Even so, he may kick over the tables – your supper with it. He'll overturn your lockers, wreck your bed and make you double-time around the barracks.'

Nicholas awoke in the middle of the night and knew the nightmare was reality. He cursed Florence until the profanity became meaningless from repetition.

The thin mat between him and the wooden bunk he lay on stank of human excrement. So did the thin blanket over him. He shivered violently and longed for the searing sun of home.

He only had on an undershirt. It was against regulations to wear shorts or trousers. If caught wearing them, the penalty was the *Bock* for the offender and an hour's double-time around the assembly area in shirts only for the rest of the barracks. Although the barracks was jammed to twice its capacity, the body heat was no match for the icy blasts that permeated every crack and crevice in the old stone building. Ice glazed the inside of the windows and long, stiletto-like icicles hung from holes in the roof.

The mildewed stone walls radiated a cold that chilled the wooden bunks. Nicholas's French companion urged him to try for the centre of the building where the rows of bunks were warmest. But even if he should be lucky enough to get the *Stubendienst* – the assistant block leader – to assign him to a centre-aisle bunk, he'd run into another hazard: if he had to piss in the middle of the night, his mat and blanket might be stolen while he was gone. Worse, he might return to find somebody had crawled into his bunk, and he'd have to use his fists to drive out the invader. And even if Nicholas were to do so, the Frenchman warned him, the ruckus would rouse the *Stubendienst*, who'd come running. Then everybody would catch it. The assistant block leader would order all of them out for a one-hour drill in bare feet and undershirts. The following evening after roll call, it would be the *Bock* for Nicholas and the man who'd tried to steal his bunk.

As he lay sleepless, it suddenly occurred to him: he'd been inside Buchenwald twenty-four hours and so fascinated by the revulsion of everything around him that he hadn't had an instant to think about escape. Until now he'd been concentrating strictly on survival.

Chapter Five

Almost none of the prisoners had ever seen a black man before.

The whistles of the *Lagerschutz* shrieked as usual that frigid January morning in 1944. They were only prisoners like the rest but their authority as the camp's security police had made them corrupt and inhuman. They clumped down the floor, screaming and swinging their bludgeons at the half-naked, emaciated prisoners in their reeking bunks, rousing them outside, across the snow and into the freezing washroom.

It was there that they saw him for the first time.

Prisoners had to wash down to the waist every morning. There was seldom any soap and the water was like ice. It piddled out of huge, perforated cylinders in streams resembling the ribs of an umbrella. For most the daily encounter with the water was a lick and a promise – unless hammered under the freezing spray by the milling bludgeons of the *Lagerschutz*.

But the black seemed to enjoy it. His tawny body didn't flinch as the astringent jets of water flayed him.

They glanced at him surreptitiously. The sight of his rippling physique made them sickeningly conscious of their own hollow chests and ribby frames. His zeal to clean himself showed them what animals they had become. Lashed by the *Lagerschutz*, it was fear and not pride that drove them to the water.

But they saw that the black man embraced the ordeal voluntarily, scrubbing himself with his bare hands as briskly as if luxuriating in the steaming shower of some pre-war public baths. If he had hummed a tune, the picture would've been complete.

They automatically resented him.

Back in the barracks they hurriedly dressed in their ill-fitting uniforms bearing the colour-coded triangles of identification. A block letter in the middle of a triangle indicated a nationality – 'D' for German (Deutschland), 'P' for Pole, 'F' for France, etc. The black wore a red POW triangle, its apex pointed upward to distinguish his patch for the down-pointing red triangle of political prisoners. The large 'A' in the triangle's centre identified him as an American. In the latrine, which was the only place where prisoners could talk without being harrassed by the *Lagerschutz*, the whispering had already begun.

'*Non, non*,' protested a French prisoner, shaking his head with steadfast Gallic resolve, 'he cannot be an American – not with his perfect French. Something is not right. We will have to keep an eye on him.'

Among the German political prisoners the same doubts were circulating.

'*Ja*,' one of them conceded to a friend, 'many in *Amerika* are of German origin. The *Deutsche-Amerikaner*'s command of the German tongue could be that perfect. It is possible, you know.'

'But a *schwartze Amerikaner*?' snickered his friend.

In the concentration camp a man might wear the criminal's green triangle, but that didn't always mean he was untrustworthy or lacked honour. The morals of many a 'criminal' were higher than those of some 'reds', the politicals. The S.S. camp commandant classified prisoners indiscriminately, so the veteran inmate knew that the colour of a man's triangle didn't necessarily reflect his true morals, character or political beliefs. Then, too, each prisoner wove a web of anonymity around himself to protect his family from possible repercussions by the Gestapo.

Thus even among themselves prisoners used false surnames, often elaborately fabricating their former occupations and lives. It was the only protection against the spies and informers that the German camp administration continually planted among them to learn what was *really* brewing behind the barbed wire.

Although under day-and-night surveillance from the ugly guard towers, the prisoners were allowed to rule themselves. They had their own government. It was not a democracy; it was an unending struggle between the three most powerful groups – the Communists, the anti-Communists and the convicted criminals. The victorious faction organized, directed and ruled every phase of life in the camp. From this ruling class the German commandant selected a prisoner he was sure would cooperate with him.

They appointed him as *Lagereldtester* – the president of the prisoner government. He, in turn, nominated the head prisoners – the *kapos* – in such departments as the kitchen, the hospital, and the crucially-important labour-allocation office, which had the most powerful leverage of all – assigning prisoners their jobs. It was through the *Lagereldtester* and his *kapo* cabinet that the Nazi commandant's orders were executed. The role of *Lagereldtester* was privileged but highly dangerous. His tenure was an endless conspiracy to blunt the harshness of the commandant's orders yet make it appear as if they were being carried out to the letter. It was a continuing masquerade calculated to reduce the murder and brutality and inhumanity – a masquerade that could be uncovered by a commandant's 'plant' within the prisoner ranks.

That was why they would wait and watch the black newcomer from a safe distance.

In the cavernous mess hall the miserable men clutched their hunks of bread. The senior of the seven prisoners at each bare, plank table sliced the bread. He used a crude wood-and-string balance scale to weigh and equalize the portions of the oval-shaped loaf. The men's anger, fermenting on their hate for the S.S. guards and their gnawing hunger, bubbled near the surface. Fingers, stiff from the long night's chill, snatched at the morsels. A fight broke out: one man, his yellowed fangs glowing dully in the light from the naked electric bulb above, shrieked that somebody else had taken a bigger piece. The two snarled at each other like hyenas scrabbling over a carcass – until the *Lagerschutz* clubbed them silent.

Nicholas studiously ignored them and ate in complete silence.

Then came the yellowish-brown soup flecked with gobs of floating grease. They slurped obscenely, clutching their precious bread in their talons, glowering at the Negro: his self-control, by comparison, reduced them to swine hoking at the trough . . .

'Three minutes to roll call! Three minutes to roll call!'

The dreaded alarm of the *Lagerschutz* detonated the customary, controlled panic. Hunks of bread were rammed inside jackets as the mess hall choked with bodies flooding toward the doors and out onto the camp streets. They stamped in the frozen snow as they formed up block by block in columns eight abreast. Almost gratefully the formations ran down the street toward the vast, open roll-call area.

The old prisoners, many of whom had arrived at Buchenwald when it opened seven years earlier, watched Nicholas suspiciously. They'd heard Negroes couldn't take the cold like whites. Yet even at temperatures which transformed the mushy, roll-call ocean into solid mud, he held himself obnoxiously erect. They chuckled mirthlessly: he wouldn't last long. The first rule of survival was to keep a low profile. It was fatal to draw attention to yourself. You survived by becoming as indistinguishable to the *Lagerschutz* and S.S. as a snowflake in a blizzard.

But a Negro didn't have a white man's intelligence, they told themselves, and this one would pay for the genetic deficiency with his arrogant, black neck in a noose one Sunday morning.

It was night. The outside work details had dragged themselves in exhausted from their pick-and-shovel projects many miles distant from the camp. The evening meal – a few grams of sausage and a cup of swill called coffee – had been gulped down. It was about an hour before lights out. Nicholas and one of the *Lagerschutz* struggled through the deep snow toward the western side of the camp. The wind sliced through them, rounding the shoulders and humping the back of the camp policeman. But the black walked tall, his arms swinging ludicrously by his sides. Except for an occasional handcart loaded with bodies and pushed by pairs of sickly inmates towards the crematorium, the streets were deserted.

Fine snow infiltrated the tight curls of black hair springing out from under Nicholas's peaked cap and clogged his eyelashes. He wiped the snow from his eyes and suddenly he was a boy again, trading absurd tales of adventure and intrigue with his buddies, promising them that he'd be rich and famous one day and that they'd read about him in the newspapers...

The large stone building close to the barbed wire bulked large as they approached it. Officially it was supposed to be the canteen where the prisoners could buy a few personal items. But it was a sham: in reality it was a huge warehouse full of provisions denied the inmates but used by the prisoner government to buy favour and maintain control. The building was windowless. Barred slits high up on the walls provided ventilation.

The *Lagerschutz* stopped in front and pulled on a weight hanging from a chain by a door. Immediately a pack of dogs inside began yelping. Shortly afterwards a peephole in the door slid back and a face glowed in the darkness. The *Lagerschutz* was dismissed and the black man told to come in.

He was led inside and down a corridor of crates, boxes and bags of untouched supplies stacked well above the level of a dimly-lit bulb. In the shadows he passed a screened pen filled with dogs. He felt their foetid odours waft to him as they barked and whined.

He emerged from the semi-darkness into a brightly lit, modern office that would have done justice to the *Kruppwerke*. Metal filing cabinets along the walls. An expensive rug on the floor. Artistically designed lamps on desks heavy with files and ledgers.

Nicholas waited expectantly, concealing his amazement. Then he heard a growl from his prisoner escort, who directed him to yet another door. Crossing the threshhold, he found himself in a much larger room. It looked like a compromise between a starkly modern living room and a traditional German *bierstube*. The sweet, heavy aroma of cigar smoke assailed his nostrils. He focused on a long conference table busy with bottles, glasses and titbits. The six men who huddled there stared up at him. They sported immaculately clean, well-pressed prison stripes. Each wore a black armband on his right sleeve.

The cabinet of Buchenwald's prisoner government, comprising the *kapos* of the camp's key departments, was in session. Nicholas was shocked. Less than five minutes away from degradation and death, humiliation and suffering, filth and bestiality, fat and fleshy prisoners held court in pomp and plenty. The ugly, two-inch-wide, scalp-deep swathe that the *harshneider*'s clippers made down the centre of each prisoner's head was absent in these men. They wore their hair fashionably long and lustrous with Brilliantine.

He instantly recognized one man as the figure in the heavy, furlined jacket he'd seen several days earlier, walking along the camp street with a plump, thoroughbred Doberman on a leash. He was the powerful *kapo* of the canteen. He introduced himself and the others in laboured, heavily accented English. 'Welcome, comrade,' he said, extending his hand.

Nicholas noted that all wore red triangles surprinted with a 'D,' identifying them as German Communists.

'Sit down,' continued the canteen *kapo* courteously.

'I'd just as soon stand,' Nicholas retorted. 'Fine,' smiled the canteen *kapo*. Then he turned to the man seated at the head of the table, the *Lagereldtester*.

'I imagine you're wondering why we've sent for you,' said the prisoner-government president in a soft, considerate tone. 'Let me explain. Your comrades on the block have told you many things about Buchenwald and you may be confused about what to expect. I'd like to tell you that our government is dedicated to fairness and justice for *all prisoners*. We extend our influence to *all* comrades to protect them from the hated S.S. guards – regardless of nationality.' He looked around at his cabinet members as if to get their agreement, then continued. 'Because you are the only American in the camp, we felt it would be comforting for you to know this.

'Besides, my staff and I make it our policy to meet all prominent newcomers personally. Some of us have been here since 1937, when the camp was started, and have never seen an American inmate.'

As the *Lagereldtester* continued, Nicholas examined them covertly. He noticed their serial numbers. Most other prisoners, including himself, had five-digit numbers; theirs were three-digit numbers. They had indeed been among the first prisoners at Buchenwald, and it was obvious from the way they held themselves that they wore their badges of longevity proudly.

It was also clear to him from the litter of food and drink, how they had survived that long.

He noticed, too, that several wore red-and-white cloth bullseye targets sown on the backs of their jackets. It was the symbol which the S.S. made a prisoner wear if he was suspected of planning to escape: it drew attention to him. But Nicholas wondered how many years had gone by since these sleek, pomaded men had thought about escape.

The *Lagereldtester* continued with his soothing dissertation, pausing tactically from time to time for Nicholas's response. But apart from a perfunctory 'thank you,' the black man remained impassively noncommittal. Finally the president, a seasoned veteran of camp politics, seemd to exhaust his store of platitudes. He turned to the *kapo* of the Political Department. This was the office maintained by the Gestapo for continued political surveillance of prisoners after their arrest and during their sentence.

The political-department *kapo* glanced at a small piece of paper in his hand. His English was better than the president's, but his manner was clipped and hurried. 'We've seen the Gestapo report on you, comrade. It indicates that you are Major Johnny Nicholas of the air force of the United States of America and that you are a pilot. Is that accurate?'

'Yes, sir, that is correct.'

'Where were you shot down?'

'Sir, military regulations prohibit me from disclosing anything more than my name, rank, serial number and date of birth under provision of the Geneva Convention.'

The *Lagereldtester* leaned forward with a pained expression and hurt in his tone. 'But we're not the enemy, Johnny. We're your friends,' he said, pointedly casual.

'I welcome your friendship, sir,' said Nicholas respectfully, 'But I'm sure you wouldn't consider me worthy of it if I disobeyed the orders of my superiors. Isn't the entire success of your government based on obedience? What would become of it if obedience was based on convenience? I'm sure you understand my position as an American officer.'

'And we hope you understand our position,' the *Lagereldtester* responded reasonably. 'It's essential for the success of our government that we know the full background and training of new comrades so we can use them to the benefit of us all. We must help one another. You've been here only a few weeks, but long enough to know that hundreds of prisoners die here every month. The German S.S. shoot them, beat them, hang them or work them to death. Your chances of getting out of here

92

alive are not good, but if you cooperate with us, they can improve.

'It's through the prisoner government that the German S.S. camp commandant's commands are carried out. But my staff and I decide specifically which prisoners work in the warmth of the tailor's shop or in the cold of the rock quarries. We assign the youngest and strongest to the quarries: they have the best chance of surviving. The old and sick we put in the tailor's shop or in the camp kitchen.

'We can't avoid the orders of the S.S., but we are able to carry them out in such a way that injuries, casualties, beatings and deaths are reduced to a minimum. It is a crucial responsibility, and to carry it out we require the co-operation of every prisoner.'

Nicholas relaxed his stiff bearing and lowered his head slightly in the silence that followed. They waited for him to respond but he didn't.

The political-department *kapo* blurted: 'It's said that your French and German are too polished for an American. How do we know that you are not an agent of the camp commandant? Or of the Gestapo? How do we know that you haven't been planted to wreck our government and leave 35,000 men of all nationalities defenceless against the S.S. butchers?'

Nicholas looked down at him and abruptly challenged in German: 'A Negro agent among 35,000 whites? Is the *S.S. Kommandant* that deranged?'

The *Lagereldtester* exchanged glances with his staff. The canteen *kapo* snapped his fingers and the prisoner who had conducted Nicholas through the building appeared with a tray. It was laden with beer, kidney beans, sausages and white bread. The prisoner set the tray at Nicholas' end of the table.

'*Sitzen sie auf dem stuhle, bitte?*' asked the *Lagereldtester*, adroitly switching to German and motioning toward an empty chair.

Nicholas hadn't seen such food in months. He knew

that none of the camp's huge population had enjoyed such delectables either – except, of course, for the president and senior *kapos*. His initial disdain for the sleek-haired men was overwhelmed by their bounty – and his apolitical belly.

He sat down and quickly snatched handfuls of food.

He was discovering that in concentration-camp society, unity didn't go far beyond a common hate for the S.S. There were those who considered themselves infinitely better than others and entitled to hoard the privileges of the camp. There were parasites who preyed on others. It was better to eat in their contemptible presence than carry it back to his block. He might be jumped on by the roving bands of Russian and German criminals who routinely assaulted and robbed the few men fortunate enough to get a parcel from home.

The *Lagereldtester* resumed solicitously in German: 'For your own protection you must help persuade us that you are who you say you are and can be trusted.'

Nicholas had reduced the heaped platter to half its original size. 'My own protection?' he queried, also in German.

'*Ja*,' interjected the hospital *kapo*, speaking for the first time. 'If your fellow prisoners mistrust you ... if they think you are a spy for the commandant, then they've been known to take matters into their own hands.' He stared woodenly at Nicholas. 'And then you are liable to wind up in my custody – perhaps permanently.'

Nicholas continued eating, his eyes fixed on the plate as if he hadn't heard the implied threat.

The political-department *kapo* still clutched the piece of paper. 'You'll begin,' he declared officiously, 'by telling us the name of your unit, the type of aircraft you were flying and your target.'

'You sound like the German interrogators in Paris,' Nicholas scolded, feeling the first effects of the beer, 'yet you're supposed to be my friend and protector.'

The *Lagereldtester* appeared to be losing his patience.

'You're playing games with words again,' he warned, his placating tone now growing brittle.

The political-department *kapo* snapped: 'Ah, so you were interrogated in Paris? Then you were shot down over France.'

Nicholas continued eating and didn't respond, although involuntarily he released a loud beer belch.

'Were you?' sternly demanded the political-department *kapo*. Nicholas took the glass of beer from his mouth and wiped his lips. 'Yes.'

'Where were you held before coming to Buchenwald? Fresnes? St. Valerian? Compiegne?'

Persistent bastards, he thought. They preyed on complacency. In the student elections at the University of Paris it was the communists who stayed up all night, all the next day, and into the following night until everyone else fell asleep exhausted or simply gave up. Then the communist students were all alone. They finally had the necessary quorum. And naturally they easily glided to victory. Nietzsche would have hated them. There was no room in the communist movement for masters. Only slaves. Well, piss on these bastards.

'Where?' repeated the political-department capo. 'Certainly your prison record before coming here is no great American military secret. It would be no problem for us to piece together an account of your activities.'

The good food filled the void in his stomach. The beer was sabotaging his will. And besides, so what? He'd humour these red sons-of-bitches. 'Compiegne.'

The political-department *kapo* smiled smugly at his colleagues, then turned once more to Nicholas. 'Where is Compiegne?'

'Near Paris.'

'How far from Paris? In what direction?'

'North somewhere. I don't know how far. They took me there at night. In a truck. I was asleep part of the time.'

'Where was your cell? On the ground floor or the second floor?'

'There aren't any cells at Compiegne.'

'Nonsense. Compiegne is one of the ancient mansions of the Richelieus. Its dungeons are full of cells.'

'Maybe so, but when I was there it was no mansion. It was an old French Army barracks.'

'Which block were you in?'

'I was moved several times. I don't remember.'

'Well, then, what was the last block you were in?'

'Block B, maybe. I don't remember.'

For five minutes the questioning continued about Compiegne and about his capture and interrogation by the Germans after he was shot down. Finally the *Lagereldtester* said: 'We're pleased you've changed your mind and have been more cooperative with us. But something still bothers us. Before we invited you here, we talked about you with one of our staff familiar with the military system of your country. This comrade tells us that your air force has trained Negroes as fighter pilots. But he hasn't heard of any Negro *bomber* pilots. So he says you are a fighter pilot.'

He took out another scrap of paper and continued. 'He says you would have been flying a Mustang P–51, a Lightning P–38, a' – he squinted to read the fine script – 'or a Thunderbolt P–47. Many of these aircraft already have been shot down and their details have long been well known to the German air force. You would not be revealing any military secrets if you agreed to describe which one you were flying.'

Nicholas stopped eating even though there was still food on the plate. His eyes were on the empty spaces where the mountain of victuals had been. He could feel the eyes of the six men boring into him.

'We can send for our air expert,' volunteered the *Lagereldtester* enthusiastically.

Nicholas pushed the plate away from him even though his instincts were to wolf down what remained. 'I can give you only my name, rank serial number and date of birth,' he announced formally.

'We already have that from the report in the Political Department,' snapped that department's *kapo* coldly. 'Which plane were you flying? Describe it in detail – engine, armament, flying characteristics. A military secret is no longer involved. All of these aircraft are already known to the Germans. By refusing to tell us you're convicting yourself as an imposter and a spy.'

Nicholas straightened up and looked at them belligerently. 'I wasn't piloting an airplane.'

The six German communists exchanged glances again.

'Then how did you arrive in Europe?' snapped the political-department *kapo*.

'By parachute,' Nicholas replied coolly. Let them be frustrated, he thought.

His response elicited a long silence. The *Lagereldtester* leaned forward confidentially and asked in a low voice: 'Are you suggesting now that you are an Allied agent? A secret agent?'

Nicholas abruptly stood up, knocking over his chair. 'I'm not saying anything more.'

'Comrade,' appealed the *Lagereldtester*. 'We're not the enemy. The enemy is outside – on the other side of the barbed wire. We are only trying to help you. What proof do you have that you are what you say you are?'

He stared at them contemptuously. 'I don't have to tell you a goddam thing! Now, is that all?'

The president and the *kapos* huddled together for a few seconds. Then the president said: 'Wait in the other room while I consult with my staff.'

Nicholas was taken back into the warehouse. The overhead bulb was not lit but light from the adjoining office shone through the space under the door. He saw shelves of flour, canned food and preserves, winter jackets, gloves, caps and shoes. He thought of the hundreds staggering around on the snow-covered, stone-hard roll-call ground with nothing but paper and cardboard wrapped around their feet for shoes.

He hated the prisoner-government. He was stunned at their command of English. They were educated, intelligent – and immensely powerful. They had the power of life and death. Little splinters of fear began to prick him. He'd always feared being a coward. As a teenager he'd purposely picked fights to prove to himself he wasn't afraid. Like the time he'd physically overpowered his high-school principal. He'd been drunk many times, gone out to the bordello, picked fights with the patrons and flattened them.

Standing once again at the end of the table, he could read nothing in their bland faces.

'Nicholas,' said the *Lagereldtester* formally. 'You present us with a dilemma. Some of us believe what you've told us. Some don't.

'Some of us think your excellent French gives you away,' said the political-department *kapo*. 'You are one of those colonials one sees in Paris all the time. Probably from one of the French colonies. Maybe an entertainer, maybe an actor or a prizefighter. When the war started you couldn't make a legitimate living, so you began trafficking in the black market like so many of your kind. The Gestapo caught you. They threatened to shoot you unless you agreed to work for them. You agreed, and they sent you here to betray us.'

Nicholas stared at the man impassively, making no attempt to respond.

'I'm sorry,' said the *Lagereldtester* apologetically. 'Until we get further information to help us resolve our dilemma, you're free to return to your block. But we'll be watching you.'

On Sunday the morning roll call was much later than usual: Buchenwald's commandant required daylight for the show he planned every week. It began as usual: Gaudily-dressed musicians with their trumpets, flutes and drums dancing out into the snow; waves of prisoners bursting from their barracks in the background and forming into an immaculately symmetrical block; then the music fading.

Only the premonitory rolling of drums continued. Then they, too, faded.

'*Mutzen ab!*' crashed the loudspeaker.

The murmuring of the voices died on the breeze at the command and caps were instantly removed and brought smartly against their wearers' right legs. A squad of S.S. marched into the assembly area convoying fifteen men – three lines of five – in their midst. They halted just to the left of the huge main-gate entrance, immediately in front of a crude wooden structure.

It had a crossbeam, and five nooses hung from it.

The guards placed a small block of wood between each man's lips and tied it in position using a length of wire knotted at the back of the head. They tied their hands behind their backs, then ordered them to step forward and take their positions below the nooses. Prisoners arbitrarily pulled from the assembly were ordered to place the nooses around the necks of the condemned men.

Seconds later the step on which the men were standing was jerked from under them.

Nicholas watched the body of his French friend writhe and twist, swaying like a lazy pendulum in space as the rope crushed his windpipe. When all the life had been choked out of him, they lowered him to the ground. His feet touched the beaten snow and his flaccid legs bent at the knees, unnaturally, like a puppet's.

It was the same for the second row of men, and then the third. And when it was over the loudspeakers exploded again: '*Mutzen auf!*'

Torn from his moorings in the civilized world, a prisoner's body and soul were doomed to extinction unless he quickly burrowed for new roots in the shifting sands of concentration-camp society. Each man had to scavenge for himself. Some, totally devastated by the initial assault, lapsed into catatonia – 'zombies' without wills, automatons who took life, torture and death with equanimity. They chose capitulation as their defence against insanity.

Others, with extreme deliberation, put their true natures in the deep freeze and became animals in order to stay alive. They case-hardened their humanity and numbed themselves against the stimul of love, horror, grief, pity and concern.

Yet a few prisoners, usually men of great moral and often religious conviction, willingly bore the burden of their humanity day after day for months and years. They shrank from any device that would have made it tolerable.

Johnny Nicholas knew one thing for certain: no matter what, he would never be cowed, never be a slave.

Chapter Six

The big black body came flying over the stone wall.

The frenzied mob milled in before it hit the ground. They hacked off the arms, legs and head and shrieked excitely as the gory torso twitched on the dusty street. Some of the women, dancing around like spastics, soaked their bandanas in the blood squirting from the arteries in the neck stump. Their menfolk, jabbering crazily, knotted a rope around the bloody mass and began hauling it through the streets.

Long into the night the drunken mobs did their shuffling, orgiastic *chairo pie* dance through the streets of Port-au-Prince, following the feet, hands, head and genitals of their 26th president on the points of swords, spears and bayonets.

The relics of President Guillaume Sam were gruesome

symbols of a new order for the tiny Caribbean island of Haiti. But it was to be an order that none expected.

From the beginning of that year of 1915 the Atlantic Squadron of the U.S. Navy had been monitoring the growing turbulence on the island. Rear Admiral William B. Caperton from the bridge of his flagship had been scanning the beautiful, verdant island daily with his binoculars, wondering how bad it might become. From the cram course he'd taken on the complexities of Caribbean history he knew just how violent Haitians could be: in the 101 years since 1804, when their national hero, Dessalines, had butchered all 70,000 French whites on the island and won independence for its blacks, they had used up twenty-six presidents – all but one of whom they'd ousted with violence and blood-letting.

A new president every four years on the average; Haiti's attempts at self-government had been a source of amusement to her North American neighbours.

When World War I in 1914 erupted in Europe, the chuckles of the Americans turned to concern. The Germans had long tried to extend their influence in the Caribbean. They had business interests and citizens in Haiti. What if the Germans, on the pretext of protecting their rights threatened by the overthrow of President Sam, were to occupy the island? True, the U.S. also had citizens and property there. But Americans were worried that Haiti controlled the approaches to the Panama Canal. If Haiti were taken over by the Germans, Kaiser Wilhelm would control entry and access to the Canal.

Word of President Sam's macabre wake reached Admiral Caperton on 14 July 1915. In the officers' wardroom, with his staff assembled, he shook his head at the news – and ordered his marines and bluejackets to go ashore the following day.

There was no harbour at Port-au-Prince. Just a stunning, white curve of beach blinding in the tropical sunlight, and in the centre a great clutter of ticky-tacky, building-block houses in pinks, yellows and blues. Amid the haphazard architecture the twin cupolas of a white cathedral gleamed, with a towering wall of deep-green mountains as a backdrop.

A mile from the beach, the scent of exotic tropical flowers clashed with the stink of human and animal waste lapping the gunwhales of the landing boats and caused some marines to gag. Here and there the inflated carcases of dead animals floated in the bay like obscene, bloated water bags.

The prows of the boats furrowed into the slime-covered sand and the Americans hopped nimbly over the side onto Haitian soil.

Under the bellowing harangue of barrel-chested gunnery sergeants to 'spread out,' they swarmed up the gentle slope of sand in their wide-brimmed Boy Scout hats, breeches and leggings with their 1904 Springfield rifles at port, waiting to blast the first *Cacos* they set eyes on.

The *Cacos* were Haiti's hereditary hill bandits who robbed, pillaged, raped and burned as a way of life. Almost all of the island's presidents had come to power by enlisting the support of these mercenaries. They owed allegiance to whoever could pay the most. When a revolution had been won, they found it hard to call a halt, continuing for weeks to occupy the cities and terrorize the population.

The tall, loose-limbed Americans moved cautiously up the trails from the beach. These gradually broadened out to become the streets of the city. They stepped over heaps of garbage and around huge potholes in the road. They held their noses because of the rills of sewage idly floating seaward down the open ditches where sidewalks should have been. As they moved further into town they twisted and turned through cardboard shacks and tin shanties, tromping everywhere on the hollow shells of rotting mangoes and oranges with their clumsy field boots. From inside the primitive dwellings, glistening black faces peered out, frightened, round-eyed.

Veteran NCOs who'd seen the slums of Peru, the

favelas of Brazil and the sampan housing of Hong Kong muttered that they'd never seen worse.

Moving up out of the *basse ville*, the lower part of the town, the marines found the stench leavened with the sweet scent of frangipani, magnolias and gardenias wafted by the breeze from the steep hills above them. The section of town where business and commerce were transacted reminded them of abandoned gold-mining towns of the American West. Unpainted two-storey wooden buildings bleached to the grey sheen of driftwood by the sun's intolerable glare, sagging perilously out of plumb. Buckled verandas and balconies supported by knock-kneed, toed-in columns. Mangy dogs scrabbling after offal in the gutters.

In the ninety-eight-degree heat the Americans sweltered under their broad-brimmed hats. Their khaki shirts were soaked with large islands of sweat.

The silence, occasionally punctuated by the sonorous rolling of voodoo drums in the hills, was eerie.

In twos and threes the frightened inhabitants crept out from behind the buildings into the blinding sun, coal-black women in voluminous Mother Hubbard-style dresses and brilliantly coloured bandanas, with wide-eyed little urchins clinging to their skirts. The kids were half-naked in filthy rags. Many had no clothes at all.

Timorously they padded up to the tall, fearsome-looking American *blancs*.

By the end of the day the U.S. Marines were being welcomed openly by the poor blacks of Port-au-Prince, who didn't seem to know who was fighting whom in their revolution-wracked country. No longer would the *Cacos* invade homes and drag off fathers and sons to serve in their armies. With the arrival of the Americans, the women could once again go to the Iron Market safely and bargain for food and fruit. No longer would their daughters be in danger from the rapacious hill-bandits.

Almost none of the U.S. invaders knew French. Even to those marines who did, the soft, liquid sounds of

welcome in the Creole tongue would defy their understanding until they'd heard it spoken for several days. But
the Americans knew joy and gratitude when they saw it
written on the shiny, ebony faces – whether they
understood Creole or not.

Other detachments of troops moved steadily upward to
the higher levels of the city and up the slopes of the
mornes, the foothills that grew up like a solid wall
immediately behind the town. After the squalor they'd
seen, they weren't ready for the lavish, Mediterranean-
style villas with their expensive terraces, gardens of palm
trees, poinsettias, breadfruit, flamboyant and exotic
Haitian roses. These were the homes of the city's
aristocratic minority, the Haitians of mixed black and
white blood who owned the country's coffee and sugar
plantations and ran its business, commerce and government.

The mulattoes were proud that they spoke French and
that they were people of learning, culture and sophistication. Many of them had lived in France and were educated
there. They were the élite of Haiti.

Their welcome to the U.S. Marines may not have been
the wild, abandoned embrace of the dirt-poor peasants in
the *basse ville*, yet it was no less genuine. Their coffee and
sugar fields had been pillaged by the *Cacos*. All work had
come to a standstill. There was neither law nor order, and
therefore no profits. They expressed their gratitude to the
Americans in the superlative embroidery of their Parisian
French and with the restraints on their emotions imposed
by their Continental educations.

Before long however, the presence of the liberators
would become *la misere*, an onerous, humiliating period
to last nineteen years during which the proud, independent Haitian élite felt that the U.S. Marine Corps rode
roughshod over their national prerogatives and made
puppets of them.

Traditionally the light-skinned aristocrats held in contempt the dark-skinned peasants who worked for them.

The peasants despised the aristocrats. Yet both classes were to unite in a hearty dislike of the Americans, who drafted the peasants into armies to build roads and bridges, upsetting their home and farm life and disrupting their ancient philosophy that what wasn't done today could always be done tomorrow or the next day.

By the time the typical young marine had spent three years in the furnace of tropical Haiti he had taken all the insults he could stomach and he was hearing voodoo drums in his sleep. He grew to despise the beautiful little Caribbean island because it loathed him. It had become to him 'just another goddam banana republic.'

It was May, 1926. The Americans had been in Haiti eleven years.

At the gates to the cathedral where he had been baptized eight years previously, Jean Marcel Nicolas, who would one day Americanize his name to Johnny Nicholas, stood with his family and thousands come to witness the formal inauguration for a second four-year term of President Louis Borno. For the second time in their generation the Haitians had gathered to witness the miracle of one of their presidents taking office in peace, at the legally appointed time, and as the result of an election conducted in accordance with the laws of the country. True, it had happened four years previously when Borno had succeeded President Sudre Dartiguenave – the first president under the American Occupation. But it was reassuring to see it happen a second time. Hopefully, thought Hilderic Nicolas and his wife Lucy, and thousands of parents like them, it meant that their troubled, tortured little island had come of age – that their vision of a viable black republic would come true.

Eight-year-old Jean's thoughts were less profound. He was fascinated by the precision of the Honour Guard of Haitian gendarmes under the command of a U.S. Marine Corps captain.

Front and centre of the khaki-clad battalion were the

red-and-blue National Colours snapping in the breeze. The men were drawn up facing the huge cathedral, their Springfields gleaming with fresh oil on the stocks and all sloped at exactly the same angle.

In the old days Haitian presidents always took the army to church with them; the favourite tactic of revolutionaries used to be to strike when the president was deep in prayer. Any leader who failed to take this elementary precaution was liable to discover he'd been unseated when he emerged through the cathedral gates.

Jean watched wide-eyed as ornate horse-drawn carriages glided up the wide, concrete driveway and deposited elegantly attired dignitaries at the bottom of steps leading up to the portico of the cathedral, an edifice modelled after the massive European houses of God. Droves of school children in their Sunday best flocked excitedly into the ceremonial area and were herded into place by harried teachers. A troop of Boy Scouts in shorts arrived and took their positions with military precision. Finally the roped-off sections on either side of the driveway were packed with the invited guests, and the hoarse sounds and shrieks of excitement lowered to a soft rumble of coughs and shuffling and whispers.

At last came the clatter of hooves. Suddenly a dozen majestic horsemen cantered up the driveway with their two columns guarding the presidential limousine. Jean watched in rapt attention as it glided to a halt and President Borno, in top hat and striped morning trousers, stepped out into the sun-splashed morning. He watched as the horsemen climbed down off their spirited, prancing mounts and escorted the President up the stone steps.

Halfway-up President Borno stopped, turned about to face the National Colours and removed his hat. In response the Colours were hoisted aloft in salute. The American captain bellowed 'Present ... Arms!' The battalion snapped their rifles to the vertical – and the brass band struck up the National Anthem, the 'Dessalinien'.

As the final chords faded across the bay, the air

exploded with the booming of a twenty-one-gun salute at nearby Fort Naçional.

But Jean wasn't looking at President Borno. He was watching with admiration the tall American marine captain who had orchestrated the ceremony, the one standing scrupulously erect with his gleaming, ceremonial sabre held aloft.

That afternoon the most impressive public building in the West Indies, Haiti's Presidential Palace, was ablaze with bunting. On the steps the newly installed Chief of State presented himself in the company of his Honour Guard and his *aide-de-camps* in their spotless white uniforms. Jean's father would note that the guard and the aides were all that remained of the 1,200 or so generals that had been in the Haitian Army before the coming of the Americans. Under the comparatively sober auspices of the U.S. Marine Corps, those ex-generals who had survived to share the glory of President Borno's inauguration day had been reduced to the lowly rank of lieutenant or captain at the most. All raised their arms in salute as their President made his second review of his army that day.

As the troops swung down the Champ de Mars, the street where President Sam's remains had twitched in the noonday sun eleven years previously, the martial strains of the band grew fainter. Finally the happy new President and his aides turned around and entered the palace for the inauguration ceremony.

Jean was too young to realize that he and his family had been invited because of their status within the island's hierarchy.

Once there had been only a single passport to that privileged caste – descent from a black-white union. When white Frenchmen in centuries past had lain with black women and become fathers, their mulatto children often inherited their money, their land and the benefits of education. As a result the ruling class in Haiti ultimately was made up of a small, light-skinned minority of educated landowners who considered themselves French, not African or Haitian. Those they ruled over were the African, the dirt-poor and illiterate peasants whose blood lines were pure, whose backs were strong and who toiled for a pittance in the plantations of the upper crust.

Jean's parents, however, had not been born in Haiti. They had come from the French island of Guadeloupe. They were French citizens; he a light-skinned man, she much darker. His colour gave him access to the élite. As for madame: her brother, Fortune Bogat, was a promising businessman who had a white wife from New York. These recommendations offset any disadvantage her darker skin tones might have posed in the couple's becoming part of Port-au-Prince's aristocracy. To his desirable complexion Hilderic Nicolas could add the high prestige of his job: he spoke excellent English and held an important post – secretary – at the British Embassy.

Clutching his parents' hands, Jean climbed the marble staircase to a spacious salon. Every few feet along the salon's walls were wide, sweeping windows that opened onto spacious balconies, allowing the reception chamber to fill with the honeyed fragrance of the tropical air. Huge tapestries hung on the walls from an unreachable ceiling. Jean was overcome by the feeling of grace, elegance and dignity of the room. Along every wall thick-legged mahogany tables were draped under glaring, spotlessly white linen tablecloths and loaded down under great pyramids of sandwiches, cakes and sweetmeats.

In a discreet, out-of-the-way corner an American-style cocktail bar did a brisk business with beautiful Haitian ladies and handsome men. Women with skins the colour of copper, gold and lemon. Men in uniform or in immaculate white-linen suits. Foreign dignitaries. Be-medalled American Marine officers. Englishmen *de rigeur* in striped morning trousers and spats. Excitable, frock-coated Frenchmen.

Glasses of Aux Cayes, Jeremie and Anse-à-Veau clicked in endless toasting. The great chamber reverberated around little Jean with bass male laughter and the tinkle of amused women. Madame Nicolas would notice the chic of the *griffe*, *quarteronne* and *metisse* ladies around her. The skin tones of the *mulatresse* and the luxuriant hair of the *maraboute*. Draped in the latest creations of Worth and Paquin, gleaming with jewellery masterpieces bought on the Rue de la Paix in Paris. Tall, erect, sinously graceful. Long shapely hands and feet. Faces that a sculptor dreams of.

They wore luxurious afternoon gowns of expensive silks, chiffons and georgettes, chic Parisian hats and gloves. Glittering sequins on net. *Cerise moire* with trains. Expensive perfumes lingering subtly on magnolia-petal skins. Soft, straight, nut-brown hair. Masses of fluffy, wavy black hair. Full red lips sensuously pouted.

Most of the men were tall, inclined to thinness. Many with the craggy, eagle features that distinguished Haiti's business and government figures. Tall, slim quadroons with tawny, dusky-yellow skins and the glowing eyes of cats. Swarthy mulattoes with crinkly, flaxen hair and pale grey eyes. Copper-coloured giants with straight, jet-black hair.

Hilderic Nicolas, sipping a thimble-sized glass of the famed but rare one hundred-year-old Presidential Rum, turned to examine the stately looking man of medium height in his mid-fifties at the head of the receiving line.

With his grey-brown eyes and aquiline nose, Louis Borno looked every inch the potentate. In his colouring he could easily have been mistaken as a native of the south of France. At the British Embassy Hilderic Nicolas had heard it whispered that while Borno was a gifted international lawyer and had the makings of a statesman, he was a little too keen on the doctrines of Benito Mussolini, the Italian fascist, for British liking.

Nicolas and the British wondered just how Borno, in his second term, might build upon what the Americans had accomplished for him in his first term. Because of the marines, the Cacos could no longer burn and pillage at will: the American-trained and American-officered Gendarmerie had seen to that. They had restored law and order, security of person and property. Prior to the U.S. occupation the tiny black nation hadn't known such stability for one hundred years. Under Borno, too, the Americans had built all-weather roads; cleaned up the streets and harbours; constructed modern docks; introduced modern sanitation and sewage-disposal systems; eliminated yellow fever; reduced the rate of malaria; reformed the prison system and installed telephones and electricity.

Hilderic Nicolas and his brother-in-law, Fortune Bogat, greatly admired the Americans; and little Jean inherited their sentiments. But the vast majority of Haiti's élite despised the occupation troops.

As a Frenchman, Nicolas could appraise the American accomplishments dispassionately, like his British employers: monumental achievements of incalculable value in equipping the island to one day govern itself. Yet he was also able to understand how his class could feel emasculated in the face of the huge, efficient American steamroller.

In the Haitian Club and in the city's private salons the mulatto aristocrats threw up their hands in theatrical Gallic gestures of disgust at the way in which the Americans had vulgarized Haitian education. They were obsessed with vocational schools at the expense of the college-preparatory schools. *Sacré bleu*! Their sons, destined to be doctors and teachers and lawyers, were being pressured to become farmers!

Nicolas knew, however, that his caste really resented something more profound. The Americans, by funnelling money into the building of trade and agricultural schools, were creating a system without precedent in Haitian society: a middle class of artisans and skilled workers. The stoic, uncomplaining, illiterate black African peasant, who could see no further than a life in the cane and sugar fields, the one on whose broad back the privileges of the ruling class were assured, could now escape by becoming a member of the bourgeoisie.

At the Institute of St. Louis de Gonzague, where Jean went to school, the dilemma of Haiti's upper-crust parents was echoed by their children. The kids were fiercely proud that the Presidential Palace was a copy of the Petit Palais on the Champs Élysées in Paris. Like Jean, they talked proudly about the military perfection of the Garde d'Haiti. Until Jean would remind them, as his father had reminded him, that the Garde d'Haiti was trained and officered by the Americans. That it was the 'Yanquis' who had built the Presidential Palace after Haitians had burned down the original structure in one of their many revolutions.

When words led to blows at the big, white three-story academy in Port-au-Prince, the good Brothers of Christian Instruction could be counted on to intervene on the side of the Americans: the Institute of St. Louis de Gonzague, like all private schools in the country, was continuing in operation at the sufferance of the Marine Corps. If the Brothers, a French order of Catholic priests, weren't careful, they might find themselves tutoring farmers instead of the country's future professional men and government leaders.

After more than a decade of U.S. occupation, most members of Haitian nobility had settled down to the humiliating belief that the *blancs* were in their little nation to stay and that the American government had written them off as unable to tie their own shoelaces. So they tolerated the occupiers with contempt veiled thinly behind French good manners and extravagances.

Jean was only ten years old in 1928 when his father sent him to boarding school in France. Even at that early age the Americans had cornered the market on his heart and imagination. The conquest would radically influence the course of his life.

Jean made the long ocean voyage with his brother Vildebart, who was four years his senior. Vildebart had been in school in France earlier, and had returned home briefly for a vacation, and was then returning.

It was too much for Jean to be brave as the family stood in farewell on the long, elbow-shaped breakwater. It was hard, too, for Hilderic and Lucy Nicolas to say goodbye to their youngest and dearest son, a handsome boy inclined to plumpness, big for his age; a boy with an agile mind, a loving heart, generous to a fault. They knew that when next they saw him their baby would be a young man.

They watched until the ship was a smudge on the cobalt horizon. When it disappeared an era had ended for them.

The French-style home of the Nicolas's was never emptier than on that night. Carmen, the fourteen-year-old daughter, was devastated. She doted on her little brother as only an older sister can. He idolized her.

His parents sat in their living room and said little to each other. Nicolas, usually a silent, undemonstrative man, was more reserved than ever. Madame cried: amid the constellation of religious pictures on the wall were likenesses of her two boys – smiling, confident, full of promise. She looked at the picture of Jean, in his velveteen suit with the knee pants, posing by an ornate chair in a photographer's salon, she thought about the dream. The tears came freely.

She'd never told her husband about it, and she never would.

Lucie Dalicy Nicolas had always consulted dreams for consolation and guidance during the crises in her life. She was also a profound believer in the supremacy of wild herbs and plants over the prescriptions of the University of Haiti's doctors of medicine. On countless occasions, when her own children or those of relatives were ill and failed to respond to physicians' treatment, she had successfully used her own potions.

While Hilderic Nicolas would be relieved that the children had been cured, he was always nervous when his

112

wife played doctor. He knew she was a perfectly sane, intelligent woman; but in an island saturated with voodoo, some might get the preposterous notion that she was maybe some kind of *boucour* – a voodoo practitioner of the healing arts.

Nor was it just Hilderic Nicolas who was nervous about his wife's dabbling as a herbalist. Her brother, Fortune Bogat, was concerned. He was just beginning to get a foothold in the business world in the early thirties after years of struggle; such rumours were the last thing he wanted.

Getting established was easier for him than for most other high-brow Haitians because he actually liked the Americans, with whom he did as much business as he could. He would find himself allied with private American interests in such ventures as sugar, railroads and communications, ultimately becoming the exclusive representative for General Motors Corp. on the island. In Haiti, even more so than in the U.S., a successful business career depended on making the right social connections and maintaining them. It could embarrass him among the Americans, who did not understand such things, to be known as Bogat, the brother of the *boucour*.

Several months before Jean's birth on 20 October 1918 Madame Nicolas had a frightening dream. In it she met a stranger who told her the quickening in her womb was a boy, and that she must name him Jean. Dutifully she had taken him to the cathedral on Armistice Day 1918 and he was christened Jean Marcel. But the warning in the dream never ceased to trouble her: the stranger said that if her new son were ever to forsake the lovely island that had conceived him in its radiant warmth, she would never see him again.

Chapter Seven

At the Aristide Briand Academy in St. Nazaire, Jean wallowed in terminal homesickness. The European winter bleached his bones. Bitter winds blew the corrosive spray of the rolling North Atlantic into every crevice of the coastal city, inflating him with gloom.

But there was more than the abrasive climate of Brittany feeding his deepening misery.

In the huge dormitory, with its alien smells and impersonal students, the two black boys kneeled on the polished floor each night just as Madame Nicolas had taught them. Prayer was their most intimate link with home. They enjoyed it. Yet on their knees they were most vulnerable to the jeers and taunts of the upper class men.

Vildebart, wincing under the sting of the taunting, was fearful – but not for himself. He knew that Jean was highly emotional and couldn't take it for long. It would do no good to tell his brother that every new boy had to go through it; that it was part of boarding-school life. He realized that although Jean was only ten, he was unusually big and strong for his age and before long would retaliate.

'Pray aloud, Jean, and drown them out,' he whispered.

It was useless. The louder they prayed, the louder the chorus of insult.

One night Jean sprang to his feet and grabbed the ringleader. The bigger boy was totally surprised at the unexpected response of the new kid to the customary ritual. He backed away, but Jean stayed with him toe-to-toe. 'You want to fight?' he screamed. 'If you do, I'll fight you!'

The French boy blanched, speechless.

Jean swirled around to the mob closing in around them. 'I'll fight any of you!' he raged. 'Come on! Who wants to be first?'

In his bed that night he wept. He was far from home, and his heart ached. This was not the France nor were these the Frenchmen of the books he'd read and re-read. They were remote from the brave, noble heroes he'd fantasized about when the French Brothers of Christian Instruction at St. Louis de Gonzague had woven the stories of their homeland.

He threw himself into the school's stiff, classical regimen of mathematics, science and languages to drown out the hurt inside. But it wouldn't go away. His bubble had been too cruelly burst. He was another victim of the innocent beastliness of the boarding-school system. He yearned for his mother's arms around him, the security of his father's presence. He longed for his own bed, for familiar food.

He awakened one morning to the familiar tolling of the first bell. A dormitory full of yawning, groaning, stretching boys in their nightshirts grumbled their way out of bed. Jean crossed to the window – and gasped.

Snow!

The first snow of the year. The first he'd ever seen. Hundreds of times he'd read about it. Seen pictures of it. Now he was about to get his first feel of the magical stuff.

The washing, the dressing, the bed-making, the polishing of his rectangle of dormitory floor that morning seemed to take forever. He hardly touched his breakfast with nervous excitement. Finally he was outside on the campus romping in the glorious, tingly, powdery, marvellous snow.

He thought of his sister Carmen and his promise at the dockside: she'd never seen snow either, and he'd told her

115

that the first time he saw some, he'd scoop up a boxful and mail it to her.

As the angry, grey waters of the North Atlantic lashed the harbour at St. Nazaire that December of 1928, Jean's memory took him to poinsettia season back home – as tall as trees, their scarlet blossoms as large as dinner plates. He thought of the wondrous trees and flowers that the boys of Aristide Briand had never seen. Breadfruit. Frangipani. Crotons.

How he missed the Haitian mornings. The breeze from the hills carrying the smell of coffee roasting in thousands of peasant *cailles*, the pungent aroma of burning charcoal. The throbbing of the drums somewhere in the towering hills, defying his sense of direction. The dank, greenhouse smell as he stepped out of the house after a heavy rainfall.

What French boy could know the lilting song of the *marchandes*, the peasant women in their colourful bandanas, their baskets of wares balanced perfectly on their heads, padding to the Iron Market in their bare feet. Ramrod straight. Hips swivelling, and their high-pitched call, telling the world what they had to sell. Leaving behind them on a hot, dusty afternoon a lingering trail of soft Creole, liquid as if it were a scent and not a language. Their laughter at some private joke sounding like water caressing a beach.

Or some of the wealthier ones riding their donkeys side-saddle, their baskets heaped with mangoes and bananas. Calabashes the size of cannonballs. The hollow clop-clop of *le shine*, the shoeshine boys, hammering their brushes on the rungs of their footrests, trying to drum up business.

And at night, as he knelt in prayer amid the foreign smell of French polish and stiff, laundered sheets, he imagined the sudden fall of night in Port-au-Prince. It was as if someone pulled down a blind. The touch of the velvet night on his face. The croaking of the *crapauds*.

In time Jean emerged from the exile of homesickness.

116

The appetite for excellence which his teachers demanded left him little time for moping. What he couldn't shake, however, was the reputation he'd gained for being a brawler. Like the 'top gun' in an American Western, he had innocently set up himself as the tough hombre to beat. For months Vildebart had managed to steer him clear of trouble. But given Jean's quick temper and boarding school ethics, it was only a matter of time before he got into serious trouble.

It happened when a seventeen-year-old senior tried to get him to join in some horseplay that both knew was strictly against school regulations. Jean refused. The senior insisted, and when Jean said no the second time, the senior slapped his face. Jean jumped back nimbly, whipped out a knife and threw it at his tormentor.

Luckily for both of them, it hit the senior in the hand, nicking a finger. What was a minor injury to him, however, turned out to be a major wound to Jean's reputation. In the sacrosanct code of the boarding school for young French gentlemen, he had committed sacrilege. Even though the student council's investigation of the incident completely exonerated him, he had nevertheless lived up to the French boys' stereotype of the black savage.

From then on they were to treat him as one.

The incident had an unusual effect. Suddenly Jean had become mature beyond his years.[1]

Until his arrival in France, Jean had been more French in his feelings than Haitian; France had more glory and heroes for a boy to look up to than little Haiti. As the son of a Guadeloupe-born Frenchman, it was very natural that he was a Francophile. He was quickly discovering at the Aristide Briand school, though, that Frenchmen – certainly young French gentlemen – were no better than his comrades back in Port-au-Prince. If anything, they were

[1]'After it happened,' says his brother Vildebart, 'Jean could be considered an adult.'

a lot worse. The hurt and disillusionment had fuelled his feelings of Haitian nationalism.

In Haiti he was on the upper rung of the social ladder. In St. Nazaire he was just another black colonial.

Jean told himself that if he were to survive he'd have to be tough and not yield an inch – no matter how big his adversaries. He would take on all comers.

In the Nicolas home, occupying the place of honour on the wall in the centre of the family pictures, was the image of the Sacred Heart of Jesus. Second only to the picture of the crucified Christ in mystical influence on Jean's life had always been the notion, of *La Belle* France. She had always been hallowed in his limitless, little boy's imagination. She was the mystery of *La Marseillaise*. The majesty of the Arc de Triomphe. The sadness of the Tomb of the Unknown Soldier. The glory of the Eiffel Tower. But at the Aristide Briand Academy he had seen her in a housecoat and curlers without her make-up.

He was a disappointed lover, angry and bitter, with a great emptiness to be filled.

At ten, he was of an age when the only place a child can find identity is in the accomplishment and honours of his parents, relatives and homeland. Haiti was soft, beautiful, endlessly ablaze with sunshine. In the face of the taunts and jeers of the academy's French-gentlemen bullies he bragged about his island. But his loud proclamations were silent evidence of his sense of rejection that France had snubbed him. Too often the Haitian glories he boasted about were the technological gifts of the Americans.

In his heart he was a boy without a country. He found himself thinking more and more about the U.S. Marines, warming himself on the memories. In reality they hadn't gone too far away, he consoled himself. Florida was just a few hundred miles across the water from Port-au-Prince. Haiti was almost part of the United States! But for a few miles of water he was an American, too, wasn't he?

He could, he supposed, call himself a North American.

His mother could read between the lines of his brave letters home. Behind his proud recitations of excellent grades in maths, science, history, English and German she could feel the struggle. After two and a half years she and her husband could take it no longer. They arranged for the two boys to transfer to the College de Garçon in Grasse.

Twenty miles from Nice, Grasse was bathed by the Mediterranean and warmed by sunshine rivalling Haiti's. It was ideal for a homesick Haitian – provided he could survive the winter of another boarding-school initiation. Here Jean was happier. But Vildebart, whose health had begun to suffer in the flinty, unremitting winters of northern France, wasn't responding to the glorious new climate. After only a term at the College de Garçon, Hilderic Nicolas told his sons to come home.

Carmen didn't recognize Jean when he stepped onto the dock at Port-au-Prince: the plump, baby-faced ten-year-old had become a muscular, poised young man of thirteen who looked and acted as if he were at least sixteen.

In the lush tropical surroundings of home Jean slowly began to thaw St. Nazaire's frost out of his bones and out of his heart. On his native soil his generosity and spontaneity began to flower again. The wonder of seeing old friends and exploring old haunts made him radiate. He was unbelieveably happy to be with his own colour again. To belong again.

Hilderic Nicolas was also happy. Privately, though, he wondered how long Jean's exuberance would last. He had seen many a Haitian return from Europe only to lead a life of discontent: three years of marinating in France, of beholding the world – and Haiti – through the monocle of the French aristocracy, could never rub off. As long as a Haitian stayed at home he could go on believing it was an island jewel in the necklace of the Antilles. But from Europe he was forced to perceive it as it really was – one of the poorest nations on the earth. For the 127 years of its existence the sun had beaten down on its green beauty, incubating in its landed gentry an indifference to its abounding poverty. A Haitian aristocrat could look out from his back veranda and not see the native *caille* seventy-five yards away – or its dirt-poor occupants. Five percent of its 4.5 million people would continue their lives of privilege and pleasure while the other ninety-five percent had to be satisfied toiling endlessly in the sugar and coffee plantations of the privileged. They'd go on gossiping in their Creole vernacular by day and at night slip off to a cockfight. Or steal away into the mountains for their *tafia* and *clairin* wine and their mystical voodoo ceremonies. For them today was the same as yesterday; tomorrow the same as today. They were content for it to remain that way.

Hilderic Nicolas could remember when there hadn't been a single all-weather road in the country. Now there were 500 miles of new roads, courtesy of the U.S. Marine Corps.

And yet for all the good the Americans brought, he knew they had caused a lot of problems. Among the peasants, where the idea of formal marriage was almost unknown, a man had several wives. It was the *placée* system which made prostitution unnecessary. Yet the Americans had encouraged brothels along with their roads and their sanitation and their educational system. Almost 150 whore-houses had sprung up in Port-au-Prince to cater to them.

Yes, it *was* disgusting, Jean's father concluded.

As for the educational system: M. Nicolas surely didn't want *his* two sons becoming farmers.

Back home, Jean was enrolled at the Harry Tippen-hauer Academy, a private school with a reputation for high scholastic standards and firm discipline.

Whenever he could sneak away, he broadened his education by slipping down to the *basse ville* to watch the Americans. They were quartered inside the Presidential Palace in a large barracks area within the palace quad-rangle. He liked to watch the big, leather-faced men

120

marching in perfect precision, doing spectacular displays with their rifles as if they were a circus troupe.

They were always so unbelievably neat. Razor-sharp creases in their pants. Shirts that fitted perfectly; and they even ironed creases in the sleeves – creases that ran vertically up the front, through the centreline of the breast pockets, over the shoulders and down the back. He'd seen them when he peeked into their barracks, sweating over their ironing boards. And their shoes! They'd sit for hours on their barracks steps, buffing a spit shine on cordovan shoes that mirrored the sun.

The *blancs* really thought they were God's gift to the world.

He laughed at their fractured English: their pronunciations would have made his English teacher cry.

Sometimes he'd go all the way down to the breakwater they'd built and watch their ships unload. Their forest-green Ford trucks plied back and forth with more supplies and equipment in one day than most Haitians had seen in their entire life's time. As they pulled away, dozens of urchins would hang from the tailgates.

Sometimes he wasn't sure if he should admire or detest the nation that could produce such mountains of material and such cocksure, confident men. By contrast Haiti was so unbearably destitute, its people so impotent and demoralized.

Another of his diversions was watching the young *Garde d'Haiti* cadets training at the Caserae Darti-guenave. For hours Jean would stare at them as they drilled to exhaustion under their American instructors. Many of the young future officers were light-skinned, he noticed, so he concluded that there were obviously other élite families who agreed that the Americans weren't so bad after all. He was surprised by the large number of jet-black cadets. Peasants from the interior, he told himself, with no learning, no culture, no sophistication. He'd heard his father's friends say that the trouble with the Americans was they carried democracy too far; that they had no sense of class. They thought it perfectly all right to mesh the light-skinned cadets and their black peasant counterparts together to enjoy the same pay and privileges and share the same barracks – and to train them to officer Haiti's army together!

Yet Jean noticed something very significant: when the stocky marine sergeant drilled them in their khaki tunics and breeches, leggings, heavy boots and wide-brimmed hats, the glaring colour difference didn't seem to affect their precision.

He wondered what his parents would say if he told them he wanted to become a cadet.

The drill and the uniforms weren't the sole attractions. The Marines had introduced boxing in the training of the young officers-to-be. Pugilism was still being taught, and Jean watched them for hours as they sparred in little groups.

The Americans had brought music to the caserne, too, by encouraging the formation of the Presidential Band.

The best time to hear it was early on Sunday mornings before the sun climbed too high.

The military musicians grouped under the canopy of a huge sablier tree growing in one corner of the parade ground. They sat on chairs and had their music on racks. In the centre stood an ancient little Haitian, impeccable in a white suit, on a raised platform. He was M. Occide Jeanty, director of the Presidential Band.

Jean liked the classical works, but he'd wait hours for the jazz melodies that the little conductor had borrowed from the Americans.

The Americans! Always the Americans! It made a Haitian boy feel very insignificant. Yet he couldn't help but admire them . . .

Haiti had its heritage, too, though, he chided himself, remembering the epics of Haitian history being drummed into him by the teachers at the Tippenhauer school.

Harry Tippenhauer, the black headmaster with German blood in his veins, found his new student who had been schooled in France a joy to teach.[2] When he explained something to Jean, even before he'd finished his explanation, the youth was far ahead of him.

Jean liked history and science, excelling in both.

He had a shotgun-blast curiosity that compelled him to learn everything he could. He could become so intrigued in history class with a revolution or a great battle that he would still be captivated in mathematics class, deafening him to the theorems of Pythagoras that day.

Headmaster Tippenhauer couldn't really hold Jean's daydreaming against him. It was more than offset by his generous nature with teachers and students alike.[3]

Outside class Jean was winning popularity with his growing repertoire of stories about life in a French boarding school.

By the end of his first year at the Tippenhauer school he had many friends. He preferred the company of crowds of other fourteen-year-olds rather than one or two close comrades. Invariably he was the centre of attention. He was fun to be around, and he was bigger and stronger than the others.

By the time Jean was almost fifteen his own identity was taking root. He was now spending more and more of his free time outside the Nicolas home at 106 Rue des Caserne near the centre of Port-au-Prince. During the long summer vacation from school in 1933 he was restless and constantly on the go. Sometimes it was close to night before his anxious parents would see him again, striding into the courtyard, smiling his wide, infectious grin and ravenously hungry.

He spent a lot of his time and pocket money at the Rex Theatre watching American movies. He enjoyed gangster

[2]Retired now and still living in Port-au-Prince, he remembers Jean as 'an extremely bright' pupil. He says the boy was 'intellectually curious about everything.'

[3]'He would help anyone,' says Tippenhauer, 'and completely forget about himself. All the time with such a good mood about him that you couldn't stop him.'

films and those about black American jazz artists and boxers. After a movie he and his friends would rendezvous somewhere to relive the exploits of John Dillinger or the Mills Brothers, parroting whatever new gangster lingo or jazz *patois* they'd picked up in the Rex that afternoon.

He had a so-called parrot's ear for dialects and languages. From his contacts with Americans on film and in the flesh, the precise, British-accented English he'd learned in France was growing lazy in a convincing American drawl. And as he got older and began to frequent bars, he delighted in striking up conversations with any U.S. Marines he might find there, pretending he was an American, too.

Among the Haitian young set of the mid-thirties, when athletics was a *cause célèbre* in Port-au-Prince, newsreels of American heavyweight champion Joe Louis regularly drew huge crowds to the Rex. The films were the inspiration for Jean himself to get into the ring. At sixteen, he was more than six feet tall and had a powerful physique. Pièrre Gabrielle, one of his closest boyhood friends, and today one of Haiti's leading sports promoters, became his manager.

Jean did well in the amateur tournaments. Boxing's chief compensation came to be a boost to another facet of his ego: the daughters of high society thronged to see the muscles ripple under his light-brown skin and to marvel at the litheness of his exquisitely proportioned body. Unfortunately his ring career came to a shameful close when, before an important bout, manager Gabrielle mistakenly rubbed him down with Sloan's Liniment instead of oil. Jean was afire – but gamely went a full round before Gabrielle threw in the towel.

Even so, the young ladies kept using their coquetry on him whether he won or lost: although Hilderic Nicolas himself might not have been wealthy, he was nevertheless distinguished in Port-au-Prince and related through his

124

wife to money. Thus Jean looked like excellent marriage material.

His disguise was perfect.

Like the typical young Haitian gallant, he was quick to recruit poetry, flattery and flowers to help him in his conquests. He worked hard at polishing the witty phrase and the penetrating observation to win their admiration. Yet unlike his friends, who unblushingly discussed their sexual exploits with one another, he kept such intimate matters to himself. They kept prattling on about their victories and their intended conquests. He kept talking about what he was going to do with his life.

As he often told Gabrielle, his ambition was to rove to the ends of the earth and to become very rich.

At sixteen, after three years at home in the beautiful island he once thought he'd never want to leave, he was ominously restless and impatient to go again.[4]

The best within the limits of his class was the Saturday night dances at the nightclubs. The Club Bellevue, the Club Cercle, the Port-au-Princien and the Trocadero were his most popular haunts.

The Trocadero was in Bizoton, an hour's drive west along the curve of the bay. Its vast vine-and-rose-entangled veranda extended to the water's edge where palm trees nodded in the soft tropic breeze. On a typical Saturday evening Port-au-Prince's beautiful people – and those who aspired to be – glided across the mirror-polish of its dance floor, while gay, multicoloured Chinese lanterns festooned from the ceiling cast whirling shadows around the room.

The best-looking *sang-mêlés* in town were there to be seen – and, hopefully for Jean and his friends – to be danced with. The girls' complexions ranged from ebony and coffee to amber and cream. As these beauties in their

[4]'Haiti was too quiet, too small for Jean,' says Gabrielle. 'He was always wanting something new, something more exciting.'

diaphanous Paris gowns tangoed and rhumbaed sensuously, waltzed gracefully or revelled in the *merinque*, white-suited musicians played spiritedly, rivulets of perspiration trickling down their faces.

Jean favoured the lighter-skinned girls. The idea of a white woman – especially white Americans like the voluptuous gun molls of the gangster movies, was the summit of his fantasy life. Here and there in the Trocadero it was possible to see a beauty with blonde hair and Nordic features. But he knew that they were still *de couleur*.

For Jean, however, there was a drawback in the nightclub circuit. It was populated by the same refined, genteel, educated and worldly people who had surrounded him all his life. Gradually the glamour and excitement of the Saturday dances faded, and he hunted for new and more daring diversions.

Down on the waterfront the nightlife lasted until dawn.

In the vast Open Market, the *Marche en Haut*, sleeping men, women and children lay with their pigs and *bouriques* full of vegetables, hugging their wares in their sleep for fear they'd be stolen. Along the Rue Nacional, scores of tiny, yellow lights gleamed. They were the stalls of the *marchandes viandes*, the teeming city's all-night restaurants. They were simply a box on the ground, an oil lamp and a barefooted woman glistening in the shadows. On the box there'd be a stack of *rapidou* cakes, the native sugar, and a few slices of coarse cassave bread selling for a centime or two.

It was a world Jean had never known.

The nights were oppressively hot. Often a storm lay over the city, with a thick roof of clouds sealing in the heat and the smells of humanity, the aroma of wood smoke and roasting coffee from the Open Market. Great black bats flitted overhead like ghostly kites.

He found the mystery and the gloom electrifying.

Sometimes he'd wander west to the poor quarter, the *Croix des Bossales*, remembering that thousands of

African slaves had once stood there in chains, waiting to be auctioned. Just behind them was the deep marsh into which the bodies of dead slaves had been pushed. Deep in the same sink-hole, he knew, were the corpses of the losers in Haiti's countless revolutions.

He roved the prostitutes' sections of the city. For Jean the shadows of the night there still crackled with the passions and tempers of a hundred years before he was born.

He wandered among the diminutive shops and cafés and sniffed the aroma of *tafia* and *clairin*, the poor man's wines, clinging to the night air. The doors of the ticky-tacky little places were usually wide open. Anyone was welcome. The dim flickering of kerosene lamps and candles illuminated ceiling and walls completely covered with multicoloured paper festoons. Amid the kaleidescope of colours and shadows, huddles of laughing, sweaty men rolled dice.

Further on in the *quartier* was the section almost exclusively reserved for the girls of Spanish extraction, the *Dominicaines*, who had come across the frontier from the Dominican Republic. The streets of the Frontier, as the Spanish girls' province was called, were shadowy, tortuous lanes. Its ladies of easy virtue batted their eyelids from flimsy dwellings that were drab and grey-bleached. The quarter was an obstacle course of sagging verandas, rotting steps and porch pillars pulled out, termites swarming in the sockets.

Jean found the disorder fascinating.

He watched the girls beckoning from behind open windows. In their violently bright colours they blazed against their drab surroundings like brilliantly plumaged tropical birds. Gowns of silk and satin. In scarlet, purple, flame and sulphur.

At La Paloma Blanca, a rambling villa on the Marquisand Road, Jean noticed that the madame corseted her *Dominicaines* to heighten their bosoms unnaturally and exaggerate the width of their hips. The Americans liked them that way, he was told. He wondered why they didn't object to their legs, which always seemed to him to be as thin as pouter pigeons'. Jean wondered why the older ones were so popular with the Americans when there were so many nubile ones available. After a little dancing, the khaki-clad *blancs* would be lead off the dance floor by the hand and up the ornate, curving stairway that had been the pride of some French colonist a hundred years previously.

He first noticed her on one of his later explorations in the Frontier.

She was magnificent, he thought, as she sat in shimmering satin on her veranda, a great scallop of pearly skin exposed by her gown cut waist-low in the back. It stopped his heart. She tilted her flawless skull as he approached, permitting him a glimpse of her sculpted profile. Then she turned and tormented him with a head-on contemplation of her pale, oval face and the crimson Cupid's bow of her lips.

As he eased closer, her delicately balanced head pivoted away, letting him explore the extravagance of her blue-black hair caught up over tiny ears and pinned triumphantly high in a Spanish twist.

He was frightened. He hurried on to the Crystal Palace, a busy bordello outside the city limits.

There tall, lithe Dominican girls rhumbaed on a tiny floor with their men-for-the-night. He stood at the door watching. Light streamed from the salon through open jalousies, and he could see that they were wearing little or nothing at all beneath their long, flared skirts.

These Spaniards had to be truly superior creatures, he reasoned, if they were able to sell what many Haitian women were willing – even eager – to give away.

He sat at his table on the edge of the dance floor, drank rum and watched the game of life go on around him. Occasionally one of the Dominicans, indifferent to the partner she had, would dance close to him and brush past him suggestively with a swish of her long, tafetta skirts. But it was the sensational lady in satin on the veranda whose beauty had frightened him, that consumed his thoughts.

Some time later, his self-confidence braced by the rum, he left the Crystal Palace a little unsteadily and made his way back to the district of the narrow streets and sagging porches. His heart beat faster with each step. She wasn't where he had left her. Instead she was inside entertaining an American marine – with several other marines waiting their turn. Crushed and humiliated, he stumbled off through the broken-down houses of the shanty town to quench his burning disappointment in the potent *clairin* wine.

All it did was escalate his anger. An hour later he staggered out of the little tavern and made his way back. Crashing into her *boudoir*, he grabbed the marine and began beating him savagely. The other two marines came to their friend's defence and attacked Nicholas. But his rage was so tremendous that he threw them through the tottering porch and into the street.

From that night on he was on the 'Most Wanted' list of the United States Marine Corps.

He couldn't hide his bloody nose and bruises from his parents. Distraught at the new twist in Jean's adolescence, they turned, as always in such crises, to Uncle Fortune. He made the pronouncement that if Jean kept it up, it was merely a matter of time before their unpredictable young son – regardless of how big, strong and fearless he was – would be found one morning in the gutter.

Jean was granted a sudden, totally unexpected reprieve: President Franklin D. Roosevelt dramatically announced that the U.S. Occupation of Haiti would end in 1934.

Uncle Fortune wiped his brow. Yet his feelings about the imminent departure of the Americans were mixed. He had made many friends among them. Because of them his business had prospered. On the other hand, he couldn't help feeling pleased to see his sister and her husband smile once again. Now, he told them, if they could just keep the boy on a tight rein for a few months until the actual U.S. withdrawal.

Jean couldn't stay infuriated with the Marine Corps forever. How could he? They'd entertained him for hours – drilling at the Presidential Palace. Unloading their cargoes down at the docks. Their mannerisms amused him. Their profanity made him laugh. Their slang intrigued him. It would be strange not to see their familiar white faces. Not to hear the 'Hup . . . tup . . . threep . . . fourp!' as they strode down the Champs de Mar. They made the town important. They filled it with a sense of action. A sense of something happening.

The new American president, in a dramatic goodwill gesture, invited Haitian President Stenio Vincent for a state visit to Washington. Stenio accepted and the nineteen-year-long sore of U.S.-Haitian relations began to heal. During its 1934 manoeuvres the American fleet anchored in Port-au-Prince and the city's high society thronged aboard the U.S.S. *Saratoga* for a gala reception. In July President Roosevelt came to Haiti. Port-au-Prince went wild in releasing its pent-up feelings. It was the most extravagant festival in the city's history. The battleships *Franklin Delano Roosevelt* and the *Houston* anchored off Cape Haitien. A model of the aeroplane in which Lindbergh had flown the Atlantic was woven in brilliant flowers and proudly exhibited downtown. The American president, saving the good wine until the last, made the momentous announcement that his forces would leave the island two months earlier than scheduled. As a farewell gesture, he made a free gift to Haiti of all Marine Corps buildings and equipment on the island!

Nineteen years of political humiliation for the islanders had come to an end.

On the eve of the departure that August of 1934, more Americans fraternized with more Haitians – and vice versa – and clinked more glasses together than in all of the

130

occupation years. When the last American vessel sailed, and its foghorn boomed a sonorous farewell all over the city, tens of thousands of delirious citizens cheered frenetically.

Jean, however, was filled with the loneliness that he'd known as a ten-year-old at the boarding school in France.

He tried valiantly to maintain the expected deference to his father's authority and his mother's love. Yet he did not deceive them. They sensed that within their submissive son was really a smouldering volcano.

The child who once had so much to say his mouth was rarely closed now estranged himself in long sieges of silence. When he spoke he couched his language *à la* the Rex Theatre's moviescreen mobsters. His father reminded him endlessly that he was misusing the language; that it was certainly not the way English was spoken at the British Embassy.

The remonstrations were useless: it was Jean's way of challenging parental authority without openly defying it.

Hilderic Nicolas wasn't the only figure of authority being challenged. He had company in Headmaster Tippenhauer.

Jean, bored with the unrelenting admonitions of St. Thomas Aquinas and St. Augustine in the classroom and in the cathedral, had begun to dip into the writings of Wilhelm Friedrich Nietzsche. In Catholic Haiti, where the greatest compliment one could pay a member of the élite was to mistake him for a Frenchman, Jean couldn't have chosen a more repugnant champion. Nietzsche was not only a German, he was also an intensely anti-Catholic, anti-Christian ex-priest.

It was not only embarrassing but disrupting to the Tippenhauer academy for Jean to slip Nietzsche's views into class discussion; for him to stand up and announce that Christianity was all wrong because it taught its followers to prop up the weak and preserve the unhealthy. They should be allowed to die off, said Jean, parroting the

131

Nietzschian dialectic. Then society would contain only the best of the species.

Even if Jean had been smaller, and even if his father's health hadn't been declining, a good, old-fashioned licking with a razor strap would have been a waste of time.[5]

Jean's iconoclasm was clearly prejudicial to good order in school, and Headmaster Tippenhauer knew that he could not tolerate the heresy forever. He had tried as long as humanly possible to contain Jean verbally. It hadn't worked, and he was forced to give Jean the only medicine he felt would cure the disease – a classical public-school whipping before his peers.

Jean was grossly humiliated when the headmaster ordered him to bend over the desk. He took the lashing stoically. When it was over, he turned upon the big, bull-chested Tippenhauer, wrestled him for the cane, forced him over the desk and reciprocated.

That, Madame Nicolas would admit thirty-seven years later, was why her son was expelled from school.

Within Port-au-Prince's small upper-class community, where almost everyone was a relative of almost everyone else, it was impossible to hide the scandal. How could the wayward boy so deeply humiliate his dignified father. *Sacré bleu*! What would he do next?

Once again the counsel of Uncle Fortune was retained. The shame was dreadful, sighed Madame Nicolas. But much worse, muttered her husband, was that Jean had wasted all his years of expensive schooling: he had forfeited his high school diploma!

Uncle Fortune rubbed his craggy features contemplatively. As one of the island's leading businessmen, he had friends in important places. He would see what he could do. So he embarked on a ticklish conspiracy to persuade

[5]'He was a very headstrong young man,' remembered Uncle Fortune. 'When he wanted to do something, he did it. His teachers were always complaining that they were having to discipline him. He didn't agree with what they said. He was very outspoken, and he wasn't afraid to start a fight with anybody.'

the bruised, ruffled headmaster to grant Jean his Baccaulaureate Part I and Part II – even though his nephew hadn't completed the required schooling. Uncle Fortune, ever the politician, brought it off! But now, they all wondered, what in the name of God were they to do with the boy?

Uncle Fortune, then in his late thirties, was the only adult who could get through to Jean. They were two of a kind. Fortune in his young days had dazzled the ladies, consumed his quota of rum and raised plenty of hell. He well knew how a hot-blooded youth could be ripped apart by puberty pulling one way and duty the other. He knew what his rebellious nephew was going through, and he empathized with him. In a society that often displayed anti-American sentiments, they were both ardent admirers of the recently departed marines. That made them even more *sympatico*. Yet their accord brought only a temporary interruption in Jean's antics.

With no more marines to throw out of the Frontier, Jean had begun to antagonize his comrades by stealing their girlfriends – and the wives of men he didn't even know. He didn't have to steal. He had what it took to win almost any young girl in the city. He could make love in any language, best of all Creole.

That really took his ladies by surprise: many upper crust families considered it fashionable to claim they knew no Creole. Being the *patois* of the peasantry, it was considered beneath them. Yet all of them had picked up Creole from the black nurses who had rocked their cradles and later had to use it to communicate with their servants, workers and market-women. In some high-born families Creole was used privately to express tenderness and intimacy. Its soft, liquid sounds had been recruited by Jean in his bedroom relationships – much to the delight of his partners. With his parrot's ear he orchestrated his romantic productions with the melody of Spanish coquetry purloined from his interludes with the Dominican *belles-de-nuit* at the Frontier. His passion for love competed with his obsession for American gangster movies; the modus operandi was always the same: the lady and her chaperone would be dropped off in front of the Rex by a considerate fiancé or indulgent husband, who would then drive off to his office or a luncheon appointment at the Haitian Club. Madame and chaperone would buy their tickets and take their seats in the dark interior. A side door always remained unlocked – courtesy of the theatre manager, who had much experience in these matters. The lady, after a prudent delay, would then leave her chaperone and exit by the side door, where 'Johnny Nicholas,' as he was now calling himself, awaited her.

A couple of hours later she would return through the same side entrance in time for the final scenes, then exit with her escort. During the short walk from the seats to the waiting car, madame would arm herself with sufficient details of the film's plot from her chaperone – just in case. Then the spouse or beau would drive them back to one of the wealthy suburbs, such as Bois Verna or Kenscoff, none the wiser.

For 'Johnny' the plot was the same; only the characters had changed: it wasn't vengeful U.S. Marines he was dodging anymore but jealous buddies and cuckolded husbands. So what? It was still the thrill of the chase – and being chased.

The theatrical and melodramatic tactics he used to avoid his pursuers warned Uncle Fortune that unless something radical was done, Jean could grow up like one of his gangster-movie heroes.[6]

The temperature in Haiti begins to climb from a daily average of ninety degrees in April to around ninety-two degrees in May. By June it has reached ninety-five. Unlike the United States, where a ninety-five-degree day can be followed by a ninety-degree day, the heat in Haiti never

---

[6]Bogat recalls: 'He'd always enter a tavern, for example, and before he sat down he'd always check for the other exits. He was always prepared for what was going to happen.'

varies during the summer. Within a degree or two a typical July will register ninety-eight degrees day after day, week after week; and August is an unyielding repetition of July.

This results in a tremendous heat mass over the island in summer. The seasonal shifting of the winds brings a humidity that makes the heat even harder to bear. It is the time of incredibly heavy rains.

Sitting on their verandas about five o'clock one summer evening, the Nicolas family, like everyone in Port-au-Prince, was perspiring heavily, praying for seven o'clock when the cool breezes would begin rushing down the mountains towering behind them, bringing blessed relief. As they glanced toward the hills they saw inky black clouds curling around the hilltops and drifting down the valleys toward the town. Yet their veranda was bathed in brilliant sunshine.

It was always that way before a violent storm...

In minutes, fat raindrops splatted their courtyard, leaving spots as big as silver dollars. They knew that up in the hills the dark clouds had unleashed a deluge and that soon the dusty little hillside trails would be raging torrents.

In fifteen minutes the gutters on the side of the road by the Nicolas house churned and hissed with water a foot deep. The burnished sun had paled to a sickly grey. Blinding flashes of lightning burned through the haze. Staggering explosions of thunder assaulted the eardrums and rocked the earth. An icy wind swept down the mountainside like an avenging scythe, whipping pliant palms almost to the ground. Massive mango trees and oaks groaned under the punishment.

Outside, the road was a raging torrent three feet deep, sweeping to the sea stones, rocks, branches, tree trunks and everything else that got in the way.

Then with a cataclysmic eruption of thunder, lightning and water, almost like the grand finale in a musical, it stopped. In the shattering silence the cobwebs of fog retreated up the valleys as if ashamed of the commotion they had caused. And once again – until tomorrow about the same time, Haiti would be its usual, scented, sun-drenched self.

The population of Port-au-Prince feared the daily summer rainstorms – even though they had become used to them. The authorities had constructed a special canal system, known as the Bois de Chêne, to drain the city quickly after the deluges.

Late that night, when the air was once again calm and the mountain breeze cool and sweet, the Nicolas family learned that in the poor section of town, several families had been swept into the raging Bois de Chêne and almost drowned: a heroic young man had dived in and saved them. It was their errant son, they later learned; and for his heroism he was awarded a medal by the authorities.

During his seventeenth and eighteenth years Johnny turned calm but obsessively secretive. Home had become a pit-stop to fill up on food and sleep. Had Fortune's Dutch-uncle talk scared some sense into him? Or had he finally realized his father's worsening health was serious and decided not to burden his mother with further anguish?

Uncle Fortune did some sleuthing. He went about it methodically, telephoning his colleagues who, in turn, began quizzing their sons. The picture of Jean to emerge wasn't clear. Apparently he was earning a living by tutoring in languages at several of the city's private schools. He'd been seen in biology classes at the University of Haiti. Further than that it was hard to say anything about him with certainty, and the air of mystery was to characterize him for the remainder of his life.

During this highly impressionable age he came under the influence of Herr Gardemann, a German embassy official whom Hilderic Nicolas came to know in the course of his diplomatic duties.

Gardemann appeared to be the typical, predictable

inhabitant of an overseas post of the newly emerging Third Reich. He had abrupt, military deportment. He spoke his native tongue precisely and efficiently and his manner was devoid of the frills Haitians were accustomed to in their ambassadorial representatives. Had it not been for the fact that Gardemann, in an inexplicable denial of Nazi racial philosophies, had taken a Haitian wife and would have three children by her, Hilderic Nicolas might eventually have decided to keep the German at arm's length. Certainly if he had even vaguely suspected the man's true purpose on the island he would have shunned him.

It would not be revealed for about five years – not until 1941 when Haiti declared war against Nazi Germany – that Gardemann, under diplomat's cover, was a secret agent of the *Abwehr*, reporting to Berlin the movement of British and American shipping in the Caribbean. It would also be discovered that Gardemann, prior to his arrival in Port-au-Prince, had spent time on the other side of the border with Haiti's perennial enemy – the Dominican Republic: he had been an advisor from the Nazi government to the staff of Dominican dictator Rafael Trujillo during the early thirties. The Nazis were wooing Trujillo to obtain a German naval base on the Dominican side of the island shared with Haiti. Anything that promised to make the Dominicans more of a threat to Haiti than they already were was automatically anathema to Hilderic Nicolas – as it was to any patriotic Haitian.

For years the two nations had disputed the location of their common border. Countless times Haitian peasant farmers, innocently wandering across the poorly marked demarcation line, had been shot at by the Dominican border guards. Many had been killed.

The two countries almost went to war in 1937, when thousands of Haitian peasants who had wandered across the frontier were brutally massacred.

Because of his job Hilderic Nicolas was aware of British intelligence reports that Trujillo had completed

137

arrangements for the immigration of 40,000 Germans into the Dominican Republic for settlement along the disputed border. In 1934 he had seen with his own eyes the German cruiser anchored for several weeks in Port-au-Prince bay. He had learned, too, that after the warship's departure the city's small German-Haitian community had split into two camps – pro-Nazis and anti-Nazis.

If Hilderic Nicolas had known of Gardemann's history and his real purpose in Haiti, the German would never have influenced Jean's life as he subsequently did. As it happened, Hilderic Nicolas had been dead four years when Haiti, on 12 December 1941, declared war against Nazi Germany and Gardemann was unmasked.

A few days after the declaration Gardemann's Haitian wife reported him missing. The police launched a search. The German's car was found on a desolate stretch of beach not far from Port-au-Prince. Newspapers reported it had been abandoned, with all four doors left wide open. The key in the ignition was still turned on and the gas tank was empty, triggering speculation that Gardemann had left in such a hurry he hadn't even taken time to turn off the engine.

Gardemann simply vanished. Police entered the Nazi embassy, which the Haitian government by this time had impounded, and found information which forced them to conclude he was an intelligence agent – not a bona fide diplomat, as he had said he was. Police theorized that Gardemann had been spirited back to Germany in a U-boat – either voluntarily or involuntarily.[7]

In the chronology of Jean's life, however, it was still 1936 and he was continuing his uneasy armistice with his

[7]The full identity of the mysterious Major Gardemann-if indeed that was his true name – has never been determined. The only record in the archives of WAST, a West German organization holding incomplete records on former members of Hitler's armed forces, that comes close, is one for Fritz Gonterman, who served in Paris Military Headquarters during 1943 and 1944.

family. The fragile truce was shattered when he beat up a policeman.

The gendarmes of the *Garde d'Haiti* remained the highly trained, professional corps that the U.S. Marines had manufactured. Although the Americans were gone, the constables and their black officers continued full of fanatical zeal for enforcing the law without fear or favour, whether the lawbreaker was the palest aristocrat or the blackest peasant.

The incident began insignificantly. Jean, curious about a crowd gathering around a disturbance in the streets, muscled in to find out what was happening. The gendarmes were already there, and were trying to disperse the crowd.

'Move along, *Monsieur*,' a coal-black gendarme told him.

Jean, doubtlessly fuelled by high-octane rum and too proud to take orders from someone he considered an exalted peasant fresh from the *caille*, defiantly refused.

'No,' he retorted. 'Why do I have to move along?'

The gendarme grabbed him.

That did it.

Port-au-Prince police paraded with rifles. While on police duty, however, the only weapons they carried were revolvers which they seldom used – because they had a much more persuasive implement: the *cocomacaque*. A stick about three feet long and two inches in diameter, the *cocomacaque* was the pride of its owner, who coated it with oil to enhance its ripe-banana colour. The wood was as hard as iron – especially at the huge, knotted business end.

Jean attacked the *gendarme, comomacque* and all.

Uncle Fortune, on his way downtown to the two-story frame building across from the National Palace, remembered what it was like to be arrested before the American Occupation. Arrest then always meant a beating. It could be one of three kinds. The sergeant might say to the guard: '*Réfléche-le petit-petit*,' which meant he wanted the prisoner 'refreshed' a little. If he wanted a good hiding administered he would say: '*Réfléche-le mais pas levez orgueil.*' This meant: refresh him – but don't arouse his pride. And if he wanted the unfortunate prisoner beaten to death, the command was: '*Fai pie le perdie terre,*' or: make his feet leave the earth.

As Uncle Fortune ascended the rickety steps to the red-and-yellow police headquarters building, he prayed that Port-au-Prince's *gendarmes* had remembered their American discipline and had not reverted to tradition.

Inside, putting on the *tour de force* of his trouble-shooting career, he literally snatched the arrogant, unremorseful Jean from a potential prison sentence and rescued the good name of Nicolas.

But this time Uncle Fortune put a price on his services: Jean had to get out of Haiti, and he would gladly pay his fare.

It was now 1937. After Hilderic Nicolas had died, Jean decided to accept his uncle's advice: he volunteered to join the French Navy. Unfortunately for Uncle Fortune, the recruiting ship wouldn't make its usual twice-a-year stop at the neighboring island of Martinique for another six months: *Mon Dieu!* With that much time on his hands Jean could plunge Haiti into a small war! Somehow Uncle Fortune would have to lodge him in cold storage. Uncle Fortune hit on it: send him to another uncle – the one who lived in Guadeloupe – until the recruiting ship arrived.

When family and friends, waving their handkerchiefs from the dock, had shrunk doll-size in Jean's vision, he went below decks and gazed through a porthole. The sun, a mammoth coral ball, slipped down into a sea of sapphire and night fell, dark and mysterious. The scream of the seagulls rose louder. In the rapidly encroaching darkness he could make out the towering *mornes* behind the city, which was a myriad of tiny Christmas-tree lights. He could see the pink glow on the twin cupolas of the white cathedral. He'd been baptized there, he reflected, almost nineteen years earlier; there, as an eight-year-old, he had

had his first up-close look at one of the fearsome looking *blancs* – stocky Marine Corps captain, with a gleaming sabre, in charge of the Haitian gendarmes' Honour Guard; and he'd become hypnotized by the might and manners of the Americans.

On the dock his mother wept, thinking of her dream.

He felt alone. He cursed the pain of leaving. He knew Nietzsche would never have tolerated his maudlin sentimentality; that was for the weak. Yet he couldn't suppress a tinge of pity for the defenceless little island as it grew smaller on the horizon.

Regaining control, he leaned through the porthole, and as the velvet night smoothed his cheeks and the phosphorescent Caribbean twinkled beneath him, he promised himself no matter what lay ahead, Nietzsche would be proud of him: he would be master of his own destiny.

Chapter Eight

The promise mocked him that winter of 1943–44, a German winter as savage as anything Siberia could produce in length and bitterness.

Each morning the thousand-man regiments of slaves trudged in the dark through the Thuringian refrigerator shouldering their picks and shovels, skidding and slipping in their all-consuming physical and mental numbness. It was a treadmill existence without beginning, without end. Sometimes the rock quarry. Sometimes grading the railroad embankment. Sometimes digging drainage ditches and water mains.

At night they staggered home carrying their rocks, trundling their dead before them.

Three months had passed since the arrival of the

dark-skinned 'American air force flyer.' Despite the 24-hour-day obsession of the prisoners with their own survival, they noticed how he always walked around with his chest out and his back straight, resolutely defying the odds stacked against him. The old-timers spat contemptuously and wondered why the stupid American kept drawing attention to himself! To his credit though, he kept his mouth shut. He spoke sparingly, said what he had to say, and that was the end of it.

An 'American' was a novelty. But this one had to be a rare breed. Not only was he black; he could speak to the English, French and German prisoners in their native tongues. Odd, they reflected, for a POW to stay so much to himself. But, then, the Dutch POWs stuck with their own kind, the Norwegian POWs with theirs. There were no other Americans, so he had no one to buddy up with. Except the British POWs.

But the British were a tight-lipped, close bunch themselves and their innate snobbery about things American forced Nicholas into an outsider's role even with his English-speaking fellow prisoners.

He'd met the camp's prisoner leaders and he wasn't buying their Communist line. They'd pumped him. In the process he'd learned about them, but they'd had almost nothing in return. Indeed, his quick grasp of the 'comrades' and their wily tactics now enabled him to play them along – just as casually as he'd played the Germans in the past.

Yet he couldn't discount the Communists' power. The S.S. camp commandant seldom got involved in details of handling the prisoners. He gave his orders to the *Lagereldtester*, who relayed them down the line. He had absolute power as long as he didn't cross the S.S. As Nicholas had seen first-hand, if you wormed your way into the good graces of the prisoner hierarchy, it could be meat and potatoes instead of dishwater soup and the inglorious rockpile.

Still, Nicholas shuddered at selling out to the Communist bastards, regardless of their undeniable power over his fate.

Nicholas rapidly caught on to the fact that he would live longer by keeping his deeply anti-Communist prejudices to himself. He also recognized that, much as he might detest their philosophy, Communists were infinitely more desirable in the prisoner government than the Greens. When the Greens had been in control for a short period, said the old-timers, they'd worked hand-in-glove with the S.S., carrying out the most repressive and brutal programmes. They demonstrated that their only loyalty was to greed and personal profit. Conversely the Reds, with their superb organization and iron discipline, had saved the lives of thousands of prisoners by working around the inhuman orders of the S.S., tampering with records, fiddling with food requisitions and manipulating manpower drafts.

He learned which cook would slip him an extra hunk of bread. Which clerk would whisper advance warning of an outside detail to avoid or inside detail to try to wangle into. Which prisoner-medic in the hospital would spare half of a sulphur tablet for an infected injury. Equally important, he learned what they demanded in return.

Gradually it dawned on him that even in a Nazi concentration camp, the most debased of human societies, there were still slaves and masters. There were prisoners who wore spotless blue-and-white uniforms and heavy jackets with fur collars to shield them from the freezing wind. There were prisoners – and he knew some of them – who freely walked the camp's streets with pomaded hair and well-groomed dogs on leashes, passing on their way bent and beaten stick-men hobbling in the opposite direction, pushing wheelbarrows of frozen corpses to the building that looked like a house of the Lord.

In the lexicon of Nazi ideology, few human species ranked below the 'N-N.' In the privations they suffered, the psychological torture of being forbidden to send and receive mail was among the worst.

Late that winter of 1944 a postman in Paris came to Vildebart Nicolas' apartment on the Rue de Charonne with a postcard. The stamp, bearing Hitler's likeness, was franked 1 March 1944. The pencilled message was couched in excellent German. It read:

> I am well. I can receive some parcels. Write to me in German. You can send me fresh or cooked vegetables as often as you wish. Send me some shaving soap and a toothbrush. I hope your wife is in good health. I would also be grateful for some tobacco.
>
> Best wishes, John

It was the only message they ever received from him.

'*Aufstehn! Aufstehn!* Outside! Outside!' roared the barracks orderly, the *Stubendienst*.

While the hollow hulks stirred in their hard bunks, a tremendous crash shattered the silence. The exhaustion-drugged prisoners, reacting to what they could only assume was some new form of S.S. harrassment, leaped onto the stone floor and threw their hands up to protect themselves.

Nicholas whirled toward the centre of the sound and saw that a sparkling chandelier of ice, a building malevolently in the peak of the roof throughout the long winter, had fallen on the floor between the centre-aisle bunks. The impact had snapped off its splendid, yard-long, crystal spikes, skittering them in all directions. Overnight the thaw had melted its frozen grip, causing it to plummet to its destruction. It would have killed a man if it had fallen on him, yet it signalled life. Spring had been born again, Nicholas realized, and the leaden weight in his shoulders seemed to ease.

It was a Sunday in March. Roll call was always later on Sundays. To Nicholas it felt like the most expensive

144

privilege he'd ever enjoyed – standing in the vast, mucky assembly area as the lemon-weak sun warmed his haggard face and chapped lips.

Half of his mind kept watch, waiting to answer his name when it was called; the other half marvelled over the fact that all his life he'd taken the sun for granted. Now it was the most precious gift he'd ever known. He closed his eyes and transported himself to his homeland. He recalled his last birthday – and the uncontrollable feeling that he would go insane if he had to stay in Port-au-Prince a day longer . . .

The Buchenwald sun bathed him with its vapid heat. He felt like a plant that had been dormant during the winter, now coming to life again. The assembly area had been threshed to filthy slush by winter's millions of footprints. The *Lagerschutz* held their clubs ready to beat anyone who marred the symmetery of the roll-call formation. The roll call leader of Block 48, to which Nicholas was assigned, was S.S. Master Sergeant Erhard Brauny, a small, handsome, blue-eyed prototype of the Aryan so eulogized by Hitler. Brauny was his usual ruthless, efficient self, snapping off the names over the public-address system.

The sunlight was working its magic on Nicholas. Great continents of cottony clouds drifted lazily through the blue amphitheatre of the sky. The air he eagerly inhaled was warm like the familiar breath of a woman loved. No spikes of cold pierced his feet. No frost scalding his lips and eyebrows. He had clung by his fingernails through a night on the face of a cliff, his grip gradually weakening, with only his arrogant, screw-the-bastards attitude to feed on, to nourish in him the certainty that one day he would escape from this revolting, subhuman existence.

He heard distant droning off to the west. Too early for bees, he thought.

The sound rose in volume, swelling gradually until it was reverberating in the cathedral of blue above.

A tingle as tactile as the peristalstis of dysentery curled

145

the guts of the prisoners. Straining their eyes, they could make out far in the distance silver flecks against the blue. Suddenly from many miles away rolled the dull thunder of explosions.

Nicholas jumped as spontaneously as a football spectator cheering on a zig-zagging halfback lunging for a touchdown. 'American planes!' he shouted hoarsely, unthinkingly.

The public-address system exploded with Brauny's scream: 'Bring that swine up here!'

Four *Lagerschutz*, snarling like jackals, quickly grabbed him, forced his arms behind his back and marched him down one of the walkways between the ranks, thumping him with their clubs.

They shoved him toward Sgt. Brauny, whose face was twisted in a scowl. When they reached the raised roll-call platform, the *Lagerschutz* released him.

He stood very tall, very erect, looking directly at the S.S. sergeant whose brutality and murdered victims were well known around the camp.

'*Was ist ihre namen*?' snarled Brauny.

'Nicholas, John,' he retorted defiantly.

'Number?' demanded Brauny, unable to read the stencilled numerals on Nicholas' grime-polished, stained and reeking jacket.

'Four-four-four-five-one!' he snapped, not bothering to begin or end his response with the mandatory and servile '*Herr* Sergeant.'

Brauny ran a gloved finger down his roll-call list and located Nicholas' name. 'You've broken the rule against talking during roll call, you black bastard!'

'Yes, sir,' Nicholas shot back sarcastically. The insult had enraged him. He was ready to kill the son-of-a-bitch and damn the consequences.

Brauny glowered in semi-shock at the black man's insolence. 'Are you aware of what happens to a prisoner who disobeys the rules?'

'Yes, sir – whatever's your pleasure,' Nicholas retorted, uncowed, arrogant.

Brauny stared at him. 'You have a clever tongue, *schwartze*,' he sneered. 'Too clever. I'm going to make an example of you.' He unsnapped the cover of his holster, slid out his Luger and pressed the barrel against Nicholas' head. Then he turned to the *Lagerschutz* and ordered them to escort him and the black man to the guard-house.

Back in the ranks of prisoners a Pole whispered out of the side of his mouth: 'That's the end of Johnny.'

'Keep your voice down or we'll be next,' came the growled reply.

Because Brauny walked behind Nicholas, the S.S. man couldn't see the smirk that transformed his prisoner's demeanour from one of cockiness to outright rebelliousness. It was a smile that said: stand up to the Nazi sons-of-bitches and they back down every time! Piss on them! Otherwise why doesn't he let me have it here and now? No, it's the little S.S. bastard who's on the defensive this time – not me.

Ever since his arrival at Buchenwald, Nicholas had consciously worked at maintaining a low profile. But it was characteristic of his personality that in spite of himself he had gathered a following among the other prisoners. Then, too, in his American-ness he symbolized the longed-for victory over the hated Germans. Also, the myths and stories about him ever since his exploits at Compiegne and on the train to Buchenwald had followed him through the main gates and grown bigger and bolder. In a society without hope he was like a magnet to the hopeless.

Brauny recognized he was martyr material; and if you were the roll-call leader and had to help keep 35,000 *haeftlinge* in line, you tried – the first time around, at least – not to blow the black's brains out.

The S.S. sergeant pushed him through the doorway of the guardhouse and ordered him to sit in the lone,

147

hard-back wooden chair. It wasn't a courtesy; he was grossly self-conscious about his shortness. A standing Nicholas made him feel like a pygmy.

Eagerly the four guards slammed him into the chair, then stood at the ready as Brauny fussed with returning his pistol to its holster. Then he strode to the corner of the office, opened a file cabinet and pulled out Nicholas' manila folder. As he perused it, he mumbled to himself and nodded intermittently. He was temporizing as he tried to come up with a ploy . . .

'It says here you are an American air force officer. You *were* an American air force officer. Now you're nothing. You're an N-N who's broken the rules. You're a piece of shit.'

'Yes, sir,' Nicholas shot back, 'but I – '

'Keep your mouth shut unless given permission to talk,' snarled Brauny, eyeing his prey hatefully. Then he laid down the file, folded his arms imperiously and assumed an officious stance in front of the prisoner. 'But what? Explain!'

He's backing down, thought Nicholas, knowing he had no other choice now but to attack, hoping to Christ he could dream up in a hurry something that would penetrate Brauny's thick skull. '*Herr* Sergeant,' he began, not knowing what the hell was going to come out of his mouth, 'those were American planes. I am – I was – a United States Army air force officer. I think – I know – that if our positions were reversed that the *Herr* Sergeant, an S.S. soldier and a symbol of the best among German fighting men, would express similar exhilaration if German aircraft were bombing the enemy . . . If not, the prisoner would be deeply disappointed.'

Brauny fidgeted.

Nicholas thought: don't touch it. Leave it alone. It's beautiful . . . You could still play the pea-brained Nazis by massaging their egos.

Brauny turned toward the window and looked skyward. The fleet of silvery B–17 Flying Fortresses had disap-

eared. The droning had ceased. If the Americans
followed form, they wouldn't return for at least twenty-
four hours. Swivelling from the window, Brauny faced
Nicholas again. He pointed his finger at him and bellowed:
If those aeroplanes ever bomb this camp, or if they ever
come near here again, I will personally put a bullet through
your fuzzy head.'

Enemy bombers had often flown over Buchenwald but
the camp had never been bombed. Unless the American
pilots had discovered the secret war plant, the so-called
Mibau factory just outside the barbed wire, Brauny
reasoned that they were not going to bomb it this time.
They would head for other targets. Then Brauny permitted himself a slight smirk. 'Return to the ranks, *schwartze
schwein*. I have something better in store for you.'

Nicholas' filthy uniform clashed absurdly with his rigid
military posture as he marched back between the packed
ranks. Every single prisoner in Block 48 trembled at the
idea of drawing Brauny's wrath. The prisoners gulped as
they watched Nicholas out of the corners of their eyes.
What was the stupid nigger trying to do? What about
Brauny? Was he ill? A healthy Brauny would pull the
trigger with delight, and by rights four of them would be
plucked from the ranks to serve as pallbearers for the late
Major Nicholas.

Roll call resumed and droned on and on . . .

It was finally over and, as was the Sunday practice, the
prisoners had some time to themselves. Most shuffled
back to their quarters, crawled into their putrid bunks and
fell off into torpid sleep. A few, like Nicholas, had the
strength to wander aimlessly through the bleak, slushy
streets of the camp, scrounging for a minute of solitude
from the filthy, craven, verminous horde that always
surrounded him.

The balmy morning lured him further from his block
than he had ever ventured before. The kitchen and the
bakery were the furthest he'd ever gone. That was when
he'd been temporarily assigned to the early-morning

149

soup-kettle detail, whose members always were first to be roused out of their bunks in the morning. In pairs they lugged the huge, cumbersome cauldrons of scalding, greasy water from the kitchen to the block mess halls. They had learned to bend their bodies at right angles when carrying the kettles. If they slipped, the impact sloshed the soup over. To avoid that they were forced to tread like tight-rope walkers. Despite their best efforts they would always slip, soaking the beaten snow with scalding liquid. The assembly area outside the block where the Russian POWs lived was rutted and filled with potholes. When a kettle upended there, the Russians swarmed into the frigid air, pulling on pants and shirts, sliding and slipping on their ill-fitting clogs and savagely fighting for a taste of the soup-snow mush.

Gradually he began to realize how close he had come to death in his confrontation with Brauny, and he began to sweat freely. The stench of his body made him want to vomit. He unbuttoned his dirty, matted jacket, wondering what the brutal S.S. sergeant meant by his threat.

He had never before roamed so far from his block. While his alarm system was activated fully, he fought the impulse to turn around and go back. Brauny could go to hell.

Gradually the familiar outlines of the kitchen and the bakery were behind him and he was now wandering in alien country, still unchallenged. Ahead was a building he'd never seen but recognized from what he'd heard about it – the *Effektenkammer*, the clothing warehouse where they kept a man's personal belongings. He paused to gaze up at the two-storey, concrete structure, wondering if his suitcase, with the picture of his mother in it, was there.

The thought snagged on his emotions. He had packed in great haste that November morning when the Gestapo had invaded the apartment. He'd tossed in a few family things, among them a dog-eared, yellow snapshot . . .

He went on walking. He choked down the fear that he

150

had strayed dangerously far. It was so strong it made the hair on his neck prickle. Damn Brauny! Johnny Nicholas was still his own master. He clopped on, stepping laboriously around potholes brimming with muddy water thawed by the sun's soft rays...

He found himself in a place remote in mood and distance from the insanity of the main camp – a small, terraced square ruled imperiously by a stately tree.

He'd never seen a tree inside the barbed-wire compound. It was an oak, nobly tall, dramatically straight and exploding in a wealth of branches. A wooden railing encircled its trunk and a small plaque hand-lettered in German said that Goethe, the great German poet, once sought inspiration here.

He'd heard the veteran prisoners say that when the oak died, so would the Third Reich.

To Nicholas it looked as if it would live for a thousand years.

The Communists secretly monitored British radio broadcasts and passed the news from man to man around the camp. Out in the rock quarry, if they had any energy left, they whispered about the long-awaited invasion of German-occupied Europe by the British and American armies. Would it really happen? When would it come? They could only guess, but the prospect kept hope alive when reality screamed at them to surrender and die.

There was a small bench in the square. He sat down and read the plaque again. What poetry would Goethe compose if he could sit here today? The thought of Goethe made him think of Neitzsche. How grievously ironic that the birthplace of the man whose philosophy had dominated his mind and actions was the charming city of Weimar, only five miles from the bench on which he, a slave, now rested his worn body.

Up on the slopes of the Etterswald, winter was still conducting a masterful withdrawal, stubbornly dumping snow on the backs of the slaves in the quarry, where

Nicholas now toiled on the top level. It had taken him months to wangle it, but now he worked among the Russian POWs. He had developed to where he could understand snatches of their conversations and make himself understood in simple phrases. It was a tough, dangerous climb to the top. For that reason S.S. and prisoner foremen policed that area as little as possible. This meant that the Russians often lay back on their tools and took it easy. They always posted spotters to warn when guards were on the way.

'Be grateful, *Amerikanets*,' one of his new Russian friends warned, during a break, 'we've only a few miles to march to this hell-hole. Any further away and the S.S. donkeys would make it into a subcamp.'

The Russian explained that a subcamp was formed when the S.S. determined they could save time and money by building a smaller camp right on the work-project site. The rock quarry was bad, he continued, but a subcamp could be even worse – although it was impossible to think of anything ghastlier than Buchenwald. A subcamp had its own prisoner government, which was often an offshoot of the main camp government but sometimes not. Buchenwald had many subcamps. Many had Communist prisoner governments because Buchenwald's *Lagereldtester* made sure that the prisoners assigned subcamps were well seeded with strong, experienced Reds capable of dominating the government that emerged.

But the S.S. subcamp commander was the final authority, the Russian told Nicholas. He could decide he wanted an anti-Communist prisoner as *Lagereldtester*, who would naturally tap other anti-Communists for key positions in his government. Or the Buchenwald S.S. commandant could just as capriciously designate a notorious Green as the subcamp *Lagereldtester*, creating a prisoner government dominated by criminals.

A Buchenwald inmate could become extremely sophisticated in camp politics, economies and intrigues. Yet transferred to a subcamp, he was suddenly a neophyte again, with an entirely new system of personalities to learn, a new chain of command to discover and a new labyrinth of intrigue to negotiate.

Buchenwald had 'outside' details, the Russian explained, as far away as the Rhine River and the Channel Islands. Before they made one of these details a subcamp, regiments of prisoners were first trucked out – usually to some wilderness – to build barracks for the S.S. While construction was under way they lived in tents, freezing in winter and sweltering in summer. When the S.S. barracks were completed, only then were the prisoners allowed to build quarters for themselves.

None of Buchenwald's fifty or more subcamps was mentioned with more dread than Camp Dora.

Every few days Nicholas heard Roll Call Leader Brauny without warning bark a lengthy list of names of men assigned to the Dora detail. These inmates were invariably stunned by the dreaded news: they said the only way you returned from Dora was feet first. As the rock-quarry detail formed ranks after morning roll call and prepared to march out of camp, Nicholas often watched uneasily as the Dora deportees climbed resignedly into the trucks.

'All we know,' the Russian POW told Nicholas, 'is it's about fifty miles away. A comrade in the Labour Records Office says it's a top-secret project. He thinks they're making it into a subcamp. He says they send the bodies back here: they don't have a crematorium yet. He was talking to one of the comrades who handles the bodies. You think we're filthy? You should see those poor bastards, he tells me. Crawling with lice. Nothing but bones. Some of them hardly ninety pounds. He tells me they're shipping them back faster than fifty a day and so tangled up they can barely pull them apart to slide them into the ovens. Another comrade is a medic in the prisoner hospital. He says the S.S. doctors have done autopsies on some of the Dora comrades. They know damn well why they died: they feed them nothing and work them 'til they

153

drop. They're so weak, he says, a bad cold finishes off most of them.

'That, Comrade Nicholas, is what you get when the Greens are in control.'

'The criminals run Dora, *tovarisch?*' queried Nicholas.

The Russian, leaning on his shovel, nodded.

A look-out whistled: the S.S. guards were returning.

The Russian hefted his shovel and joined a large group which had suddenly returned to work furiously.

As Nicholas swung his pick, the dread of Dora made him shiver. In his imagination he heard his name boom from the loudspeakers as they tagged him for Dora. He had to escape from the quarry detail: they were always drafting men from the quarry for Dora.

No, he thought, that wasn't really so. True, many Dora draftees were from the quarry, yet he'd known men who had been sheetmetal workers in civilian life. And plumbers. Carpenters, too. There'd also been university professors and scientists who had gone.

So whatever they were up to at Dora, it involved common labourers and skilled tradesmen. Even scientists. In one way it sounded like a soft detail – except that he knew there was nothing soft about *rigor mortis*.

He told himself he'd better start immediately manoeuvring and manipulating to get out of the quarry and into the relative safety of the Mibau factory, a mysterious facility located just outside Buchenwald's barbed wire.

The Mibau detail fell out every morning after roll call, formed up and marched about a quarter of a mile to the thirteen huge sheds comprising the factory complex. There they worked all day long in heat and comfort. Lucky bastards. Their supervisors were German civilians and the work was so sensitive that the prisoners had to shower and wear clean uniforms each day!

'Tell me,' whispered Nicholas the next chance he got, 'how do you get into the Mibau?'

154

The Russian spat contemptuously. 'If I knew I'd be there myself.'

'What do they make there?'

'Some kind of radios, they say. There's a lot of Frenchies working there as engineers and technicians. That's the only way you can get in: if you know something about radios.'

'Radios?' repeated Nicholas. 'I know a lot about them. Our planes have very complicated radios.'

The Russian didn't respond.

Nicholas swung his pick vigorously, edging closer to the Russian. 'Remember that time I was on soup detail and slipped outside your block?'

'The first or second time?'

'The first time, when you tried out your English on me and said I ought to slip more often.'

'*Dah*, I remember.'

'The first time it *was* an accident. But the second time? Well, I remembered how much you seemed to enjoy licking up that slop.'

The Russian cast him a shrewd, sidelong glance. 'You don't know any more about radios than I do, Comrade *Amerikanets*, but you bluff well. Maybe you might have a chance. I could talk to my friend in the Labour Records Office.'

Nicholas felt a ripple of elation. 'Will you?' he queried casually. 'For a price, comrade. What have you got to offer?'

Nicholas continued swinging his pick, occasionally turning his head slightly to keep an eye out for the guards and foremen. When it was safe, he slipped a hand into his jacket and produced something.

The Russian snatched the bribe and quickly stuffed it into his jacket. 'Two carrots?' he sniffed diffidently.

Upping the ante, Nicholas dealt him a single cigarette.

'*Ochen Hawrashaw*,' the Russian conceded. 'Very good ... But a post in the Mibau is worth more than a cigarette and two wilted carrots, Johnny.'

Nicholas' anger rose. He slipped the Russian another cigarette and furiously slammed his pick into the rock. 'How do I know you'll deliver, *tovarisch*?

'You don't,' the Russian said belligerently. 'But I have connections. I got you up here to the top level, didn't I?'

'*Dah*,' Nicholas agreed.

'Also, I happen to know you're N-N, but you smuggled out a postcard and received a parcel, didn't you? So you have a few connections yourself.'

Nicholas felt his anger well up again. 'I know you, *tovarisch*, don't I?' he said softly, hoping the flattery would have the desired result.

'If I get you into the Mibau,' continued the Russian, 'it will also cost you half of the vegetables and tobacco you got from your brother.'

Nicholas got madder. He'd heard old-timers boast about the smooth efficiency of the vast intelligence service operated by Buchenwald's prisoner government. Now he was a victim of it. Goddam the Russian bastard!... But he knew he'd never get into the Mibau on his own, so he'd have to take his chances with the Russian. 'Agreed,' he finally said, sensing he'd been manipulated by an expert. But he was still worried: if this fellow were so influential, why was he begging for peanuts? 'Don't forget, comrade, I'll know when you get the package – maybe even before,' warned the Russian.

18 May 1944 was a day for rejoicing among the Poles on the top level of the Etterswald. A BBC broadcast heard on the Communists' secret radio and spread by word of mouth among the prisoners, reported that soldiers of the Free Polish Army fighting alongside the American and British armies in Italy had raised the Polish flag atop Monte Cassino. The Catholic monastery, which had been turned into an impregnable fortress by the Germans, had

held up the Allied advance for months. It was finally destroyed and the glory went to Poland.

The broadcast also told of thousands of Allied bombers from Britain smashing major targets in Germany and Occupied Europe by day and night.

As the prisoners swung their picks and shovels their hearts pounded with the promise of the long-awaited Allied invasion of Europe. The thought of freedom coming closer and closer made them slightly drunk.

But Nicholas was not in the quarry that morning to catch their mood; a week earlier, on 11 May, Brauny had stepped up to the podium with an enigmatic smile on his face, bellowed the American's name and banished him to Dora.

Chapter Nine

Five-hundred feet below the earth, Nicholas was one of the human ants staggering under burdens of rock blasted from the blind end of the tunnel. They trudged deliriously with their massive armloads or pushed their carts through the chaos of boulders for a mile to the outside, where they dumped their cruel cargoes on the slope of the Kohnstein, a hill in the Harz Mountains of central Germany.

The dynamite blasts, amplified a hundred times in the subterranean cavern, shattered their eardrums. Clouds of chalky dust, riding the shock wave, buffeted their bony bodies and floured them with a grit that burned their lungs and scoured their eyeballs. Each detonation rippled through the hill and shook loose ceiling boulders that crashed down on them, crushing dozens to death and mutilating scores.

'*Mach schnell! Mach schnell!* Hurry up! Hurry up!'

roared the S.S., ramming them with rifle butts. '*Heraus!
Heraus!*' screamed the prisoner foremen, the criminals,
scourging them with lashes made of electrical cable.

If they ran too fast they tripped and smashed themselves between the loads they carried and the boulders
obstructing the tunnel floor. Because they couldn't see
more than five paces in the swirling dust, the stronger
were continually bumping into the weaker, slower-moving
men. Prisoners with armloads of rock kept colliding,
spattering blood and splintering bone. Some collapsed
with their burdens halfway to the tunnel exit and never got
up. Those who made it to the tunnel mouth found their
hearts thumping wildly, their breath rasping, their thin,
knobby knees quivering uncontrollably like fiddlers'
elbows. They schemed endlessly to malinger at the rock
pile, gulping in great drafts of clean, mountain air. And all
the time they squinted like frightened ferrets at the *kapo*
in charge of the rock pile – and his sinister length of cable.
It was the last trip for some. They slithered to their knees,
doubled up, vomited their breakfast of greasy soup with
the chunks of sausage still undigested in it. They were
immune to the stench of the vomit puddled in their
crotches. They were beyond the blows of the rifle butts
and the steel-cable lashings raining down on them.

Clutching a small boulder to his chest, Nicholas lurched
through the billowing dust. The space between his
eyeballs and eyelids felt raw with grit. He could open his
eyes only for an instant and then had to close them. He
could feel the grit in the back of his throat. The
detonations intensified the perpetual dust storm, blotting
out the vapid, yellowish lights strung along the centre line
of the ceiling. Without them as a guide he was temporarily
blind, not knowing if he was heading for the exit or about
to crash into the craggy wall of the tunnel.

Ten hours gone. Two more before relief by the night
shift.

When the shift changed, they staggered into four short
caverns off Tunnel A and collapsed into four-tiered

wooden bunks still warm from the bodies of the night shift. Sleep was impossible. The explosions ripped on and on through the night. The fractured wedges of ceiling never stopped thundering to the rubbled floor. The air hammers never ceased their chatter. Thousands of shovels went on scraping and scratching like the endless washing of the tide on a vast beach. The ravished men screamed in their nightmares. Their bodies cannonaded all night long, belching putrid waste into the bunks where they lay. They coughed and hacked until globs of phlegm leaked out between their limpid lips.

In the ghoulish hour before they were hammered and cursed to their swollen feet to start the nightmare all over again, the stronger, like human carrion birds, slipped from their bunks to scavenge on the weak and the dead, robbing them of their shoes and their rags.

He was stronger than any six of them combined, Nicholas told himself. But for how long? His arms felt as if they had been torn from their sockets. The weeks and weeks of rock-carrying had worn great bruises on his chest. His knuckles were battered bloody. In the total darkness of the tunnel he could sense the shapeless hulks scattered around him. The wasting of their bodies revolted him because he knew that in a very few months he would be indistinguishable from them. The physique he was so proud of would be ruined. His iron will would turn to putty. Typhus and tuberculosis would devour his insides. He would stink disgustingly of dysentery, and he would be loathed and despised as he now loathed and despised those around him. The prospect was hideous. It stunned him.

If he didn't waste away he would be clubbed into eternity by a *Lagerschutz*! Or he could slowly bleed to death in a ditch from a head bashed in by an S.S. rifle butt!

He pictured himself at the bottom of a mound of bodies; prisoners, indifferent to all except their own exhaustion, one at his feet and the other at his head, swinging his stiffened carcass into the back of a dump truck as if he were a side of beef. Him landing with limbs askew on a pile of stiff bodies. The truck creaking on its way to Buchenwald where its cargo box is tipping and he is sliding down and out in a huge mound beside the building with the tall smokestack. He imagined the long-armed metal tongs gripping him around the neck and ankles and dropping him into the metal stretcher, sliding him into the oven . . . He imagined heavy black clouds pouring out of the smokestack, and he wondered which particles were him and which were somebody else . . . Would they notice his brown skin among the fish-belly-white mound of dead? Would all his hopes and dreams, his glorious vision of himself, turn to smoke over the Harz countryside? The whimpering, snoring, coughing, spitting and flaccid farting all around was becoming unbearable. How long before he'd become like the rest? Never, by God! Never! While he remained master of his own mind, the guards were nothing. The barbed wire was nothing. The beatings were nothing. But the instant he let the bastards conquer his thoughts, he'd become a pitiful slave like all the others.

'I noticed this big black man on the parade ground at roll call one morning,' recalls Cecil Jay, an English prisoner at Dora. 'I asked the block *Eldtester* who he was and he told me he was an American from Buchenwald.'

Jay, who lives in Springe, West Germany today, had arrived at the Kohnstein from Buchenwald in September 1943 with the first shipment of 300 prisoners. Luckier than most, he had escaped the incredibly brutal labour in the tunnels because he was a carpenter. He worked in a construction detail outside in the open air, building wooden barracks for a subcamp.

By March 1944, when Nicholas arrived, Jay's detail was close to completing the barracks for the S.S., who had lived throughout the bitter winter in plywood lean-to structures at the base of the Kohnstein hill. The S.S.

personnel had risen to full strength. Jay's detail then began building barracks for the prisoners, who numbered four thousand and whose ranks were increasing daily with fresh shipments from Buchenwald.

The Englishman had been a prisoner for five years. He became curious about the presence of an American Negro at Dora and excited by the possibility of talking with someone in English for a change. He manoeuvred himself close to Nicholas at a roll call and managed to exchange a few words. 'He said he was completely fed up with the S.S.,' recalls Jay, 'and he asked me if I was able to get him some bread.'

They met routinely after that but Jay found the black man reluctant to talk much about himself. Jay, a veteran 'concentrationary,' knew why: Nicholas was keeping his mouth shut in case Jay turned out to be a Gestapo or S.D. stool-pigeon.

'The sort of things we talked about,' says the Englishman, 'were life in the camp and the work we did. But he did tell me that his parents were pretty well off and that if he could only write them a letter, he would be all right.'

It was May. The sky was a dazzling blue. Birds twittered ...

'*Mutzen Auf!*' roared the assistant roll call leader.

Hardly had the caps snapped back on again when Master Sgt. Brauny walked across the field with a clipboard under his arm, taking care to keep the mud off his gleaming jackboots. He stopped beside the assistant roll call leader and let his eyes roam over the prisoners. 'Sloppy!' he shouted. 'Very sloppy. We will try it again ... *Mutzen ab!* ... *Mutzen auf!* ... *Mutzen ab!* ... *Mutzen auf!* ... *Mutzen ab!* ... *Mutzen auf!*'

He continued to scrutinize the haggard assembly. As he did he unconsciously moved up and down on his toes, boosting his sawed-off stature each time. He was immaculate in his well-fitting black S.S. uniform with the silver

161

lightning-flash emblems on the collar and his high-crowned peaked cap. His expression was that of someone overcome by an objectionable odour. 'Some of you know me,' he continued. 'Some of you don't. My name is Brauny. Master Sergeant Brauny, your new roll call leader, and you will address me at all times as *sir*.

'This is supposed to be a protective-custody camp – not a stable. You are filthy pigs. Discipline is intolerable. The output of work is far below what is required. All sense of punctuality has vanished. As the new roll call leader I intend to make drastic changes.

'First, you will strip off all your clothes. Shake your clothes out and lay them at your feet. The sunlight will delouse you.'

There was no move among the prisoners.

'*Schnell*!' shouted Brauny.

The *Lagerschutz* began to strike out wildly at the prisoners.

The men needed no further encouragement and rapidly stripped, baring their bleached, shrunken bodies.

'Second, you have been getting away from good discipline ever since this camp was established almost nine months ago. You have been permitted the decadence of one roll call a week, which is a Sunday morning roll call. From now on there will be the traditional two roll calls a day, morning and evening. Previously the dead were permitted to stay in the tunnels. From now on *all* prisoners will be present at roll call. If not, the ten men whose serial numbers are closest to each of the dead men's serial numbers will be held personally responsible.'

Brauny flipped back a page on his clipboard and examined the next page. When he resumed, his voice had a sneering quality which made it clear that he was disgusted with what he was to read: 'I am directed by the medical officer, Dr. Kahr, to inform you that as soon as it is practicable, the prisoner hospital will be moved out of the tunnels into a new wooden barracks which

162

Kommandant Fourschner has generously provided for that purpose.

'I am also directed by Dr. Kahr to inform you that when the transfer is made, there will be the daily sick call – as was customary at Buchenwald, where most of you came from. Prisoners examined and found too sick to work will be given a convalescent slip which will exempt them from work for one or several days.'

Brauny looked up from the clipboard. 'But I'm telling you that these slips must be handed to me *before* morning roll call – or they are useless!' His blue eyes roved the sullen, silent ranks as if searching for any hint of rebellion to his comment . . . '*Herr Doktor* Kahr, unfortunately, will be faced with the customary problem of weeding out malingerers! You swine don't know how to behave when we Germans treat you with decency. I will be giving him the benefit of my many years of experience in dealing with that problem! Do you understand?'

He resumed reading from the clipboard.

'This camp has come to the end of Phase One and is now commencing Phase Two. I am directed by the Labour Allocation Officer to inform you that all prisoners with technical and scientific training are ordered to step forward and identify themselves. They will be given special training that will be of great value when they return to civilian life.

What a pile of crap! thought Nicholas.

Brauny started calling the roll.

'Aachen! ... Asche! ... Banaczek! ... Boule! ... Carre! ... Carruthers! ... Czaplynski! ... Dakunchak! ... Delacorte! ... Dobrinin! ... Dortmund! ... Eberhardt! ...'

Nicholas trembled.

It was not the still-cool mountain air of the Harz that caused it. It was the obscene human spectacle all around him. Bellies bloated by malnutrition. Buttocks shredded by whipping and eroded by starvation. Necks and backs knobbed with ripe carbuncles, purplish and pulsating.

Torsoes furrowed by whip and cable and oozing pus. Where the lice had bitten in, crotch and armpit rashes of yellow-headed boils.

He slid his hands to his backside and cupped his buttocks. It had already started to happen to him too . . .

In the old days when Gabrielle had put on the tournaments the girls reached out to touch his body. He could remember the way they used to look at him. The roundness of Florence suddenly flashed in his imagination. For an instant he thought he could hear the swish of her skirts. He remembered the smell of the perfume she wafted into his apartment. In another few months he would be just like them. How he hated her.

'. . . Kirkwood! . . . Kirsch! . . . Kleist! . . . Koplov! . . . Kurilik! . . .'

He stared at Brauny. Four thousand naked men shivering in dread of a little German with baby-blue eyes. One single Nazi, all of five feet, four inches tall. He could squash him with one hand tied behind his back – even in his condition. Christ, why hadn't he killed the bastard back at Buchenwald? Brauny – the miserable son-of-a-bitch who won Round One by sending him to Dora – was now well ahead on Round Two . . . '*Hier*!' he shouted automatically as Brauny called his name.

He ached to beat him to a pulp in front of everyone. He could picture himself doing it. It was like a motion-picture running on the screen of his mind: Brauny blinks. Incredulous. Claws at his holster. Manages to get his pistol out, but there's a scuffle. Nicholas disarms him and points the gun at Brauny's temple. Lay down your weapons, Nicholas hears himself shout to the S.S. guards, or I'll shoot him. Brauny is whining now, pleading for the guards to obey so he can save his skin. He hears the rifles thump on the mud-soaked field. There's a storm of exultation from the prisoners, who come surging forward to retrieve the weapons. Nicholas can see them grabbing him, hugging him, kissing him, trying to hoist him on their shoulders, But he's saying no, no. Suddenly he's at their head and leading them in a charge through the newly built barracks, dragging out startled S.S. with their hands joined above their heads and shouting '*Kamerad*!' He's banging with his fist on the door of Commandant Fourschner and –

'... Zafarana! ... Zajac! ... Zamler! ... Zaspaloff! ... Zator!...'

The harsh sounds of the roll call jerked Nicholas back to reality. He was crushed by his impotence and inflamed by the vividness of his wild daydream. It would be the last thing Brauny would ever expect because he was absolutely certain he was their master. Any notion to the contrary would have been totally absurd to him.

So why not try it? Nicholas reproached himself.

He told himself that he would have the two best weapons possible – surprise and total lack of logic, for a sane prisoner would never try it. Outrageous, but it had worked for Nicholas on other occasions.

It would work. It would work because it was the kind of madness that always worked. In a month or two his will and his buttocks would be wasted away. So it had to work! Now!

His trembling persisted, but now the cause was anger, gathering force like a storm. Reason nagged him, reminding him that the *Lagerschutz* would beat him to death before he got fifty yards.

Goddamn the *Lagerschutz*!

There had to be a way of getting close to Brauny while rage made avenging vices of his quivering fingers.

'Zawicki! ... Zdabosz! ... Zellner! ... Ziebach! ... Ziegler! ...'

... before he would be forced to look down and see his manhood shrivelled between his thighs...

'... Zollweg! ... Zuckerman! ... Zylinski! ... Zywicki! ... Zywiec!...'

The abrupt silence as roll call ended, plucking him from his trance.

'Dress!' roared Brauny.

The act of climbing into his stinking rags rammed home to Nicholas how far the Germans had come in stripping him of his dignity. He discovered that he embraced his sleazy jacket with more zeal than he had ever lavished on any of the elegant suits left hanging in his wardrobe in Paris.

Brauny had made him utterly dependent on his shit-soaked rags.! He'd kill him for it! That very moment!

'All prisoners with technical or scientific training: front and centre!' shouted Brauny.

The prisoners hesitated. They knew the unspeakable risk of volunteering.

The S.S. used tricks like that to weed out 'undesirables and shirkers' seeking "soft" details, regarding such prisoners as morally unfit for a protective-custody camp and prime candidates for liquidation. Sometimes they shot those who stepped forward. A prisoner never knew what to do when they called for 'volunteers'.

But often the appeal was genuine, as it had been when the S.S. at Buchenwald asked for prisoners with technical training to work in the Mibau factory.

What was the S.S. up to *this* time?

A few men gambled and stepped forward. A few more. Then a trickle more . . .

Nicholas walked erectly between the ranks toward Brauny and the assistant roll call leader, and took his place in the line of volunteers . . .

The roll call was finally over.

'*Mutzen Ab!*' shouted Brauny. '*Mutzen Auf!*'

The main body of prisoners hobbled back inside the tunnel, leaving Nicholas and the others standing at attention before Brauny.

Nicholas knew he could reach out and touch the sergeant. He felt the blood rush to his head as if he had suddenly downed a large draft of Haitian rum. He fixed his eyes on the holster. He noticed the way the sergeant's left thumb was hooked like a claw over his pistol belt – a

166

few inches from the holster. He stared down at him, telling himself he'd never have another chance.

He had no weapon. Not even an old messkit knife. Not even a-sharpened tent stake that some prisoners used to defend themselves. There were stones stuck in the gobbed mud like chocolate-chips in cookie batter, but he'd have to bend to get one. No, he would have to use his hands. His big, powerful hands. With the right leverage he could snap the bastard's spinal cord in one twist – with luck even before the bullets started ripping through him.

'Sound off names and numbers!' shouted Brauny to the volunteers. 'Front rank, left to right!'

The tension stretched Nicholas' stomach. He wanted to throw up. He was mesmerized by the small, black-uniformed figure strutting down the line, pausing before each prisoner, challenging him for name and number and quizzing him on his credentials.

Nicholas' mind drifted. He was in school again and Headmaster Tippenhauer was about to cane him before the entire class. He could feel the hot rush of shame to his face and the anger make his body tremble. He could feel the memory of his stinging backside, but it was not the pain that was making his body shake; it was the decision he had made that he was going to shame the huge, barrel-chested headmaster as he had been shamed. He was counting off the strokes, having sworn to himself that when the appointed number had been delivered, he would attack.

Chapter Ten

Hans, a diplomat's son living in the sprawling port city of Hamburg, loved to spend his summers with his relatives in the little village of Salza. It was just a mile from Nordhausen in central Germany. The big cities of the middle 1930s teemed with uniforms and worried-looking civilians, but in the rural areas like Salza life seemed to stand still. It was reassuring, comforting to go back year after year and find the same old friends, the same old haunts.

Most of all he looked forward to climbing the Kohnstein. It was the favourite diversion of Salza schoolboys rummaging for a way to kill the long, idle hours of summer vacation. Locally the Kohnstein was known as a mountain. In reality it was a foothill of the Harz Mountains, 1,144 feet above sea level and measuring 450 feet from base to peak.

There was a tunnel that ran into the south side of the hill. It piqued his boyish curiosity and his sense of adventure, but there wasn't much he could do about it. It was always guarded. Why? There never seemed to be much activity there. So the ten-year-old Hans and his friends dutifully but reluctantly kept their distance.

On a typical hot summer day they would leave the home of Hans' aunt, whose parlour window offered a postcard view of the conifer-covered hill, then hike or thumb a ride several kilometres to the outdoor swimming pool just a few hundred meters from the tunnel entrance. There they'd cool themselves by taking a long, lazy swim. Finally, motivated by the mountain-climbing craze that was sweeping German youth of that decade, they would

168

take on the Kohnstein, trying a different path to the summit each time.

Hans would never return to Hamburg in the fall without indulging himself in his favourite experience: his last climb of the season, when he'd pay a visit to the grizzly-faced Hermit of the Kohnstein, as he was known locally. This was an eccentric character who pressed his own cider from apples and gave the delectable juice to Hans and the others – but who sold it for a good price to adults.

As British bombers continued their systematic razing of Hamburg during 1943, Hans and his mother returned to Salza for the first time in many years. Although eighteen and a young man, he could hardly wait to wander the Kohnstein again, taking a dip in the pool, dropping in on the old hermit – maybe quaffing a scoop of his peerless cider.

But for Hans they would never again be more than memories.

Unlike the bucolic vision that he had nurtured on the train from Hamburg, Salza and Nordhausen had been transformed. Military vehicles, equipment and soldiers everywhere. The hill, once freely accessible, cordoned off by miles of high fence. The tunnel he'd known since boyhood artfully camouflaged to blend with the hillside. New wooden buildings constructed not far from the tunnel mouth and more were being built. Truckload after truckload of men in zebra-striped uniforms riding into and out of a large compound behind the fence.

What was going on?

What had happened to the idyllic playground of his early youth?

That same summer of 1943 Nordhausen was celebrating its 1,000th birthday. By coincidence, he thought to himself at the time, that was the longevity Hitler had predicted for his Third Reich.

Besides its long history, Nordhausen was also distinguished for its excellent *Korn Schnapps* and its Roland's

Column. This civic monument was a symbol of the townspeople's dedication to the freedom which industry and commerce enjoyed in the fruitful Golden Plain nourished by the waters of the Helme River.

The cobblestone streets and steep-roofed houses of this regional trading centre of some 39,000 persons provided a quaint and picturesque setting. Its upper and lower sections were connected by flights of steps. And it boasted two impressive monuments to religious freedom – its Roman Catholic cathedral, renowned for its Romanesque crypt, and its Protestant cathedral, the Church of St. Blasius.

The old world of the industrious burghers of Nordhausen ended one day in 1938, the same year that twenty-year-old Johnny Nicholas left Haiti to join the French Navy. On that ominous day a team of experts from I. G. Farben, the huge German chemical combine, descended upon the town.

For centuries the townspeople had dug calcium sulphate in almost pure form from open-cast mines in the dome-shaped spurs extending south from the main body of the Harz Mountains. Farben saw a profit to be reaped by bringing method, money and mass-production techniques to what had been a cottage industry.

For its pilot operation Farben selected the Kohnstein. A more luxuriously forested, pine-scented setting could hardly have been found in all of Germany's majestic mountain scenery.

So the year prior to the outbreak of World War II, a Farben subsidiary known as Ammoniak began operating a calcium-sulphate pit inside the Kohnstein.

Simultaneously an economic research company of the German government with the abbreviated name of WIFO[1] was formed to scout the Third Reich for bomb-proof storage facilities to store gasoline and oil reserves. It was actually I. G. Farben, which was losing money on its

[1] *Wirtschaftliche Forschungsgesellschaft.*

170

calcium-sulphate mining venture, that brought the Kohn-stein's possibilities to the attention of WIFO. If tunnels were bored in the hill, Farben suggested, it would make ideal storage.

WIFO was interested, and Farben proposed a deal: the giant chemical company would give the hill to the German government – if the government would share half the cost of tunnelling. In that way WIFO would have its bomb-proof storage and Farben would obtain huge amounts of calcium sulphate at half the mining costs.

WIFO engineers drew up a blueprint: two large-bore tunnels running parallel through the width of the hill and interconnected by forty-six smallbore parallel tunnels.

Using advanced machinery and equipment, engineers succeeded in boring one large-diametre tunnel completely through and the other part way. They had also drilled twenty-three of the planned forty-six interconnecting tunnels when Farben withdrew, complaining that even though the government was paying half the drilling costs, Farben was still losing money on the calcium sulphate.

Thus the commercial-mining project was abandoned.

WIFO, grateful for the tunnels that had been bored, crammed them with petroleum reserves that a year later would help fuel and lubricate the German war machine as it rolled across Western Europe and later into the Russian heartland.

But in the same year of 1938 infinitely more specific plans for German world conquest were taking shape about 180 kilometres to the northeast of Nordhausen.

The location was the little Baltic Sea fishing village of Peenemünde. It was a highly sophisticated military research complex on the island of Usedom, near the mouth of the Oder River. Here, crowded into a 700-acre site, more than a thousand scientists, engineers and technicians had been labouring since the early thirties to perfect Hitler's so-called secret *Vergeltungswaffen* ('revenge weapons').

These were the V-1, a pilotless, flying bomb; and the V-2, the world's first guided missile.

The V-1s flew as fast as the speediest Allied fighter plane of the time. About the size of a typical fighter aircraft, they were launched from a long ramp pointed toward the centre of London. Dubbed the 'buzzbomb' or the 'doodlebug' by Londoners, they flew at a preset altitude with enough fuel to take them over the heart of the British capital. When the tank emptied, the engine stopped and the V-1 glided steeply to its target, exploding on impact.

The V-2, a frightful weapon for its time, made the V-1 by comparison look like a mere nuisance. It had an explosive warhead that excavated a thirty-foot-diametre hole almost twenty feet deep when it hit its target. It stood forty-five feet high on its launching pad and blasted off spewing clouds of liquid oxygen in its wake. Arcing across the English Channel faster than the speed of sound, it gave no warning of its approach and zeroed-in silently on its target under gyroscopic control.

There was no defence against the V-2 as there was against the V-1, which could be shot down by fighter planes and anti-aircraft artillery. Hitler was convinced that if enough V-2s could be produced and launched in time, he would eventually be able to strut down the Mall at the head of a German victory parade in London. His grand vision of triumph was shattered, however, on the night of 17 July 1943, when 571 Royal Air Force bombers plastered Peenemünde with incendiaries and high explosives.

The news detonated a fury in the German leader. He had believed his High Command when it had assured him that Peenemünde, the Nazi equivalent of Cape Canaveral, was invisible from the air because camouflage experts had artfully woven it into Ruegen Island's thick, pine forest. He had believed his security chiefs who had insisted that Peenemünde's seven-foot-high, 600-volt, barbed wire fence could not be penetrated. Yet British agents had done it and radioed the news of the V-2 terror weapon to London.

The German antiaircraft defences had hosed the sky with flak that night. When the big, four-engined, Halifaxes and Lancasters had droned away from the target area, they had left forty-six of their number scattered across the North German Plain.

But it had been worth it. Peenemünde, which had cost the Germans $120 million to build, was heavily damaged. The death toll included 572 technicians and 178 scientists; and while the research could continue there, production and testing had to be moved to a safer location.

From Hitler's convulsion over the loss of Peenemünde came his apoplectic command: get V-1 and V-2 production started again – immediately! Disgusted with what he conceived as bungling on the part of his army and air force, he turned to the head of his own personal army, S.S. Reichsfuehrer Heinrich Himmler, to raise Peenemünde anew from the ashes.

Tapped for the assignment was General Walter Schreckenbach, head of the S.S. Construction Branch.

The engineer on the job was an officer with the tunnel vision and fanatic dedication of a typical S.S. officer, Col. Hans Kammler, a former architect.

The new production facilities, Kammler told himself, would have to be invulnerable to Allied bombers. Thus it was pointless to go back to Ruegen Island. A new site would have to be found, so secret that no spy could ever find it; so well protected that no bomb could ever touch it.

One of his very first acts in his new command was to fire off teletype messages to all S.S. regional headquarters in Germany ordering a search for such a site . . .

It was a sizzling summer day when Kammler's Fiesler-Storch touched down at the Luftwaffe field on the southeast corner of Nordhausen. His brightly shined boots had hardly touched the tarmac when he was whisked away amidst a caravan of large, black cars. They raced across the bridge over the Helme and tore out of the city, northward toward the Kohnstein.

In the back seat, Kammler, a handsome, virile man in his late forties with grey streaks in his black hair, leaned forward impatiently, tense with urgency: Hitler had charged him with the single most important strategic mission of the war.

The Kohnstein was exactly what he was looking for.

The Ministry of Economics? To hell with them! They would have to find somewhere else for their massive inventories of petroleum and lubricants!

Back in Berlin Kammler worked around the clock on the WIFO blueprints.

It was simplicity personified. Extend Tunnel B so that it runs completely through the base of the hill as does Tunnel A. Next, double the existing number of connecting tunnels from twenty-three to forty-six. Finally, pave the floor area with concrete.

The result: a vast underground factory. Completely secret. Totally bombproof.

Even in peacetime, with unlimited manpower and equipment, Kammler would have been challenged with an awesome undertaking. But in the late summer of 1943, with Germany's men and material stretched the width of Italy against the Anglo-American armies and from the Baltic to the Black Sea against the Russians, Kammler's was a wild, impossible visionary scheme. Exactly the challenge for a man of his personality. He would have to proceed at top speed.

His work force would cost him nothing: the slaves in Buchenwald, only sixty-five miles away, provided a ready, plentiful, and expendable supply.

Less than six weeks after the last British bomb had exploded on Peenemünde, a convoy of trucks whined up the slope to the base of the Kohnstein and dumped off 200 of Buchenwald's scarecrows in their filthy, zebra-striped uniforms. They'd been told nothing. They stood amid the trees in the August heat without food or water. They stared at the plywood tents of the S.S. and the two huge, circular holes in the side of the hill, fearing the worst.

The inexhaustible S.S. colonel-engineer had worked a miracle and Hitler would shortly make him a general.

On the wall map of S.S. Construction Branch Headquarters in Berlin 'Closed Area B' was still an innocuous rectangle coloured green. When, during that first snow of the winter of 1944–45, *Luftwaffe* pilots flew over the territory, it was the same Christmas-card iydll.

Camp Dora – as the Kohnstein outpost had first been codenamed – was a malignancy that had metastisized well beyond the hill itself. Now officially called Camp Mittlebau, it was supported by a complex of thirty-one subcamps[2] crammed with some 32,000 slave labourers, all within a convenient twenty-mile radius of the main camp.

Under the hill's dome located at map co-ordinates D 09-53-10 Kammler had wrought order out of rubble. The boulder-strewn tunnel floors had been paved with concrete, making the Kohnstein the largest manufacturing plant under one roof in the history of the world.[3] Electricity, illumination, air-conditioning and plumbing had been piped in. The cross-tunnels had been outfitted with gleaming, well-oiled machinery for making the components and sub-assemblies. Along Tunnels A and B ran standard-gauge German railroad track plus an assembly line, and overhead, massive gantry cranes rolled smoothly.

[2]Harzungen, Ellrich, Boelke Kaserne, Kelbra, Klein Bodungen, Wieda, Blankenburg, Rossla, Osterode, Ilfeld, Hohlstedt, Quelinburg, Trautenstein, Regenstein, Wickerode, Gross Werther, Artern, Rottleberode, Nixei, Osterhagen, Woffleben, Bleicherode, Tettenborn, Mackenrode, Walkenried, Klaissingen, Sonderhausen, Ilsenburg, Ballenstedt, Sollstedt and Niedersachswerfen.
[3]Approximately 2.3 million square feet. Even today, more than thirty years later, the second largest single manufacturing plant under one roof is 2.1 million square feet. It is owned by Boeing Co. in Everett, Wash. U.S.A.

In the cavernous immensity the space of forty-five football fields, Kammler had raised a new Peenemünde from the ashes of Reugen Island in exactly one year's time. Indeed in May 1944, a mere nine months after he had launched the gigantic undertaking, the partially completed complex had produced 300 V-2s for experimental testing.

At least a month before the final design was set, and when more than 1,000 rockets had been built, an excited Hitler ordered the awesome weapon into military operation.

In Holland the German 15th Army Group was training crews to handle and fire the weapon. The basic instruction manual, the 'A-4 Fibel (Primer),' was an unorthodox document for the *Wehrmacht*, with brief homilies and inspirational verse illustrated by buxom *frauleins* in negligées and swim suits – or Christmas-card sketches of German villages, whichever the occasion demanded.

The slim volume was required reading for the soldiers encamped in the heavy woods of the Hague's biggest city park, the Haagsche Bosch, which was within the necessary 200-mile range of London. But there were other sites, too. Designed to be fully mobile, the V-2 was hauled around on a long road-trailer. It could be emplaced quickly in any location with a hard surface; an aircraft runway or a highway intersection for instance. Immediately after firing, the crew march-ordered their equipment and were gone in minutes, which meant that the mobile units were almost invulnerable to retaliation from the air.

On 6 Sept. 1944 the Haagsche Bosch crews loosed off their first shots into the heart of Paris, which had been liberated a month earlier by the Allies.

Two days later, emboldened by their success, they adjusted their firing orders and lobbed the first one into the heart of London.

It wasn't until October, though, that a fully satisfactory working model was approved. At that point Alben Sawatzski, director of plans and operations, received an urgent order from the Kohnstein's managing director, Dr. Georg Richkey: tool-up for a production quota of 900 a month.

A month later, in November, Camp Dora and its thirty-one subcamps clustered around the *Mittelwerke* underground factory broke free from the influence of Buchenwald and became the sovereign slave empire of Camp Mittelbau.

But apart from official S.S. memoranda it would never be anything other than the dreaded Dora.

The English were terrorized by the monster missile.[4]

Hitler was elated. He wanted to escalate the terror to avenge the terrible night-time fire-bombings of major German cities by the British, and he ordered Albert Speer, his Minister of Armaments, to deliver 5,000 V-2s to the army for a mass assault on London scheduled for February or March in 1945.

The German leader had no desire to slight the Americans, whose devastating daylight air raids were pulverizing Germany's industrial capacity. For them he had in mind a deluxe V-2, the A-9/A-10 rocket.

The A-9/A-10 was no *Fuehrer*'s fantasy; it was Dr. Wernher von Braun's dream.[5] Von Braun was the designer of the V-2. The A-9/A-10 was the summit of the V-2 concept – a missile that would soar to an altitude of 110 miles, sprout wings and glide into New York City at more than 3,000 miles an hour.

It was on the drawing boards in the winter of 1944–45. All that was needed was time.

---

[4]The German V-1 and V-2 campaigns against the British Isles lasted approximately seven months. In all, 5,823 flying bombs and 1,054 rockets landed; in addition, 271 bombs and four rockets fell into the sea. Total casualties were 33,442, with roughly half of all bombs and rockets falling in London.

[5]In 1974 Von Braun (now deceased) resigned as Director of Manned Space Flight at the army's facility at Huntsville, Ala., and went to work for Fairchild Industries. He was the foremost of a cache of German rocket experts captured by the Americans at the end of the war and brought to the U.S. to work in the nation's guided-missile programme.

All orders to his army commanders in the field to hold the line were expedients to buy time. He communicated the frenzy to all around him – especially to Kammler.

'Never mind the human victims,' the S.S. architect screamed as he stormed into the Kohnstein that winter of 1944–45. 'The work must proceed and be finished in the shortest possible time!'

Chapter Eleven

Crystal goblets tinkled in the officers' mess and a hand-crank phonograph megaphoned the tinny sound of a Wagnerian opera through the cigar smoke. *Kommandant* Fourschner, host of the party to introduce Mittelbau's managing director, Dr. Georg Richkey, to his ten civilian colleagues[1], had tapped his private sources in Nordhausen for the best.

The ping-pong tables had been pushed together and draped in linen. They sagged under the weight of china, gleaming cutlery and culinary seductions most Germans hadn't seen in $4\frac{1}{2}$ years of war.

The civilians and S.S. men drank *Korn* schnapps and mingled as sociably as if it were parents' day at the Officers' Academy in Brunswick.

The forty-six-year-old *Herr Doktor*, an owl-eyed, steep-shouldered little man, appeared in the green, military style uniform of a *Gau-Amtsleiter*, with a Party decoration prominently displayed. Even though he had an

---

[1]Director Rettler, chief technician; Director Sawatzski, planning and operations; Director Rudolph, in charge of V-2 production; Dr. Winkler, in charge of V-1s and jet turbines; Dr. von Bovert, anti-aircraft rocket development; Dr. Friederik, electrical controls; Dr. Bruhms, V-1 assembly; and Dr. Geitenstuker, V-2 assembly.

Johnny Nicholas as a boy in Haiti

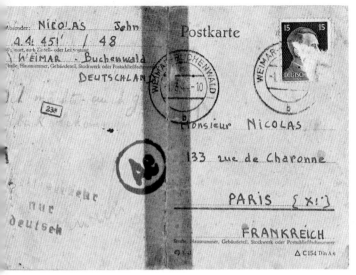

Absender: NICOLAS Sohn
4.4. 45!' / 48
Wohnort, auch Zustell- oder Leitpostamt
WEIMAR - Buchenwald
Straße, Hausnummer, Gebäudeteil, Stockwerk oder Postschließfachnummer
DEUTSCHLAN

[23]

mehr
nur
deutsch

Postkarte

Monsieur NICOLAS

133 rue de Charonne

PARIS {XI']

FRANKREICH
Straße, Hausnummer, Gebäudeteil, Stockwerk oder Postschließfachnummer
△ C 154 Din A 6

ostcard, written in German, sent by JN from Buchenwald
his brother, Vildebart, in Paris

ohnny in Paris, around 1939

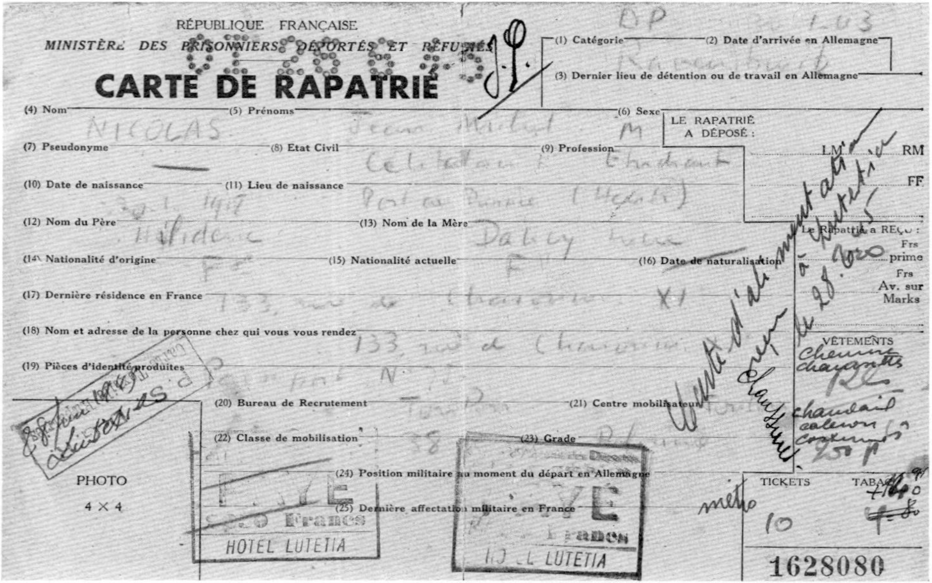

RÉPUBLIQUE FRANÇAISE

MINISTÈRE DES PRISONNIERS, DÉPORTÉS ET RÉFUGIÉS

CARTE DE RAPATRIÉ

(1) Catégorie DP (2) Date d'arrivée en Allemagne

(3) Dernier lieu de détention ou de travail en Allemagne

(4) Nom NICOLAS (5) Prénoms (6) Sexe M

LE RAPATRIÉ A DÉPOSÉ : LM RM FF

(7) Pseudonyme — (8) Etat Civil (9) Profession

(10) Date de naissance (11) Lieu de naissance

(12) Nom du Père (13) Nom de la Mère

Le Rapatrié a REÇU : Frs prime Frs Av. sur Marks

(14) Nationalité d'origine F (15) Nationalité actuelle F (16) Date de naturalisation

(17) Dernière résidence en France 133, rue de Charonne XI

(18) Nom et adresse de la personne chez qui vous vous rendez 133, rue de Charonne

(19) Pièces d'identité produites

VÊTEMENTS

(20) Bureau de Recrutement (21) Centre mobilisateur

(22) Classe de mobilisation (23) Grade

PHOTO 4 × 4

(24) Position militaire au moment du départ en Allemagne

(25) Dernière affectation militaire en France

TICKETS 10 TABAC

HOTEL LUTETIA

1628080

Johnny Nicholas's
French repatriation card

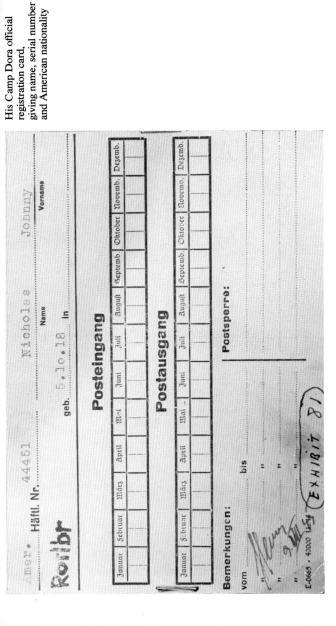

His Camp Dora official
registration card,
giving name, serial number
and American nationality

Amer. Häftl. Nr. 44451

Rohbr

Nicholas — Name

Johnny — Vorname

geb. 5.10.18 in

Posteingang

Januar	Februar	März	April	Mai	Juni	Juli	August	Septemb	Oktober	November	Dezemb.

Postausgang

Januar	Februar	März	April	Mai	Juni	Juli	August	Septemb	Oktober	November	Dezemb.

Postsperre:

Bemerkungen:

vom   bis

"   "

"   "

"   "

L-0665 · 40000 1454

(EXHIBIT 81)

The camouflaged entrance to the tunnel system
inside Kohnstein mountains

Gardelegen: the barn after the massacre, 1945

The remaining wall of the barn now forms a shrine-sculpture in memory of the victims; Gardelegen, 1969

Photographs and documents courtesy of Hugh Wray McCann

excellent production-engineering reputation, there was a real question in Col. Kammler's mind about just how far Richkey, whose two brothers and two sisters were U.S. citizens living in the enemy country, could be trusted[2] in helping to destroy the United States of America. So Richkey, partly out of self-defence but chiefly out of production zeal, quickly developed a cannon-fodder appreciation of Dora's limitless pool of slave labour.

It was May 1944, and Richkey and a coterie of intelligent and theoretically civilized German specialists had been appointed to save the Fatherland from imminent disaster. The V-2 was Germany's ace-in-the-hole. Richkey was gambling for time and he was losing. Pressured on all sides by Hitler, Himmler, armaments minister Speer, and Kammler, who was now a brigadier general, he closed off his mind to all but one consideration – building rockets.

Kammler, Richkey's *bête noire*, had a self-aggrandizing ego alarming even by S.S. standards. He could swing from building gas chambers in Auschwitz to tunnelling a rocket factory under the Kohnstein and never miss a beat. Coming from outside the S.S., he privately harboured no allegiance to the uniform; it was an expedient disguise for his unscrupulous ambition, which was one day to hob-nob with Hitler and Himmler. He had been a civil servant for much of his career. Then in 1941 *Reichsfuehrer* Himmler, the head of the S.S., had appointed him a colonel in the

[2]Richkey was one of scores of German V-2 experts captured by the U.S. Army and subsequently brought to the U.S. He voluntarily cooperated with his former enemies, placing at their disposal forty crates of blueprints which, contrary to Gestapo orders, he had not destroyed. When he defected to the American forces, Gen. Kammler issued orders that he was to be shot on sight. He was returned from Wright Field Engineering Division, Dayton, Ohio, in 1947, where he was working for the U.S. Air Force, to stand trial in the Nordhausen War Crimes case. His sister, Aenne (sic) Richkey Schumann, wrote an appeal for clemency on her brother's behalf: '. . . May I also state that we are here (sic) two brothers and two sisters. We are all (U.S.) citizens . . . During the last war we all did our share to assure victory for the land of our adoption . . .'

S.S. and given him command of Amtsgruppe C. in the S.S. Economic and Administrative Department. There he was responsible for a nationwide building and construction programme which, by 1942, had pressed into service 175,000 slave labourers and prisoners-of-war.

Richkey stood in dread of Kammler, as well he should have. As a result, Mittelwerke's managing director and his staff were forced to live only half-lives, permitting their technical duties to drown out any vestige of pity for the slave labourers in the tunnel toolrooms, workshops and assembly lines. Armaments Minister Speer would argue after the war that to hit rocket-production targets, he was forced to use labour wherever it was available. There was a superabundance of it to be found in Germany's concentration camps.

Von Braun, creator of the V-2, was in his early thirties. For more than $1\frac{1}{2}$ years after Peenemünde was bombed in mid-1943, von Braun continued his work there because the research and development facilities had not been hit during the raid. However, the time soon came when he, too, was to see with his own eyes the stories of human degradation in the Kohnstein. On 23 January 1945 Gen. Kammler ordered complete evacuation of Peenemünde because the Red Army was coming closer and Russian military intelligence had put a high price on German scientific brainpower. By mid-March, when the Russians were twenty-five miles away, all the centre's personnel and their families – more than 5,000 people – had been relocated in the towns and villages around Nordhausen, 240 miles southwest.

Von Braun, a bachelor, installed himself at Bleicherode, eight miles southwest of Camp Dora: the umbilical cord linking him with his creation had shortened drastically, but mentally he could keep far away from the crimes against humanity occuring daily in the Kohnstein. In May 1944, ten months before von Braun arrived, Richkey could calmly sip his *schnapps* and sample banquet delicacies while six miles northwest a starvation-mad Pole in Subcamp Ellrich ate the testicles of a dead comrade.

Of the 52,000 workers Richkey would have at his disposal, about 12,000 were German civilians, most in supervisory and technical positions over the slave labourers. In the furious rush to buy more time, Richkey teased the civilians with production bonuses that ran as high as fifty percent of their base pay. To the 40,000 prisoners, almost all of whom were foreigners and who worked sixteen- and eighteen-hour days, he gave nothing. If they fell behind in their quotas he reported them as saboteurs.

The punishment for sabotage was always execution.

At the Nordhausen trials that would take place in 1947, Dr. Richkey would be charged with production speed-ups so demanding that they killed thousands of slave labourers.[3] He would also be charged with 'making accusations of sabotage for the most trifling incidents which resulted in the hanging inside and outside of the tunnels of hundreds of workers.' The indictment said that 'by failing to use the power inherent in his position (he took) a consenting part in the death by exhaustion and other means of many hundreds of prisoners.'

During the horrendous first six months when approximately 10,000 slave labourers were carving out new tunnels and expanding existing ones, the 'official' death

---

[3] A German prisoner, Josef Ackermann, testified in the Nordhausen War Crimes Trials: 'The physical condition of most of the prisoners – one could almost say ninety percent of the prisoners – was so bad that ... the bones were showing. A large part of the prisoners were suffering on their legs, which was due to the insufficient amount of ... shoes ... and through the long period of standing during the twelve-hour work period. The bad physical condition of the prisoners may be judged from the fact that even though they didn't have any disease or ... were not actually ill ... they were so weak and in such a weakened condition that they were unable to do any work. The physical condition ... was to such an extent that many of the prisoners on the way to work and on the way from work collapsed and died. The autopsy of the bodies did not show any disease, but it showed a complete weakness of the body ... (visualize) a prisoner who for ... years never sees an egg, never saw butter, never saw meat, never saw milk ...'

rate was 2,882 – which meant that the actual rate was probably fifty percent higher. After the machinery was installed and production got under way, conditions improved. Still, Richkey was so unremitting in his punishing speed-ups that the death rate jumped instead of dropping!

From 1 November 1944 to April 3, 1945 Dora records show 8,936 deaths. True fatalities were conceivably around 12,000. Most died of exhaustion and malnutrition. Many were executed for sabotage – real or imagined.

In every German concentration camp organization chart there was a small rectangle of space containing the word 'Revier'; the word is used to mean an infirmary or hospital for prisoners. In many camps it existed in name only.

At Camp Dora the Revier was instituted when prisoners scrounged an old tarpaulin and fashioned it into a tent outside the entrance to the main tunnels. Had it been left to Dora's camp commandant, Major Otto Fourschner, it would have remained in that state of wretched primitiveness; he had no concern for prisoners' lives. Every scrap of lumber he could lay his hands on was going into building the Kohnstein factory for V-1 and V-2 production. But the Revier at Dora, despite incredible difficulties and dangers for the prisoners, expanded gradually in size and sophistication under the benign conspiracy of a newcomer to the camp – an S.S. medical officer, Dr. Karl Kahr.

In the mounds of concentration-camp literature that have accumulated since World War II ended, the term 'S.S. doctor' is synonomous with quack and charlatan; it evokes visions of men who used prisoners as human guinea pigs for horrendous medical experiments. But Dr. Kahr was the exception that proves the rule. When Johnny Nicholas, his striped uniform begrimed with the filth and dirt of the excavations in the tunnel, dragged himself into the doctor's office and announced that he, too, was a physician and that he wanted to be a prisoner-doctor[4] in the Revier, the new S.S. medical officer accepted the offer.

Kahr and Nicholas were among the major architects of a grand plot involving the prisoners to pilfer and steal materials and equipment. The audacious scheme would ultimately result in a Revier enjoying such unheard of luxuries as an organized sick call, convalescent slips that carried not merely his signature in ink but the weight of his authority, extra food for the sick – and three, gleaming, new military-style barracks.

Dr. Kahr, an S.S. first lieutenant, arrived in Dora in February of 1944 and discovered that the death toll for the previous six-month period had been 2,800. If the slim, thirty-year-old Austrian had been the typical S.S. medico – of the ilk, say, of Hoven and Schiedlausky back at Buchenwald, the statistics wouldn't have surprised him. But he wasn't.

A product of the universities of Graz and Vienna, Kahr was a newly graduated physician at the outbreak of the war and was anxious to do his patriotic best for the Fatherland. He wouldn't settle for anything less than the most prestigious outfit in the German armed forces – the elite *Waffen* S.S., whose combat units would trample the Polish Army and romp through the French and English on the Western Front. But practicing the healing arts as a battalion surgeon amid the snowy wastes of the Soviet Union soon purged him of his romantic notions about war.

---

[4]Dora's first prisoner-doctor was a 36-year-old Mennonite-Dutch physician, Dr. Hessel Louws-Groeneveld, of Nymegen. He set up his tarpaulin hospital with twelve cots secretly made by an English prisoner who was a carpenter, Cecil Jay. Dr. Groeneveld had no medicine or equipment and performed amputations with a carpenter's saw. Frequently during the first summer of Dora's existence he would return to examine an amputee and discover the stump quivering with maggots. From fifty sick prisoners a day in August 1943 his patient load soared to three hundred daily as the weather turned cold; but he was forced, because of lack of facilities, to send three-quarters of them back to the tunnels. Dr. Groeneveld survived the war and returned to Holland to practice medicine. Later he wrote a book about his wartime experiences. He died in 1973.

The obscene, brutal and inhuman conduct of the Waffen S.S. against Russian men, women and children numbed and shocked him. What kind of Germans were these? What kind of a Germany was he fighting for?

Russian shell fragments that pierced his head and his left leg during an artillery duel snatched him away from the insanity of it all and put him in a hospital bed back in Germany, where men still ruled their lives by common standards of decency and honour . . . or so he hoped.

His wounds healed but he walked with a severe limp. 'Unfit for Combat' was stamped on his dossier and he was posted to a branch which the Waffen S.S. men despised almost as much as they loathed the Russians – the Concentration Camp Branch: it was said to be the dumping ground of 4-Fs, perverts, psychos and cowards.

In Berlin, where Kahr reported after his nine-month absence from duty, the Chief of Medical Affairs for the S.S., Dr. Lolling, told him: 'You are now going to come (sic) to a camp where very bad conditions reign. But I call your attention to the fact that the man in charge of administering the camp (Major Fourschner) is not very interested in improving the life of the prisoners.

'Because we do not care if 1,000 or 10,000 people die. The most important thing as far as we are concerned is the armament mission . . .'

Dr. Lolling's callous admonition didn't prepare Kahr for his first visit to the tunnels.

Air choked with dust. The clamour assaulted the eardrums. Shrivelled men coated in white, limestone dust squatting in the rubble to relieve their bowels. Pissing in their hands to wash their faces. The rockfalls. The screams of agony. The stony indifference of the S.S. The prisoners' bunks sprayed with liquid excrement. Blankets mobile with lice. The cannibalistic ritual of the dead being stripped of their clothes and wooden clogs by their friends.

Back at his quarters Kahr recalled with grim irony that

day he had returned from the Fatherland, to what he felt was a semblance of civilization . . .

The clothing situation was impossible: thin cotton stripes year around. No socks. Half the prisoners without shoes.

The food was enough to keep a prisoner's heart beating and little more: a half-litre of coffee at 6 a.m. – really warmed-up beet juice; one piece of bread; and twenty grams of margarine. Clear turnip soup at noon. At 6 p.m. turnip salad and maybe a bite of sausage.

Less than 2,000 calories·were supposed to fuel a man for twelve hours of pick-and-shovel swinging. Fifteen hours if you counted roll calls. At some of the distant subcamps it was nearly midnight before they marched back and were dismissed from roll call. Three hours later it was '*Aufstehen! Aufstehen!*' again as the *Lagerschutz* bludgeoned them out of their bunks to start another frightful day in the tunnels.

The death rate was averaging 850 a month when Kahr arrived that February.

'You! *Schwartze schwein!*' Brauny shouted. 'You're the *Amerikanisher* bastard who gave me trouble at Buchenwald.'

Nicholas felt his comrade jab him in the ribs. It jerked him back from his daydream of the humiliation he felt when he'd been whipped before his classmates in the Tippenhauer academy. 'Sir!' he stuttered automatically, rapidly marshalling his wits. 'Sir! . . .'

Brauny gritted his teeth. 'You'd better not be trying to squirm your way into a softer job, because if you are –'

'I am a physician,' interrupted Nicholas, trying to restrain the hate in his voice.

Brauny stared back at him. '*You* a physician!' he sneered. 'I think you're a slippery black bastard!'

Nicholas knew he couldn't hold on much longer. He should have strangled Brauny at Buchenwald. He couldn't stand there now without putting his hands around the little runt's neck and wringing the life from him. Everything else, every other consideration, was fading with blinding speed. All he could see was the pompous S.S. sergeant with the baby-blue eyes and the finely chiselled face. He longed to pound the life out of him and make it a prayer to God.

'Fall out, *Schwartze*, and report to the labour allocation officer!'

Nicholas' emotions, damned up for the horrific revenge he had contemplated, flooded over and swirled through his mind like a toxin affecting his brain. He fumbled for his sanity but it was like clutching for fog. The parade ground didn't seem real.

'*Schnell!*' screamed Brauny. '*Mach schnell!*'

His addled reflexes, stung by the high-pitched yell, jerked his legs, stepped him clumsily out of ranks and marched him off.

By the time he'd walked the eighth mile back to the main part of the camp his rage still simmered. It was no longer explosive and uncontrolled. Now it was cold and calculating. In the sunlight, so bright that he had to close his eyes, he reflected on what had happened.

He had always prided himself in his total composure, yet Brauny had almost provoked him into completely abandoning his self-control. By merely attempting to strangle the S.S. sergeant he would have dug his own grave. It had been close. If the tunnels didn't kill you, he thought, they drove you mad – mad enough to try the unthinkable and invite your own execution.

The labour allocation officer was S.S. Technical Sergeant Wilhelm Simon, a supercilious, balding S.S. man whose big ears on his long skull jutted out like handles on a jug.

Nicholas wondered what the hell he could expect from Simon, whose joy in life was assigning weak and helpless prisoners to the very heaviest work and watching them die at it. Once Simon had stood two Jehovah's Witnesses on the edge of the quarry excavation. After two days they'd

186

collapsed and fallen over the precipice. No, Simon wouldn't do him any favours, unless he could do Simon a favour. Like most of the S.S., the brute always had deals going with key members of the prisoner government – the criminals, or Greens. Simon would ask the *Kapo* in the tailor shop to make him some fancy civilian suits; the S.S. man, as payment for the suits, would offer to assign Greens to the comparative warmth and safety of the tailor shop. The Kapo would agree to the highly illegal suit-making proposal on orders from the prisoner government, which ceaselessly ferreted out ways to compromise S.S. personnel. Once they'd found a way, then they'd use it to blackmail the S.S. into playing ball with the prisoner government.

If Commandant Fourschner were to find out about it, however, Simon would be finished – even though Fourschner surely had the same deal or better going somewhere else.

There was one place in Dora where the Greens didn't rule; that was in the *Revier*, which was dominated by Communists.

Nicholas, who had learned camp politics with great speed, knew that the Greens wanted other criminals, not an American POW, infiltrated into the *Revier*. So what was the point of going to see Simon, he asked himself, other than to obey Brauny's command? Simon would turn him down and slip a Green in. For Nicholas and his chances of getting into the *Revier*, it was like being called out before stepping into the batter's box. There was only one man who could appoint a prisoner to the *Revier* without owing anything to anybody: Dr. Kahr.[5]

---

[5]Dr. Kahr, a soft-voiced, compassionate-looking man now in his sixties, still walks with a pronounced limp as he goes on his rounds in the beautiful Austrian town of Graz, where he practices medicine. Of the war years he says: 'We had good times and we had bad times. When I was a physician with the troops in Russia and France, it was a good time. My work in the concentration camp was the worst. In the camp it was the worst time of my life. You could see so much misery – but you couldn't help. You felt helpless.'

The custody camp leader, First Lieutenant Hans Moeser, held the power of God over every prisoner in Dora. Moeser had to bow only to Fourschner, who wielded sovereignty over prisoners *and* S.S. personnel combined. Moeser was suspicious when the new medical officer came to him and announced that he wanted a very specific prisoner on his staff. Moeser decided he would have to take a look at this prisoner himself.

Nicholas stood in Moeser's office, his arms stiffly by his sides, cap in hand, staring fixedly at the blank wall above the custody camp leader's head.

Inwardly he ridiculed himself for trembling in the presence of any of the black-uniformed imbeciles who ruled his life. But how could he forget that Moeser was the son-of-a-bitch who shot the hanged men, still twitching, in the back when they were cut down from the scaffold – and smiled while he was doing it?

In his peripheral vision he could see Moeser's cruel face. The man's left eyelid half-covered his eye because of an injury or birth defect. His lips were thin. His mouth was so wide that when he was viewed head-on it looked

As camp medical officer for the Mittlebau complex Kahr was responsible not only for Dora but also for the medical facilities – poor as they might have been – at Dora's thirty-one subcamps. Since the bulk of the prisoners were at Dora, he necessarily spent most of his time there. His duties were primarily administrative. 'I didn't actually treat the prisoners myself,' he recalls. 'But I was interested in the kinds of injuries and how they got them. We had first-aid stations in the tunnels and I would check on them.' Four days a week he inspected the tunnels. Conditions were 'very, very bad,' he remembers. 'The problem was there wasn't enough food for the prisoners and they were worked too hard. Their resistance was so low that the medicines and vaccines didn't work. They had very little food for the prisoners. I hoped that in my position I would help improve it.' Dr. Kahr remembers that Nicholas came into the *Revier* one day. 'I think he had some wounds from working in the tunnel. He said to me: "I'm a physician. Can I work here? I'm not a political prisoner. I'm an American prisoner-of-war." I was very pleased, but I wondered what people would say about a Negro in the *Revier*.' After talking it over with the kapo of the *Revier* and some of the prisoner staff, he discovered that they were in favour of the idea because, he says, 'he was a Negro. They wanted a Negro. He was the only one in the camp and (apparently) he was a sensation with them.'

as if it had run out of face on both sides. His left ear stuck out at right angles, and two crescents of baldness at his temples had encroached upon his sparse, black hair.

'What's going on between you and the camp medical officer?' he demanded in a high, reedy voice. He was sneering and the innuendo was obvious.

Nicholas opened his mouth to reply but Moeser cut him off. 'You disobeyed the order of Roll Call Leader Brauny to report to Labour Allocation Leader Simon. You disobeyed camp rules and regulations by approaching the camp medical officer without permission. You know the punishment for breaking camp rules, don't you? Do you think I make them for my own amusement? I won't tolerate a subhuman like you making me a laughing stock. How would a smart American bastard like to be shot next Sunday? Or is hanging your choice?'

It was the old S.S. technique of bombarding a suspect with abuse and threats to make him snivel for his life. Somehow Moeser had to be jarred out of his complacent attitude that this was just another prisoner standing before him. Nicholas' intuition told him that powerful as Moeser was, Dr. Kahr was equally powerful.

'The *Herr Obersturmbannfuehrer* has asked the prisoner five questions. Should the prisoner to reply to all five or merely the last two, which the prisoner believes the most important?' His reply was in rapid, faultless German calculated to startle the S.S. officer.

Moeser stiffened. 'You speak German,' he declared, as if Nicholas were guilty of another breach of camp rules. 'Where did an American *Schwartze* learn to speak German?' he demanded.

'It was the prisoner's favourite language in high school, *Herr Obersturmbannfuehrer.*'

Moeser looked at him suspiciously. 'What other languages do you speak?'

'*Herr Obersturmbannfuehrer*, the prisoner also speaks English, French, some Spanish, a little Russian . . . That is one reason why *Herr Doktor* Kahr thinks the prisoner

189

would be of use to him in the *Revier*, where many languages are spoken.'

'By the time I have finished with you, *Schwartze*, German will not be your favourite language any more.'

'*Herr Obersturmbannfuehrer*. The prisoner is very fortunate to have the opportunity of hearing someone speak German as it ought to be spoken.'

Moeser didn't know if Nicholas was being sarcastic or not. He wasn't used to being addressed by a prisoner as the American POW was now talking to him. 'You went to *Herr Doktor* Kahr to get out of the tunnel work!' he yelled.

'*Ja, Herr Obersturmbannfuehrer*. That is correct. If there is one thing the prisoner has learned from his study of German it is that Germans are logical people. It is logical for any prisoner working in the tunnel to try to get out of the tunnel. It is logical for the *Herr Obersturmbannfuehrer* to deduce this truth. If the prisoner tried to conceal that fact, the prisoner would be insulting the *Herr Obersturmbannfuehrer*'s intelligence – which the prisoner believes would be regarded as a crime worse than those that he has already committed.'

Moeser blinked. Prisoners didn't talk to custody leaders that way! It irritated him that a Negro could have such a superior command of the German tongue. 'Why did you study German? There must have been a reason?'

'*Ja, Herr Obersturmbannfuehrer*. There was.'

'And what was it?' Moeser demanded angrily.

'The prisoner was interested in the great German philosopher, Wilhelm Friedrich Nietzsche, *Herr Obersturmbannfuehrer*. *Herr* Nietzsche believed that the weak must be allowed to perish so that the strong can flourish without the burden of supporting the weak. He believed that there can only be two classes in the world – the strong and the weak. *Herr* Nietzsche is not popular in the United States, *Herr Obersturmbannfuehrer*. There was always the possibility that the English translators had tampered with his message. The prisoner decided to learn the *Herr*

Obersturmbannfuehrer's mother tongue so that the prisoner could understand *Herr* Nietzsche's thoughts as if they were coming directly from his mouth.'

Moeser shuffled with several index cards. He looked at one for several seconds, then as if one chapter of their conversation had ended, he began: 'How do you feel about murdering innocent German women and children with the bombs your American planes drop on Germany?'

'The Geneva Convention, *Herr Obersturmbannfuehrer*, permits the prisoner to give only his name, rank, serial number and date of birth.'

'Shit on the Geneva Convention! According to these records you are a doctor. You have taken the Hippocratic Oath. You have been trained to preserve life, not to destroy it. A man like you would be no possible use to *Herr Doktor* Kahr. You have gone back on your oath. You are not worthy to be called a doctor. That is why you are a *Nacht und Nebel*: you are a terrorist who masquerades under the cloak of a doctor!'

Why was Moeser baiting him? Was there something he hoped to get out of him that the Gestapo back in Paris hadn't? Or was he just doing it for his own amusement? There were a dozen ways he could answer the tight-lipped S.S. sadist. One or two of the answers would keep him alive. The others would get him a bullet or a noose. He was feeling very tired. The heat in Moeser's office made him want to close his eyes. It was becoming an effort to concentrate. The wrong answer could mean his early funeral.

'It would never be tolerated in the *Luftwaffe*!' shouted Moeser. 'A doctor who squanders his skill by learning to fly an airplane and drop bombs. If you are a doctor, then you are a medical whore.'

Nicholas clenched his teeth. He felt like a blind man walking a tight-rope, wondering when he was going to put his foot down and discover he wasn't on the wire. He remembered the prisoner-medics at Buchenwald. How they were envied. Never stood roll calls. Clean clothes. Soap and water. Extra rations. He remembered the S.S. doctors at Buchenwald, most of whom had been failures in civilian life. They'd taken shortcuts to their medical degrees via their S.S. rank. Most had been sadistic butchers. Even when S.S. were sick, they preferred to be treated by prisoners-doctors rather than by S.S. doctors.

Was Kahr *really* different? Or did he just appear that way? He'd acted human, civilized when Nicholas had talked to him. But you never judged by appearances – not in the warped society of a concentration camp.

Moeser read from another card. 'It says you are from Boston.'

'*Ja, Herr Obersturmbannfuehrer.*'

Moeser waited for Nicholas to elaborate. When he didn't, the S.S. lieutenant added: 'I haven't seen an American before. And I have never seen a Negro. I have been told that Negroes are persecuted in the United States. How does one of them become a doctor in America?'

Nicholas' eyes felt like leaden trapdoors and he bit on his tongue to repress the urge to yawn. 'In the same way, *Herr Obersturmbannfuehrer*, that he becomes a pilot in the air force.'

'How is that?'

'Only after the greatest struggle, *Herr Obersturmbannfuehrer*. It is very difficult. He must want it very much.'

'Where is Boston?' asked Moeser, examining another card.

'It is north of New York City, *Herr Obersturmbannfuehrer*.'

'Does it have a university?'

'*Ja, Herr Obersturmbannfuehrer.*'

'Is that where you studied medicine?'

'*Ja, Herr Obersturmbannfuehrer.*'

Nicholas was inexorably succumbing to the fatigue and the heat of Moeser's office. The S.S. man seemed to be going around in circles. He was either asking aimless questions to satisfy his own curiosity – or he was fishing for something. About Boston? Medical school? Could Doctor Kahr have put him up to asking such questions? If not, then what possible interest would the answers be to a camp custody leader? Or could it be the political department of the camp that was behind it – the Gestapo *still* double-checking on the story he'd given them in Paris?

A prisoner hadn't seen the last of the Gestapo when the camp gates slammed behind him. Through the political department, Gestapo agents posing as prisoners reported on what went on inside the camp. It was the exact parallel of the Greens continually trying to slip their people into jobs in the S.S. offices, barracks and mess halls to find out what the S.S. was up to.

Could *that* be why Moeser even bothered to give Nicholas the time of day instead of kicking him in the balls and throwing him in the bunker? To make him a Gestapo plant? They seldom pressured a prisoner on his first day to become a stool pigeon. They usually waited until he'd become totally seduced by *Revier* life – no roll calls, extra food and straw for a mattress instead of rocks.

'You are a *scheisskopf* to want to work in the *Revier* with all those Communists,' said Moeser. His voice had lost its nagging, punitive tone. It was almost conversational. 'An officer of your education and intelligence should know better: they don't like the Western democracies. They would make life very difficult for you. Do you think that because you're the only Negro and the only American they will treat you as a mascot?'

Nicholas forced himself to stay awake and sound rational. 'The prisoner has not considered that possibility, *Herr Obersturmbannfuehrer*. The prisoner is a doctor. If he can assist the custody camp leader in his work, he would prefer to do the work of a doctor.'

'Maybe you think the comrades will not notice the

colour of your skin,' persisted Moeser, his words soaked in sarcasm.

'The prisoner had not considered it, *Herr Obersturmbannfuehrer.*'

'How could you? You are an American. You think everybody but the Germans love you. Don't be stupid! The Communists hate you. But they love your guns and your tanks and your airplanes.'

Nicholas was so exhausted now that it required tremendous effort for him to plumb the depths of Moeser's convoluted interrogation. What was he after?

'It is just an alliance of convenience,' the S.S. man continued. 'The minute they don't need you Americans any more they will cut your throats.'

Was Moeser trying to keep him out of the *Revier*? Or was he trying to build hatred of the Communists so that once Nicholas was in the *Revier* he'd be willing to inform on them? Supposing he agreed to spy on the Communists in order to get into the *Revier*, then simply not produce anything worthwhile. No, Moeser would have the last word: the S.S. man would simply leak the information to the *Revier* that Nicholas was a plant – and it would be curtains for him. He found it almost impossible to keep his eyes open and his brain tracking the complexities of it all. He felt like a caged animal suddenly released in a maze: he continually found openings and escapes – but they kept leading back to where he'd started out. If Moeser could help the Gestapo infiltrate the *Revier*, it could be a promotion for him, for the Gestapo had tremendous influence. But the last thing Nicholas wanted was to be indebted to an animal like Moeser; it would be a vice the S.S. officer would never stop squeezing. His mind spun as he tried to think of a way to extricate himself. He longed to go to sleep. In his borderline state the thought of going back to the tunnels sent his heart racing. He tried desperately to unscramble his thoughts.

He knew that Dr. Kahr wanted him in the *Revier*. He had to take him at his word. He knew that Moeser was the second most powerful officer in the camp. He knew that Dr. Kahr was also enormously powerful because of his independent status in the camp. He reasoned that in a stand-off between Moeser and Kahr, the doctor would prevail; that if Kahr really wanted him, then nothing Moeser could do would change that. So the only way to get out from under the threat of indebtedness to Moeser was to pretend he had changed his mind; that he didn't want to go to the *Revier* after all.

'With German soldiers and American equipment,' Moeser continued, 'the Bolshevists could be wiped off the face of the earth, Major Nicholas.'

So now it was 'Major Nicholas!' The slimy bastard. Who did he think he was dealing with? Some horse's ass from the Ukraine? 'Do you,' he began, brazenly dropping the obligatory use by a prisoner of an S.S. man's rank when speaking to him, 'really believe that the Russians despise the Americans?'

'*Natürlich*!' retorted Moeser with a slight glint in his eyes. He leaned forward as if some degree of confidentiality had suddenly been created between them.

'Then,' Nicholas continued, cautiously feigning innocence, 'their talk about all men being equal under their system – regardless of colour or creed – is that just propaganda?'

'*Ja, Ja*. Utter propaganda. They have fooled you as they have fooled all Americans. And unfortunately many of those are German-Americans. Even though we are at war, there are still very close ties between the American people and the German people. Are there many German-Americans in Boston, Major?'

'Not many.'

'But there is one city, Major, where there are many Germans . . . What is it?'

Nicholas felt as if he was back in the ring again with his boyhood friend Gabrielle calling out encouragement: he was punchdrunk. He could hear the words clearly but his faculties seemed to be anaesthetized. Yes, there was a town famed for its German population – but what was it? He could remember the U.S. Marines at Port-au-Prince bragging about it. Christ, what was it? He'd come this far as an American and it had worked. To have it all fall apart now because of something so insignificant, so casual, that he could never have figured on it . . .

Moeser was now clearly suspicious. He scanned the index cards before him.

Nicholas had nearly reached the point of capitulation. He desperately needed rest to be a match for Moeser. But Moeser wouldn't give him any rest.

'They say this American city makes better beer than German beer,' continued Moeser, watching him very closely. 'But that's not possible.'

'In Milwaukee they will tell you it is possible,' Nicholas said conversationally, trying to hide his exhaustion and the profound relief that flooded through him.

'*Ja, Ja*, Milwaukee! You've been to Milwaukee?'

'*Nein*.' He realized he couldn't keep up the mental battle – that he had to draw it to a close as rapidly as possible but without tipping his hand. 'You are right about the Communists. They are just using my country and the sacrifices of its people. At any moment they will turn around and bite the hand that feeds them.'

'*Jawohl*, Major,' said Moeser enthusiastically. 'They cannot be trusted.'

'That is why I want to withdraw my request to work in the *Revier*.'

Moeser's jaw slackened. 'What?'

'You have convinced me of a serious error in judgment. An American would be unpatriotic to want to associate with them. They are only pretending to be our allies.'

'You cannot withdraw your request!'

'But they are liars: they care only for the equipment we give them. You said so yourself.'

'*Ja, Ja*,' declared Moeser vigorously, 'but –

' – and you have helped me to see their deceit and treachery. I would rather return to the tunnels than –'

196

'*Nein*!' shouted Moeser. '*Nein! Nein*! You do not understand!'

Nicholas feigned the confusion of an innocent. 'The prisoner begs that you forgive him. He has seriously misjudged the *Herr Obersturmbannfuehrer*, who has indeed been a friend of the prisoners and concerned for their better interests. The prisoner begs that you inform *Herr Doktor* Kahr that you have helped the prisoner to see the error of his thinking –'

'Shut up!'

'*Ja, Herr Obersturmbannfuehrer*!'

Moeser looked away. He was incensed that his subterfuge had backfired. He had baited his hook skilfully only to snag it embarrassingly in his own lip. He gripped the arms of his chair until his knuckles turned white.

Nicholas knew that at that moment Moeser longed to put a bullet in the back of his head. Yet he wondered if there weren't perhaps a few more lines to be delivered to make his theatrical performance irrevocably convincing. His own *coup de grace*, perhaps. '*Herr Obersturmbannfuehrer*! The prisoner wishes to thank –'

'Shut up!' screamed Moeser, bounding from his chair.

Nicholas stood stock still, chest out, chin in, arms stiffly by his sides.

Moeser walked around behind him.

Nicholas could feel the hair prickle on the back of his neck: what was Moeser up to now? He didn't dare look around. His imagination told him that the custody camp leader was unbuttoning the flap on his holster, sliding out his pistol. Any moment he expected to hear the click as he cocked the weapon.

But instead there was a thin, quiet voice very close to his ear. 'You will report to the *Revier* tomorrow morning after roll call. *Verstehen sie*?'

'*Ja, Herr Obersturmbannfuehrer*! I understand.'

'And you will not breathe a word to anyone of what we have discussed in this office. Not to *Herr Doktor* Kahr. Not to anyone. Understood?'

197

'*Jawohl, Herr Obersturmbannfuehrer!*'

'It was only for your own protection that I gave you the advice I did.'

'*Ja.*'

'Now get out!'

He clicked his heels, turned about and faced Moeser. '*Danke, Herr Obersturmbannfuehrer*,' he said, trying to suppress the smile of exultation beginning to curl the corners of his mouth: he had achieved his objective of getting into the *Revier* – with an unbelievable bonus: now he had something with which to blackmail First Lieutenant Moeser, who the moment that he realized it, would have him killed.

Chapter Twelve

Day after day Dr. Kahr shuffled about the base of the Kohnstein, where the barracks of Camp Dora were taking shape. Tyre tracks rutted the muddy grass and the terrain was littered with timber, construction equipment, mining supplies and uncrated machines. He kept his eyes open, his mouth shut and his mind in gear.

Gradually and grudgingly he was coming to the conclusion that Dora was a landmark example of German stupidity. From Managing Director Richkey, through *Kommandant* Fourschner, down the lackeys like Roll Call Leader Brauny and Labour Allocation Leader Simon, all suffered literally and metaphorically from 'tunnel vision.' They hated Jews and foreigners so passionately that they were blinded. Couldn't they see that if they fed the prisoners more, clothed them better, treated their injuries and diseases, they could get much more work out of them? How incredibly ironic that the very officials charged with meeting Hitler's delivery date on a V-2 rocket fleet were actually sabotaging his plan by their short-sightedness!

Kahr used his authority to enforce the terms of the convalescent slips he gave to seriously ill prisoners. The jealously coveted pieces of paper allowed them to stay in their bunks for one, two or three days and rest. Under the previous post medical officer, Brauny and Simon had thought nothing of ripping the slips in pieces and screaming at prisoners with 104-degree temperatures to get back to work. If the pathetic men wavered, they'd beat them savagely. But when Brauny and Simon tore up Kahr's slips, the doctor threatened them with court martial for insubordination.

Kommandant Fourschner, on the other hand, was much more difficult to deal with. As a lieutenant, Dr. Kahr could only try to cajole the major into change. It was almost impossible. Fourschner regarded the presence of a medical officer and his paraphernalia as nuisances. Why spend time patching up Jews and foreigners? Let them die. There are boxcar-loads more where they came from.

They would last a little longer in the bitter Harz winter, Dr. Kahr suggested mildly, if they had better clothes. There were thousands of brand-new uniforms and unused shoes in the warehouse, he told the major. *Nein, Nein*, replied the *Kommandant* wearily. Didn't Kahr realize regulations dictated that a commander must always have a specified supply of clothes and footwear in reserve as a percentage of his prisoner population?

Couldn't he requisition more from Berlin? *Nein*. There were no more to be requisitioned. Now was there anything else the *Doktor* wished to discuss? If not, the *Kommandant* was very busy.

Because Fourschner continued to ignore his pleas,

Kahr started by sending memoranda[1] to higher headquarters demanding soap so that the prisoners could wash themselves and their clothes.

The *Revier*, by this time, had been upgraded to a small, blind-end tunnel inside the hill, and two tents on the slope outside, each with twelve beds. The *Revier* staff, which in the beginning had carefully kept its distance from Dr. Kahr, now began to feel he was not a typical S.S. doctor. His efforts to improve conditions couldn't be ignored; and while career *Revier* men were too old and too cynical in the ways of camps and S.S. men to want to clutch him to their bosoms, even they felt he was definitely not on Fourschner's side.

Kahr demanded the strictest personal cleanliness from his prisoner-doctors and medical orderlies. Their new access to soap and clean uniforms changed the way they carried themselves. And S.S. NCOs, like Brauny and Simon, bristled when they saw them; haeftlinge[2] were supposed to look haggard, beaten, meek, hopeless.

Kahr soon realized that he was a child lost in the administrative jungle of the S.S. rear echelons. Since his arrival in February 1944, he had knocked on official doors and cranked out sheaves of reports about the abominable conditions until he was finally persuaded that what he must do in Dora couldn't be done through official channels. He discovered that behind the rules and regulations and formal procedures was another mechanism – one based on the privilege of rank or position, the extending of a favour and the reciprocation of that favour. It was a mechanism that crossed the lines of politics,

[1]Josef Ackermann, a German prisoner who actually typed the memos, recalled that Kahr 'wrote repeatedly to the administration requesting that better clothing be issued to the prisoners.' At Subcamp Ellrich, for example, the doctor found out that the regulation forbidding the use of soap to wash uniforms had led to a torrential outbreak of vermin. He fired off a message to Berlin informing them that unless fresh clothing was brought in immediately, there would be an epidemic of typhus at Ellrich.
[2]Literally persons in arrest.

religion, nationality. It even bridged the barbed wire between prisoner and guard.

As he changed his tactics, Dora was changing too. About 10,000 prisoners who lived in the tunnels were being moved out into barracks in a permanent camp near the tunnel mouths. By May the tunnels had been completely paved and equipped with machinery, and Richkey would proudly telephone Minister of Armaments Speer that he had produced 300 experimental V-2s for testing in Poland.

It was an achievement to make German hearts burst with pride – as long as they didn't know the cost in human life.

To gear up for the mass production, which would begin in the autumn, Richkey was installing new equipment every day in his amazing factory inside the Kohnstein, and Fourschner was under pressure to bring in more slaves, build more barracks for them and train them to operate the machinery.

One day in May, Kahr limped through the camp on his way to see Fourschner. As he picked his way past the foundations of half completed barracks and through massive piles of lumber and building supplies, a wild idea formed in his mind. The idea mushroomed as he stepped over huge, recently felled pines and detoured around large stocks of concrete bags and rows of prefabricated roof trusses.

The *Kommandant* wasn't especially pleased to see him. Why didn't Kahr just go into Nordhausen and get drunk as the previous medical officer had done?

The conversation began with a lot of window-dressing.[3] The time was ripe to praise the *Kommandant*: 300 V-2s ready for testing in nine months! Incredible! Then he adroitly deployed the conversation into the area of the health of the prisoners. Fourschner grimaced. Kahr

---

[3] 'Fourschner had few redeeming characteristics,' Dr. Kahr said after the war, 'but he would listen to me, and I learned how to handle him.'

persisted. What would be the possibility, the doctor inquired, of allocating materials for three barracks for use as hospital facilities?

Fourschner was shocked: had the doctor lost his mind?

Indeed he was serious, he assured the major; and he familiarized the Kommandant with his conclusion that lack of prisoner medical attention was actually delaying the day when the Kohnstein could go into mass production. More drugs and dressings and expanded hospital accommodation, he continued, would not be pampering of *haeftlinge*. Just the reverse. Skilled workers were dying off every day and the S.S. commander was continually burdened with the task of shipping new workers from Buchenwald and training them to take over their jobs. A very minimal upgrading of their medical treatment would get them back at work and ease the pressure on Fourschner.

As the doctor picked his way back to the *Revier*, which was now a wooden hut located in an abandoned quarry up the mountainside, he shook his head in disbelief. Fourschner had bought it! He had given Kahr his three new barracks! But nothing could slow down the hectic mass-production preparations; the prisoners would have to build them in their own time.

The news of the miracle of the barracks filtered out through the prisoners' intelligence network. For days it buzzed through the sinuous sick call line that wound down the slope from the quarry hut. It helped them forget their miseries.

The construction of the barracks was an epic event in the prisoners' lives. It represented a victory – however small – over their black-uniformed overlords. Every foundation completed was another defeat for the Germans. Each time a wall went up they celebrated in their minds.

First they sank deep holes in the tough, mountain terrain. Then they drove thick tree trunks into the holes, leaving eighteen inches above the surface. Next they squared off the tree trunks and bolted them to heavy timbers supporting the floor.

A quarter mile east was the railroad siding where the boxcars of lumber and building supplies came in via Nordhausen. The prisoners had to walk to the siding to pick up their materials, then carry them back to the quarry area. For the undernourished, emaciated men the ordeal would have been torture – if it hadn't been a hospital that they were building.

Camp Dora had two types of barracks. One type was used to quarter enlisted men on *Luftwaffe* bases; the other was used to house German Labour Service workers. Both barracks came in prefabricated parts which a crew of healthy men could assemble into a finished building within a few days. For the twenty emaciated prisoners who made up the construction crew, the job took weeks.

The first barracks, with room for 200 beds, wasn't ready until September. Getting the beds to furnish it proved almost impossible. Dr. Kahr scrounged, begged and pleaded. Finally, in the autumn of 1944, the sick began to trudge from the suffocating blackness of the tunnels into quarters where at least a thin ray of hope shone through the windows. And shortly afterwards Nicholas joined the staff of the *Revier* as a *Helf Arzt*, an assistant doctor.[4]

Now Dr. Kahr had to connive to get the rest of the hospital staff[5] he needed. He was appalled to learn that all

---

[4]Johnny Nicholas was not the only blackman in the Nordhausen area in those days. Hans, the boy whose recollections form the basis for the opening of Chapter ten is Hans Massaquoa, currently managing editor of *Ebony* magazine. He grew up in Germany where his father was a Liberian diplomat. His mother was German. In wartime Nordhausen Massaquoa found a job as a turret-lathe operator for Schmidt-Kranz, a metal-fabricating firm. When Nordhausen was liberated by the Americans in April 1945, he quickly befriended the conquering GIs, learned to speak English and eventually made his way to the U.S. He is an authority on blacks in Germany.

[5]In addition to some twenty prisoner-doctors, Dr. Kahr would ultimately have under his jurisdiction S.S. doctors Kather, Kurzke, Rindfleisch and Gaberle.

jobs at Dora – not just those in the prisoner-hospital – were assigned on the basis of politics; not training, ability or experience. Here the Politicals, the prisoners wearing the red triangle, were dominant. Here, he learned to his horror, Communists who had been plumbers in civilian life were performing surgery. Communist lathe operators were pulling teeth. Communist street-car conductors were handing out pills. Communist painters were giving injections.

And all the time, he discovered, there were qualified doctors and men with medical training among the thousands of non-Communist political prisoners. Like the medical talents of Johnny Nicholas, their's were being utilized in *tunnelling*!

From Kahr's logical but naive standpoint, it was intolerable. But to the Communists, it meant continuing control over one of Dora's primary centres of power. As long as the Reds held on to the *Revier*, the Greens were denied control of the entire camp.

As prisoner-medic Nicholas wielded immense power. He could detour innocent prisoners out of the fatal-injection line and into some other line where they'd emerge to live another day. He could hand out – or deny – the slips that authorized a prisoner a day's 'convalescence' in his barracks instead of another twelve hours of agony in the tunnel. He often could lay his hands on extra rations, which he could use to keep one man alive or bribe another.

The hospital *Kapo*, who commanded the prisoner-doctors, literally held the power of life or death. If the Reds wanted to get rid of a particularly troublesome Green, the hospital *Kapo* could arrange a *Revier* visit for him under some innocent-sounding pretext. Once the Green appeared, they could diagnose his ailment as typhus and put him in the typhus ward, where he was sure to get the disease and die.

This was the kind of power that the Greens wanted for themselves. Without it they weren't the complete masters of the camp they hungered to be. Willi Stimmel, a Green, was the *Kapo* in the Labour Records Office; he had the job of infiltrating Greens into the *Revier*. When Dr. Kahr requested a list of candidates for the expanded prisoner-hospital he was planning, Stimmel had predictably picked a list of Greens.

As his education in concentration-camp intrigue progressed, Kahr also discovered that a camp medical officer possessed unique power. Nominally he took his orders from Fourschner. But this was an administrative convenience; Dr. Kahr actually was responsible to Dr. Lolling, so he had some independence. Even so, because the doctor ate, worked and as infrequently as possible socialized with Fourschner, it was just good politics to offer deference to him.

The first time he really tested his power was when Stimmel, a tough, hardened criminal, handed him the list of Green candidates for the *Revier*; the doctor tore up the list and dropped it in the waste basket, thereby earning the enmity of the Green government.

Kahr[6] moved briskly into his new barracks assigning one for internal diseases, one for surgical cases and a third for contagious diseases. He was totally unaware of the threat to his work and his life.

He re-organized the original hut beside the quarry as a hospital-administration building, a place to keep records and a dispensary for the daily sick call.

It was a magnificent victory – while it lasted.

By late autumn of 1944 events on the Russian front directly affected the health of Dora. Several large concentration camps in eastern Poland, including Auschwitz and Gross Rosen, were squarely in the path of the Russian advance. S.S. *Reichsfuehrer* Himmler had declared that no concentration-camp inmate

[6]He was 'the best of all the S.S. people, a man with feeling and a human heart,' testified former prisoner Julius Bouda of Loyny, Czechoslovakia, before the Nordhausen War Crimes military tribunal.

was to be captured alive by the enemy; they were to be liquidated. He ordered that prisoners who couldn't be killed quickly enough be evacuated to camps inside Germany.

Just when Dr. Kahr had managed to cajole Fourschner into making some important concessions, boxcars loaded with evacuees were dumped on his doorstep. Riddled with vermin and disease, most were automatic candidates for the hospital. They also represented thousands of new mouths competing for the same limited stocks of rancid beet juice, slimy turnip soup and mouldy turnip salad. It was the old story of the patched-up lifeboat that will make it to shore if it takes on no more survivors: the gaunt hordes from Gross Rosen and Auschwitz had piled aboard and the boat was slowly going under.

The desperate situation screamed for desperate remedies. After a spring and summer in Dora, Kahr had matriculated in a bureaucratic shrewdness for getting things done. He fired off a barrage of memoranda to the S.S. hierarchy. Behind it he detoured around the system in an orgy of reciprocal back-scratching in low places to acquire more hospital barracks illegally![7]

Kahr's dangerous scheme was premised on the fact that in the concentration-camp society everything was done under orders. Nothing happened unless it had been ordered.

When his crew brazenly began carting construction materials from the railroad siding to the quarry, nobody questioned them. When the material became foundations and walls and roofs, S.S. men and prisoners alike passed-by uninterested – totally unaware that the material

---

[7]The co-conspirators were Cecil Jay, the English carpenter, whose job at Dora was to build barracks; and the totally unpredictable, temperamental S.S. master sergeant in charge of barrack construction, Rudolph Jacobi, who swung like a pendulum between acts of sadism and compulsive generosity to the prisoners.

had been 'requisitioned' from Fourschner's precious supplies.[8]

Dr. Kahr built four additional barracks[9] illegally – and Kommandant Fourschner was completely oblivious to all this.

Kahr placed Nicholas in charge of Dora's dispensary.

The dispensary occupied the east end of the three-room hut that, until the doctor's amazing coup, had represented the entire hospital. He had a crude desk, a chair and a table. Behind the desk were several shelves of bottles and jars of ointments and salves. A corner window allowed him to see up the slope to the quarry, which the S.S. used when they performed executions by firing squad. He could also look east toward the S.S. camp and the tunnel entrances about an eighth of a mile beyond.

Kahr had adapted the centre room of the dispensary, which was really the building's entrance lobby, as a bathroom. It had wash basins clustered in the centre around a single bathtub.

Dora's daily droves of sick prisoners reported to the dispensary.

Nicholas treated them, then sent ninety percent back to work in the tunnels; the others he assigned to beds in the hospital. Dr. Kahr had ordered that every prisoner admitted had to have a bath. In the centre room, if water – it was always cold – and soap were available, Nicholas and others on the prisoner-hospital staff worked to scrape the filth from the scrawny, fevered bodies. Then they were lodged temporarily in the dispensary's third room, at the west end of the building, where Kahr had installed

[8]All around Dora, said Dr. Kahr after the war, there were 'enormous quantities' of construction materials. It was 'entirely possible' to walk off with them without being challenged. Amazingly, he remembers, it was even possible to commandeer a steam shovel to level off the site for a barracks!
[9]In April, 1945, when the U.S. First Army liberated Dora, investigators would discover that of the camp's forty-five completed barracks, eight were in use as prisoner-hospital facilities.

about ten bunks. It was a transition ward where the most seriously ill waited until a cot was empty in one of the three new hospital barracks.

From the door of the dispensary, sick call stretched down the snow-covered slope.

They waited, mute as penitents at a place of pilgrimage. Each time Nicholas looked at them he felt guilty about his own incredible reprieve from certain death in the tunnels; he knew these men and had carried rocks alongside them. He felt as if he had to gag when they struggled up the steps, shrugged off their rags, then bowed and scraped before him as if he were some Oriental potentate before his subjects. He'd see their eyes glisten in the belief that he could conjure some elixir to remove their ills, but all he could do was slip them a sip of the milk that Dr. Kahr miraculously scrounged from a secret source.

It was too late, of course, to help most of them medically; at best it was a delaying action. Nicholas knew it – but he couldn't tell them the brutal truth. He'd tried a few times but the prisoners lingered on with eyes as docile as a whipped dog's, begging for sulphur tablets he didn't have: he'd just palmed his last one into the trembling hand of someone more sick. Others pleaded for a convalescent slip that he *could* give them – if he didn't have to consider Brauny's rage when a prisoner handed him a slip.

The pilgrims languished by his door in Job-like patience. The sight of them worked on his conscience. He lay awake at night, cursing the stupid lessons of his parents and teachers about doing onto others. That's what had landed him in the mess he was in. Camp Dora was an alien planet. Up was down. Left was right. Good was bad. Bad was good. And the Ten Commandments were Thou Shalt Preserve Thyself repeated ten times a day.

Only in the surgical barracks were conditions remotely close to those in a normal hospital.

It consisted of six separate rooms with a total of 120 beds. Amazingly they weren't the typical, rough-hewn wooden bunks. Somehow Dr. Kahr had pilfered steel, hospital-style beds for his surgical patients. With mattresses, too.

But elsewhere in the *Revier* it was a medieval charnel house.

In the contagious-diseases barracks, 200 dying men competed for 250 sulpha tablets a day. In the internal barracks 700 men lingering between life and death were squeezed into 350 beds. Paradoxically it was worth it; some were dying on clean, straw mattresses and occasionally white sheets.

Even with all of Dr. Kahr's authority, ingenuity and stubborn medical discipline, he was swimming upstream against a swift current. With the same food supplies now being eked out to fill thousands of new mouths, malnutrition became a plague. 'Healthy' prisoners were being wiped out by the common cold.

Among the *Revier* staff, life – although crucifyingly frustrating – was still paradise compared to the tunnels. Clothes were clean. The influence of position could pry open a kitchen *Kapo*'s stranglehold on bread and vegetables. There was still the luxury of inside work and protection from the sub-zero temperatures . . .

Nicholas's guilt fattened as the sick-call line thickened, coiling obscenely down the slope. For weeks he had rationalized that the *Revier* staff had a burden other prisoners didn't have: the grinding, mental torment of deciding who to give sulphur and charcoal tablets, aspirin and paper bandages. Yet the scrawnier the bodies, the bigger and more purplish the carbuncles, the wider the festering sores, the more his rationalizations revolted him.

Sick call was an elegantly produced, extravagantly choreographed sham. He knew it. As long as he did and they didn't, then he was a cheap trickster in the charade. There were no cures. There never had been. All any prisoner-doctor could do was to temporarily postpone the inevitable death of tomorrow. He was the padre of death row, handing out convalescent slips as last rites.

To visualize that tomorrow he needed only to look out his window and see the tiers of naked bodies inside the wire corral waiting for the crematorium.

Chapter Thirteen

Sustained coughing hacked the predawn calm.

At the dispensary door a heavy-set *Lagerschutz* grumbled, occasionally admitting another batch of prisoners. 'Shoes off!' he shouted periodically like a barker at some grotesque circus sideshow. 'Get your damned shoes off!' He stepped off the porch and walked along the ragged, sinuous line, poling the beam of his flashlight at this man, then that man. 'You goddamed loafer!' he roared at one man, hammering him with a club. 'You're not sick, you bastard! You're malingering! Get the hell out of here!'

Terrified prisoners scrambled for safety down the slope. Some fled back to the tunnels. Others sought refuge some distance off in the trees, peering out like errant children, returning furtively only when the *Lagerschutz*'s tantrum had subsided. It was an excellent way of weeding out the malingerers. Yet it also discouraged the genuinely ill and was another reason why Dora's monthly death toll was climbing toward 1,000. The line reformed after the onslaught. The wretched men, suffering their injury and agony in silence, waited their turn.

'Ten more!' bellowed the *Lagerschutz*, opening the dispensary door. 'Single file and get your filthy shoes off!'

They struggled to mount the steps. Some made it on

210

their own. Some clung to a comrade. Others were carried bodily by friends.

The Kapo of the prisoner hospital was a German criminal named Schneider. Despite Dr. Kahr's efforts to keep the Greens out, they had managed to wedge Schneider into the most powerful job in the hospital.

'Line up and strip!' commanded Schneider. 'Clothes will be properly folded and placed on the floor in front of you so I can see your triangle and read your number! *Mach Schnell!*'

The sick men complied dumbly. In half a minute they were arranged before the big German *Kapo*, stark naked.

Their bodies were scarecrow caricatures. Carbuncles as big as goitres bulged purplish under their mottled skins. Chilblains ruptured from winter's frost festered on their hands and feet. They coughed rhythmically and deeply, their barren rib cages ballooning hideously as if they might burst. Terrified to spit, they gulped down stringy sputum only to cough it up again. The flesh on their faces had wasted away, hollowing their eyesockets and lending them the wide-eyed expression of surprised children.

'Injured to the left! Ill to the right!' shouted Schneider. 'C'mon! Move! We don't have all day!'

They shifted turgidly as if invisible mud gobbed their feet and minds, scraping up their clothes and shuffling through the door into Nicholas's office.

He wore a white armband on his striped jacket with the red letters '*Helf Artz.*'

'Line up by the table,' he said civilly.

The men meekly shuffled into place.

There were a dozen glasses on the table filled with a white opaque liquid. Each glass contained a cylindrical wooden plug drilled down the centre and fitted with a thermometer. Several feet of string connected the end of the plug to a row of nails hammered into the wall behind the table.

Nicholas dipped one of the plugs into a can of oil. 'Bend down,' he said.

He went down the line of men, taking their temperatures.

While Nicholas waited for the mercury to register, he sat down behind his makeshift desk. 'Names and numbers, please,' he asked. Then he proceeded to question them about their symptoms, making notes on a sheet of paper. They were so comical looking with the strings dangling from their arses that in other circumstances the black prisoner-physician would have exploded with laughter at the sight of them.

Finally he removed the plugs, put them back in the glasses and recorded the temperatures.

Dr. Kahr had given him plenty of latitude to give pills, salves and convalescent slips; however, his medical prerogatives were severely limited by the meagre supplies and equipment on hand. But he could not admit a patient to the hospital ward without consulting Dr. Kahr – and then only after thorough examination.

The ward's twin-tiered bunks held eighty patients, but it wasn't uncommon for two or three times that number to be shoehorned into the creaky structures. The mattresses were the same excrement-stiff, straw-filled bags used in the tunnel. There was little sulphur. No morphine. Few bandages or surgical dressings. The scalpels were dull and rusty.

The thought that he himself might one day become sick or injured preyed on Nicholas' mind. If that ever happened, he'd be at the mercy of Hospital *Kapo* Schneider, who was plotting a Green takeover of the *Revier*.

But he tried not to think about it. He concentrated on the incredible change in his lot since wangling his way out of the tunnels three months earlier: clean clothes. Extra food occasionally. Remittance from the daily purgatory of roll call. The daily miracle of news from the outside world

212

via the hidden radio that the hospital Communists had assembled from stolen parts.

These components came from inside the tunnels where, by midsummer of 1944, the cross tunnels had been fitted out as production and assembly plants. Shipments that looked as if they belonged in radio receivers arrived every day from the Mibau factory at Buchenwald. Prisoners, trained by German civilians to do electronic-assembly work, didn't know what they were making or the purpose of the device. They were ordered to keep quiet and not to ask questions. If they talked about their work, they risked execution on the spot. But what effect did another death threat have? They not only talked shop, they blithely smuggled bits and pieces of the Mibau parts into the *Revier* when they went on sick call. It didn't take the *Revier*'s highly disciplined and resourceful Communists long to assemble the parts into a workable radio.

Because Nicholas was identified as an American POW, the *Revier*'s Reds regarded him as an outsider. They were formal and correct with him, but they never invited him into their privileged klatsch of regulars who listened to the British Broadcasting Corporation and American Armed Forces newscasts. They passed along to him their versions of the news of the Russian victories on the Eastern Front and the progress of the Allied invasion of Europe on the Western Front.

Access to such news was worth all the other *Revier* privileges combined. It was like the promise of a life after death; a faith invulnerable to the daily horror all around him.

Yet the daily parade of the walking dead gnawed at his conscience. The guilt festered. They limped in with only a glint of hope in their dull eyes. When they came to him, they were already beyond the repair of the finest medical treatment in the world. So he was just as much a part of the prisoner-doctors' conspiracy of pretence as any of them. In the privacy of *Revier* bull sessions they voiced

213

their own hopelessness in a cynical rule-of-thumb: 'Above the belly – aspirin. Below the belly – castor oil.'

Heavy, officious footsteps slammed on the unpainted wooden floor of the barracks.

Nicholas looked up and saw Schneider clump in. He ignored him and went on with his work.

Schneider crossed to the table and examined the prisoner and the records Nicholas had made out minutes earlier and stared fixedly at one sheet of paper, then picked it up. 'This temperature is only one hundred, Nicholas!' He stared at the six naked prisoners. 'Which of you bastards is the malingerer?' he rasped.

The prisoners stood mute, their Adam's apples ratcheting.

Schneider glared down at their neatly arranged clothing, read off their numbers and checked them against the sheet of paper. 'So you're the shirker!' he crowed triumphantly, walking up to a wisp of a Frenchman.

The prisoner trembled. His throat constricted. He could barely talk. '*Herr* Schneider, *Herr* Schneider,' he quavered. 'Dr. Johnny told me if I felt –'

Schneider rammed his fist in the man's spongy belly.

The Frenchman croaked and sagged to the floor, curling up like a snail plucked from its shell. He puked violently. Schneider began kicking him. The man rolled over evasively, squeegeeing his stinking bile across the floor with his body. Clawing for his rags, he staggered and crawled out of the dispensary.

'Let that be a lesson,' Schneider growled to the five remaining prisoners. 'You, too, *schwartze*!' he said to Nicholas. 'The *Revier*'s no place for slackers.'

He launched into a tirade against the black man for babying the prisoners with too many convalescent slips.

Nicholas stood and took it. He knew Schneider was just handing down the drubbing that he had taken from Stimmel, the Labour Allocation Office *Kapo*, about keeping the work force at a maximum by slashing sick-call

214

to a minimum. Stimmel, in turn, was getting it from the labour allocation leader, S.S. Sergeant Simon. Simon was getting it from S.S. Master Sergeant Brauny, the roll call leader, who was driven insane by empty spaces in the roll-call ranks; he knew that this infuriated Camp Commandant Fourschner.

It was a vicious, circular chain of intimidation, each link pulling on the next to protect its privileges.

Nicholas knew that with Dr. Kahr in his corner, he needn't cow-tow to Schneider, even if Schneider were the top prisoner in charge at the *Revier.* 'Wait just a minute!' he warned, startling the German. 'These people have been standing for hours! You're getting in the way! Maybe we should get Dr. Kahr in here?'

Schneider was smart enough to know when to back off and when to stand up and fight. Nicholas was humiliating him before the rank-and-file, but he would settle that score later. He glowered, then stamped out, leaving the dispensary in shattering silence.

When Schneider was out of earshot, Nicholas returned seriously to the matter at hand, only to be confronted by a gaggle of grinning faces.

He smiled widely. 'Now, where was I?' he inquired absent-mindedly.

Together they exploded in a grand guffaw at Schneider's expense.

His patients' knew that, by slighting Schneider, the black man was putting his neck in a noose.

Most of the time, however, Nicholas had little more than conversation and an occasional aspirin. All suffered from slow starvation. All were in constant, low-key pain – even if they didn't have any overt disease symptoms. Awarding an aspirin was more a sign of Nicholas's good will than a remedy. At least a sick man could walk away knowing he had that.

Almost all suffered to some degree from dysentery. For them Nicholas had dark-coloured charcoal tablets which

Dr. Kahr purloined from Buchenwald in large quantities.

Nicholas tried to save the precious sulphur tablets for the prisoners with open wounds; the injuries in the tunnels, for example, and especially the scourgings on the *bock*, where a man's buttocks were flayed into a stew of blood and flesh. After a session on the *bock*, a prisoner had to remain immobile for several days if the massive damage was to begin healing, so the convalescent slips allowed him to lie motionless in his barracks.

Whether Nicholas could give them a pill or not, to all he gave his time and a salve of the banter and blarney for which he was gaining a reputation. He got to know their names and personalities, where they worked and more about their personal lives than they realized. He got close enough so that he could kid them and in a concentration camp society that implied a rare relationship. His warehouse of yarns always remained well stocked. He was always good for a piece of malicious gossip about the S.S., and once a week or so he could be depended upon to whisper some exciting news on the war – the liberation of Paris, the German cities that the Allies had bombed that week, the progress of the Russians armies.

'You're sure it's true, Johnny?' they'd persist, as ravenous for the ultimate morsel of news as they were for the final crumb on their mess table. 'Where'd you hear it?'

He would smile his characteristic, enigmatic smile and deflect their questions with some facile blandishment.

Beneath his easy-going, unruffled exterior, however, the mental pressure of the daily sick call was grinding him down. The news would leak from one day's sick call that he'd given this man a sulphur tablet and that one a convalescent slip. The next day he'd have to swim against a tide of supplicants for the same life-savers.

Who to give to? Who to deny? Life or death, and 'Dr. Johnny' the unwilling judge.

Somehow, with his glib good humour, he kept the line

moving, and soon the dispensary became an oasis in a desert of misery where Nicholas's baritone levity and hyperbole slaked the prisoners' parched existence.

Dr. Kahr was impressed with the 'American's' skill in cleaning wounds and injuries and improvising bandages and dressings. His black prisoner-doctor was highly adept at excising the huge islands of dead tissue – known as phlegmones – with his ancient scalpels. He dipped his pathetic instruments in alcohol pilfered from the tunnels, where it was being used – the prisoner who stole it told him – as some kind of fuel.

Jean Septfonds, a Frenchman who worked in the tunnels, limped in one morning with three huge phlegmones on his right leg. He'd fallen a year previously and pierced himself on rusty barbed wire. The infection had persisted all of that time, and he knew that the stubborn plugs of pus were slowly draining his life away. When Septfonds showed up at the dispensary, Nicholas knew that the Frenchman wouldn't last long. He cut away the infection, swabbed it with the alcohol and bandaged it with paper, then granted him a few days' reprieve from the tunnels by issuing a precious convalescent slip.

Each morning after sick call was over and the *Revier*'s prisoner-doctors had made their customary but clandestine pot of soup, Nicholas would secretly set a can of it on the sill of the dispensary's rear window for Septfonds.

The Frenchman's phlegmones eventually healed and he went back to his work in the tunnel.[1]

Because Nicholas spoke French and because of his success in nursing Septfonds back to health, his reputation spread among the French prisoners. Some of them were so seriously ill and injured in the tunnels they were

---

[1]Septfonds survived the war and returned to his home in Auxerre. 'If I had not gone to the *Revier* and to Johnny,' he says, 'I would not have returned to France.' Because of Nicholas, he continues, 'I was very often able to slide secretly into the infirmary, and that way I was able to be saved.'

afraid to report to sick call – especially if they had gold fillings in their teeth. When Dr. Kahr was away in Buchenwald scrounging for more medical supplies, Corporal Maischein, the drunken medic in charge of the S.S. troops' dispensary, staggered over to the prisoners' dispensary and tagged the seriously ill and injured for the crematory; his two-fold purpose was to reduce the prisoner-patient population and line his pockets with gold.

Frenchman Jean Berger[2] of Angers often went on sick call to plead with Nicholas for bandages and medicines for his grievously ill comrades back in the tunnels, who feared that they might fall victim to Maischein if they were put in the *Revier*.

Gabriel Boussinesq, another Frenchman, had worked eighteen hours without relief one day. He was desperately weak; if Nicholas hadn't given him a convalescent slip, his demise was certain: Boussinesq was scheduled for a second eighteen-hour shift when he staggered into sick call.

The grateful Frenchman, a nonsmoker, gave Nicholas cigarettes, which functioned as one of the forms of currency in the camp; he knew that the black man handed out cigarettes to patients when he had nothing else to give them.

Walter Pomaranski, a Pole, was deep inside the Kohnstein when it happened. He was toiling at the intersection of Tunnel A and Cross Tunnel No. 42 when he saw the scowling S.S. face under the pudding-bowl helmet rushing at him. The guard's rifle arched down and the butt-plate smashed into the seventeen-year-old Pole's head.

Why?

Who knows? There were a hundred innocent things an

---

[2]At the war's end he returned home to Angers. He says of Nicholas: 'He was dynamic and convinced of final victory ... He rendered numerous medical services to everybody.'

218

unsuspecting prisoner could do to provoke a predatory guard. When the S.S. man was through with him, the Pole's leg and skull were fractured. His Polish comrades left him for dead amid the shadows ... When he opened his eyes, he saw a tall, black-skinned man looking down on him.

'Who are you?' Pomaranski asked weakly in German.

The black man smiled, showing glistening white teeth. 'Ever heard of Dr. Johnny, Pomaranski?' Nicholas replied, also in German.

'No,' said the Pole groggily. 'How do you know my name?'

'Your friends. They brought you here. You must be a big man among the Poles, Pomaranski. They slipped out of their barracks, sneaked back into the tunnels and brought you out. They figured you were dead but wanted to be sure. So they waited until lights-out and smuggled you over here.'

'Where am I?'

'In the dispensary.'

'What time is it?'

'Midnight?'

Pomaranski realized that they were both breaking strict camp regulations about medical treatment, which by edict was rigorously restricted to the morning sick call. 'I'm sorry to put you to this trouble. They should not have brought me.'

'Well, if it wasn't you lying here, it'd be somebody else, so forget about it.'

'Am I hurt badly?'

'Let's put it this way: if Maischein finds out how bad, he'll be looking for you. Know what I mean?'

Pomaranski knew.

But he wasn't feeling much pain: Nicholas had given him a shot of an almost unheard of drug at Camp Dora – morphine – to ease his suffering. Using the crude devices available to him, the black man sewed up the gouges in the Pole's skull, then put a cement-bag splint on his leg.

All the while he kept up an unending flow of conversation.

'I'm an American air force officer, Pomaranski. The only American in the camp. I'm also a doctor. If this were a dispensary back in the States, we could really do a job on you. Look, I'm not going to kid you. You're in tough shape and you're going to hurt for a long time. But for Christ's sake don't let anyone know about that skull fracture.'

Pomaranski nodded. 'How did an American air force officer get into a slave-labour camp?'

'From a plane. Engine trouble over France and I had to bail out . . . But the war'll soon be over. You know that, don't you, Pomaranski? The Americans took Paris in August. They'll be across the German border by the end of the year. The Russians liberated Warsaw – in October. The United States air force and the RAF are bombing every major city in Germany. We'll all walk out of here through the front gate pretty soon.'

When Nicholas had done all he could do medically, he slipped Pomaranski some food and cigarettes, then he carried him out of the dispensary and laid him in an empty bunk in the washroom ward. 'Just remember, Pomaranski,' he whispered, careful not to awaken the occupants of the other nineteen bunks, 'you're a Pole. There are thousands of Poles fighting with the Allies all over the world. Keep your spirits up. Don't give up hope. We're all going to go back home one day. You wait and see.'[3]

Pomaranski's recovery had a strange, disturbing effect on

---

[3]Pomaranski lived to see the accuracy of Nicholas's predictions. After the war he emigrated to Canada, and resides in Terrace, British Columbia. He has a claim lodged with the West German government for reparations for his sufferings in German concentration camps. In an effort to document his injuries, he wrote the U.S. government asking them to help him locate a U.S. air force doctor, a Major John Nicholas, who treated him in Camp Dora in 1944. He received no reply. 'If it wasn't for him,' says Pomaranski, 'I might not have gotten out of Dora alive. He was either a very sincere man or a good actor.'

Nicholas. After years of playing at doctor, of parroting its language glibly and surrounding himself with its practitioners, he had suddenly discovered what it was to save a human life. He'd saved those women and children from drowning in the Bois de Chene years ago, but this was different. It was indefinable. Impossible to put into words. Suddenly all his medical pretension of the past seemed cheap. He felt elated and disgusted.

He hadn't always been infatuated with the power to heal. Most of his teen years had been consumed with the hero-worshipping of American heavyweight boxer Joe Louis. He'd seen all of the 'Brown Bomber's' fights on newsreel half a dozen times over. He had revelled in physical power. But the humiliation of the Sloan's Linament deflected his ambition. He began to think about capitalizing on his way with words and his growing awareness of the magnetic attraction he held for people. Maybe he'd go into acting or entertaining: he learned piano and became good at it. But that, too, was a phase duly supplanted by a precocious patriotism that enticed him into trying his sea legs as a naval officer.

In Left Bank haunts he found himself drawn to the medical students. A breed apart, it seemed to him; special even in the malaise of poverty that afflicts students the world over. It took the highest possible intelligence to diagnose disease accurately. A doctor was a scientist and a detective. The combination fascinated him, captivated him.

Many long hours he'd spent with Pape and Coicou, quizzing them on the profession that was hungrily monopolizing his interests. The two medical students, yawning long after midnight, regurgitating for Nicholas what they'd learned in class that day. Nicholas, with his ruthless curiosity and endless questions, on the edge of his chair, soaking it all up.

While Nicholas was winning the admiration of the prisoners, Dr. Kahr was gradually captivating Nicholas, who had always believed that no man was his equal

221

physically or intellectually. The young Austrian physician was a magician; he'd conjured something out of nothing at Dora. Indefatigable as a wind-up toy, immune to the impossible. Polite, humane, heroic.

Saving Pomaranski's life had another profound impact on Nicholas; it gave him a new kinship with Kahr. He felt as if he had touched the mystery of what drove the doctor to do what he had done. To heal was to have power. Not Neitzsche's concept of power, but power from the fulfillment born of salvaging life from death.

Yet the doctor disturbed him: Nicholas couldn't put him in one of the mental pigeon holes where he automatically slotted everyone. It wasn't simply that he still found difficulty in disciplining his knee-jerk reaction to the doctor's S.S. uniform. It was much more. What made Kahr tick? What was in it for him? Everyone had an angle. Nicholas had his. Survival. What was Kahr's? Why did he take such risks in the care and feeding of a herd of *Stucke*? And now that he had, why was he so modest about it? Why did he try to give the impression he wasn't really doing anything extraordinary?

He was one hell of a guy, S.S. or not; he'd conned Fourschner out of his shorts. If the commandant ever caught on, Kahr would be a *Stucke* himself.

For the first time in Nicholas' life he experienced the depression of feeling inferior.

For all Nicholas' admonitions, the Pomaranski incident leaked out among the other prisoners. The betrayal of the trust was out of gratitude, not malice. But that didn't help; there were S.S. stoolpigeons planted among the prisoners. How long before the story worked its way to Brauny and Custody Camp Leader Moeser? Both itched to settle the score with him because of the way he'd manoeuvred himself out from under their thumbs and into Kahr's protective embrace.

The Pomaranski episode was backfiring. On the strength of the 'miracle' he'd wrought, the prisoners in sick call were now plaguing him incessantly for his food scraps, special favours and recovery slips. Sick call was becoming an exhausting emotional ordeal. With the complicity of Kahr he'd secreted Pomaranski in the typhus barracks. Sure, there was a good chance the Pole would catch the disease. But the chance had to be taken: the S.S., terrified of typhus, never went into the dreaded typhus ward. So if Pomaranski didn't contract typhus, he'd be safe there until his injuries healed.

To bring it off, however, required dextrous scheming and creative cheating. The conspiracy to keep the S.S. from finding out about Pomaranski was a crucifying ordeal for Nicholas. The concessions he had made to the Pole were impossible to duplicate for the mob now besieging him.

Didn't they realize what they were asking? Yet they kept on begging. They also pressured him relentlessly to admit sick friends at midnight. 'You're a good man, Johnny. Okay, Johnny? Please, Johnny?'

Too dangerous, he'd try to tell them. Sure, he did it for Pomaranski. But that was a special case. What was special about it, Johnny? Well, he just didn't have enough medical supplies to go around, and if Schneider, the hospital *kapo*, were to get wind of it, he'd kick him out of the *Revier* and back into the tunnels. That would ruin it for everyone.

'Come on, Johnny! We've heard how you can handle Schneider. Just for my comrade. Please, Johnny. He's in bad shape. He's going to die, Johnny, if – '

'God damn it no! No! No! It can't be done. You've got to get out of here!'

They'd leave sullenly as if Brauny had just beaten them, clutching the potato scrap he'd pressed on them as consolation. He cursed himself for having let Pomaranski's comrades talk him into it. He'd let himself go soft. He'd never make it now if they threw him back into the tunnels.

At noon the stench of diseased bodies was replaced by the

irresistible smell of rabbit soup. To comply with the concentration-camp manual, which decreed that a *Revier* must make some contribution to medical science, Major Fourschner had ordered a small cubicle set up for producing and testing antityphus vaccine. Prisoner-doctors injected blood samples from their typhus patients into the lungs of live rabbits to incubate. When the rabbits had served their purpose, they cut out the lungs and made soup of the rest.

After four months the aroma began to stink in Nicholas' nostrils. His life and that of a tunnel rat were worlds apart – even further, he reflected, than between Haiti's élite and its ignorant masses. He'd never been a peasant but he had been a rat in the bowels of the Kohnstein. He had lived that hell. He knew in his bones and belly the misery that being a prisoner-doctor spared him.

He tried to stifle his guilt by luxuriating in contempt for the spineless, whining way the sick-call prisoners scraped and scrabbled for his meagre favours. Still it nagged him like a stone in his shoe. Even worse, he knew that he had become an addict to the *Revier*'s privileges. Despite his most extravagant rationalizations he began to despise himself.

The *Lagerschutz* overseeing sick call yelled out: 'That's all! That's all! Report to the *appelplatz* for roll call!'

All but a few in line trudged away dejectedly toward the tunnels. The remainder, as if in a trance, stood rooted to the spot. They were desperate for some alleviation of their miseries.

They scattered when the *Lagerschutz*'s club started whirling.

Nicholas watched, from the porch of the barracks, his insides churning. He slumped at his desk. Again the smell of rabbit soup filtered through the building. Goddam! Couldn't they even wait until the poor starving bastards had left?

Precisely at six a.m. Brauny's voice, metallic over the loudspeaker, commenced the roll call . . .

An hour and a half later the wind had changed. The loudspeaker sounds, originating from the dispensary, now gusted intermittently against Nicholas' eardrums. By catching the names he could tell which part of the alphabet Brauny had reached. He knew how far the roll call had progressed. Finally he heard the names at the end of the alphabet and waited for the premonitory 'Mutzen ab! Mutzen auf!' He thought to himself that in a few minutes the funeral procession of which he had once been a member, would again be swallowed in the gaping maw of the Kohnstein.

Dismissal didn't come. Instead the wind carried a garbled torrent of loudspeaker sounds. Long, sizzling stitches of profanity. Brauny seemed to be making a speech and somebody was obviously being seared by his wrath.

For a few seconds Nicholas permitted himself to pity the poor devils on the receiving end, then banishing it all from his mind, he busied himself with his thermometers . . .

'Nicholas!!!'

He whirled around.

Brauny stood at the door. Schneider, the hospital *kapo*, was a step behind him.

'Believe me, *Herr Hauptscharfuehrer*,' Schneider was saying, 'I have warned him repeatedly but he refuses – '

'Shut your mouth!' snarled the little S.S. master sergeant, his clean regular features florid and puffed like a puff adder. 'Nicholas! Thirteen convalescent slips!' he screeched, his arm extended with the offending pieces of paper in his fist. 'What do you think we're running here, you black swine? A health spa? You'll cross me once too often.'

Nicholas jumped to his feet and stood smartly at attention, fuming.

Brauny stepped closer to him until their faces were

225

inches apart. 'Did – you – hear – me?' he yelled, pausing between each word.

Nicholas once again found himself stifling an overwhelming compulsion to reach down and strangle Brauny. '*Ja, Herr Hauptscharfuehrer*, the prisoner heard,' Nicholas said with iron self control. 'But the prisoner has been authorized by *Herr Doktor* Kahr to use his discretion in these matters. In the prisoner's opinion these thirteen men are too sick to work in the tunnels today. If the *Herr Hauptscharfuehrer* would examine the slips he would recognize that on each of them the *Herr Doktor*'s signature appears below that of the prisoner.'

Brauny's boot caught him in the fork of the torso. His knees buckled and his big body hit the floor with the sound of a door slamming in an empty cathedral.

'Thirteen is a very unlucky number,' sneered Brauny, kicking at the jack-knifed body. 'You should know that.' He ripped up the slips, held out his hand and allowed the pieces to float down like confetti over Nicholas' twitching body. 'Pick up the pieces, you *schwartze asel*!' he commanded. 'The dispensary floor shall be spotless at all times! Isn't that right, *Doktor* Nicholas? Nothing's too good for the vermin who come in here. Right, *Herr Doktor*?

'Subhuman swine!' spat Brauny, aiming a final kick that knocked Nicholas over on his side again.

The pain between his crotch and his throat gestated slowly. Three days passed before he had the courage to explore the damage. His fingers curled in recoil at the Zeppelin-sized mass . . .

His hate for Brauny so inflamed him that his rationality was almost completely consumed. It didn't matter to him that he shared a ward with TB-ridden spectres whose hacking filled the air with disease. All he could think of was killing Brauny. For hours his skull boomed with schemes. Only the balm of his planned revenge made pain bearable.

Two weeks later he could walk naturally again. It was night. He tip-toed out of the dispensary. The floorboards squeaked. He stopped abruptly, fearful that someone had heard him. He peered into the shadows. Was someone following him? For a moment memories of his noctural excursion in Compiegne flooded his mind.

The only sounds were the laboured breathing of the men in the washroom ward. Occasionally one would groan in a nightmare or bump as he changed position. Otherwise it was peaceful.

He padded through the washroom and peered through the windows in the main door. He checked to make sure the canvas bag was securely on his shoulder, then opened the door, eased it shut behind him and moved into the darkness.

As he stole along the slope he could hear the distant whir of machinery in the tunnels. It was after twelve o'clock and the night shift was half way through its ordeal.

He walked quietly across the rain-dampened grass through the trees, heading for the movable barricade in the barbed wire where he knew he'd find two guards. Nearing them, he stiffened into the straightback military-style carriage that distinguished him from all the other prisoners. He could smell the tobacco smoke before he could make out the glow of their cigarettes. He could hear the occasional click of their equipment and the scuff of their boots.

He slid his hand under the flap of the bag and explored the contents. 'Psssssssst!' he called. 'Psssssssst!'

He continued walking with his exaggerated gait. He could hear the Russian voices: Ukranians recruited into the S.S. to fight against their old Russian oppressors. They'd performed abominably in combat and had been shipped back to Germany for concentration-camp duty.

'Psssssssst! Zylanski!'

'*Hande hoche!*' came the growled reply in heavily accented German.

'Kiss my ass, Zylanski!' Nicholas called out softly in passable Russian.

A flashlight clicked in the hand of the other guard, a huge, moustached bear of a man. '*Ke-toe tam?*'

'Who the hell do you think it is?' chaffed Nicholas. It's the *Amerikanetz*! Tell him, Zylanski!'

Zylanski had been secretly receiving treatments for syphilis in the dispensary from Nicholas. The soldier was afraid to report his condition to Dr. Kahr for fear the S.S. might discipline him. Nicholas kept giving him useless medicines so he'd keep coming back, giving the black man a chance to strengthen their relationship.

Nicholas walked unhesitatingly toward the barricade while the other guard's flashlight shone on his face.

'What are you doing out here?' demanded Zylanski nervously. 'You almost got drilled between the eyes!'

'After all I did for you?' bantered Nicholas. 'Ukranians are supposed to be grateful for favours.'

The giant Ukranian looked on threateningly, not about to be taken in by Nicholas' casual approach. 'Get this *chernozhopy*[4] back to his quarters,' he snapped to Zylanski.

'Back to the *Revier*, Johnny,' growled Zylanski uneasily.

'Hell, no! I thought I'd go for a stroll into Nordhausen and see the frauleins like you do, you big Ukranian stallion.'

The other Ukranian prodded him with his machine pistol. 'Get back where you came from!'

'Sorry, friend. Brauny's orders.'

'He never told us anything about it,' Zylanski's partner shot back.

'He never told anybody about it – except me. He doesn't want anybody else to know about it. Understand?'

[4]Russian for black donkey.

228

The big Ukranian cocked the bolt on his machine pistol.

'Jesus Christ, Zylanski,' pleaded Nicholas. 'Your dumb comrade here doesn't get it?'

Zylanski slowly pushed aside the barrel of his partner's weapon.

'You mean Brauny's got the pox, too, Johnny?'

'You didn't want anybody to know you were coming to me when you had problems! Right, Zylanski?'

Zylanski shuffled uncomfortably.

'If Brauny finds out you know . . .' Nicholas purposely didn't complete the sentence. He preferred the two guards to get the idea for themselves.

'All right,' said Zylanski, pointing to the cluster of newly built S.S. barracks several hundred yards away. 'Over there. You know which barracks?'

Nicholas nodded.

Zylanski slid the barricade open and let him through. As he entered the narrow opening, the other guard prodded him again with his weapon. 'Let's see the bag?'

Zylanski snapped: 'Never mind the bag! Let him through!'

But the big Ukranian was adamant. He hung his weapon on the barricade, grabbed the bag and began combing through it with one hand, holding his flashlight with the other.

The bag was full of bottles, small tins of ointment, bandages, scalpels, scissors.

'What are you going to do?' sneered the guard. 'Cut Brauny's damn prick off?' He tossed the bag back at Nicholas.

Nicholas slung it over his shoulder and stepped forward. The guard stopped him again with the barrel of the machine pistol. 'I didn't say you could go.'

'For Christ's sake!' snapped Nicholas, appealing to Zylanski, 'Doesn't this idiot catch on? It's Brauny's orders!'

Zylanski's partner bristled. 'No black pig can talk to a Ukranian like that and get away with it.'

Nicholas held up both arms theatrically in surrender. 'Okay! Okay! Never mind. I'd rather be back in bed, anyway. I'll just tell Brauny in the morning one of his Ukranians – '

'I didn't say you couldn't go,' acquiesced the Ukranian.

'Okay, then!' said Nicholas, striding through the barricade opening.

As he did, Zylanski's comrade expertly snapped the watch from Nicholas' wrist, grinning mischievously.

'You bastard!' spluttered Nicholas. 'Hey, Zylanski!'

Zylanski, obviously intimidated by his huge comrade, was afraid to intervene. 'Hurry, Johnny. We're off at three o'clock. If you're not back before –'

'Take it easy, Zylanski. I've got two and one half hours – unless he invites me to stay for breakfast.' He wasn't as blasé as he tried to sound: the wristwatch was vital to his plan. But what could he do. He'd come this far. There was no turning back. '*Dos vidanya*,' he said.

When the guards could no longer see him, he changed direction and moved directly up the slope of the Kohnstein. For the first few hundred yards the terrain was a mixture of long grass and gorse. Beyond that he entered the thickly forested dome of the hill.

Progress through the tall trees was slow. They were packed together. Broken-off branches stuck out from the trunks like daggers in the dark. The ground was soft with rotting branches and leaves. Each time he stepped his foot sank into the spongy debris up to his ankles . . .

After half an hour of tough going, he stopped. Three hundred yards down the slope from where he stood gaped the entrance to Tunnel B. He stole from the safety of the trees and began to work his way slowly down the slope. In his feet he could feel the reverberations of the excavation work going on inside the hill.

Closer and closer he crept to the mouth of the tunnel,

feet first, his backside sliding on the wet grass, palms of his hands taking his body weight.

At any moment his heels would slide over the rim of the thirty-eight-foot-diameter hole and touch the huge canvas awning extending horizontally from the slope. He had the sudden, wild fear that he would slip on the grass, slide down uncontrollably onto the awning and burst through onto the ground thirty feet below.

Slowly he moved, probing in the inky blackness with his heels . . .

Finally he touched canvas.

Despite the chill he was lathered in sweat. He felt tipsy – as if he'd had too much champagne. It was the feeling that fear and exhilaration always generated in him. He told himself he was crazy; that he could still turn back. But the agony from Brauny's kick in his crotch fed his recklessness.

He squatted in silence, breathing in the pungent smell of pine while his heartbeat returned to normal.

If he dropped a pebble from where he sat – where the awning touched the hill – it would hit a wooden guard shack manned by four S.S. men with a heavy machine gun. They guarded the entrace and also prevented the escape of those working the day shift, now slumbering in the dormitory cross-tunnels, which were further back into the main tunnel.

Yes, it *was* crazy. Yet he'd promised himself. And he couldn't break a promise to himself.

But he didn't have a concrete plan. Back at the dispensary he'd assured himself that once out on the hill, something would work out. It always did . . .

A half hour later he was still groping for a workable scheme.

He glanced instinctively at his wrist and cursed the Ukranian. Without a watch he had no way of rationing his time for the madcap notion that had catapulted him from his bed. He had to make it back through the barricade before Zylanski went off duty, otherwise . . . He wondered how much time he had left as he peered back in the direction of the *Revier*. It seemed miles away. Between him and the *Revier* the S.S. barracks, with 500 of the sadists slumbering in them, bulked in the darkness.

He was getting edgy; nothing was coming to him. His scintillating imagination wouldn't ignite. All he could think of was to use the vertical poles supporting the awning: Cut a hole in the canvas and shinny down a pole? Yes, and what would the four S.S. guards at the bottom do as he slid down the thirty-foot pole?

While he ran this bizarre notion through his mind, he heard the sound of a distant truck engine. The undulating whine meant that it was labouring up and down hill. A load of equipment and supplies from Nordhausen, he thought. He looked south, intermittently glimpsing slits of light piercing the low, black underbelly of the clouds. The engine sound gradually rose in volume. Soon the truck's black outline appeared in the cleared space leading up to the tunnels. As it turned toward the Tunnel B entrance, he realized the headlights could reveal his location. He rolled over on his face and pressed himself against the slope. He could feel the light bathe him as the truck rolled forward. Then the vehicle moved under the awning. He stuck his finger in a rip in the canvas, widening it gingerly so that he could see through.

Looking down, he watched the truck disappear from his line of sight and enter the tunnel mouth. The guard shack was not directly below him as he'd thought; it was further back into the tunnel. He listened raptly and heard the truck stop. Although the diesel engine idled noisily, he could hear voices. Chit-chat. Laughing. The guards, too, were starved for news from the outside.

Another idea hit him. Not a very good one, he told himself. But he had to do something. He'd let too much time slip by. The three o'clock deadline ticked closer . . .

He retraced his steps up the slope into the trees. Momentarily he glanced west toward the *Revier*, then began walking east. He moved fast; time was running

232

short. He tripped several times on fallen tree limbs and slammed onto the forest floor. He was breathing hard and sweating freely. He had no clear way of knowing how far he had come. Whatever the distance, he still had not run into the high fence which, they said, completely encircled Dora. He emerged from the trees and cautiously ventured down the slope, searching for the vague outlines of Tunnel A's awning.

He couldn't find it. He'd never been out at night before. He was confused by the darkness. How long had he been walking? How far had he come? It seemed to take him an inexplicably long time to descend the slope and reach level ground. Still no sign of Tunnel A. Still no sign of the fence. He continued to forge south, his dew-soaked pants clinging to his legs, until something told him it was time to head west again – toward the camp . . .

He was sweating heavily when he intersected his objective – the north-south road linking Nordhausen to Dora. There wasn't much time left.

He stood on the unpaved road. His plan was to get into the Kohnstein by sneaking aboard the next supply truck. He'd have to find a hill or a bend in the road, a spot where the truck would slow down. But he couldn't find either. Maybe he'd find something further on down the road.

He started walking south again, wondering when he'd come to the fence.

What time was it? Goddam Ukranian! It seemed hours since he'd left the dispensary. He licked his lips nervously and broke into a jog.

Occasionally he stopped, listening for a truck engine, trying to ignore the pounding of his heart, then he'd start jogging again. God almighty! Where were all the hills and bends? He'd seen many of them when they'd trucked him in from Buchenwald.

Where was the massive barbed-wire perimeter fence he'd heard about?

Then it struck him sudden as a club. Could he possibly be out of Dora? Had he escaped from Dora? Maybe he was mad. Or maybe it was just more S.S. bullshit about the huge, high-voltage, barbed-wire fence. 'Keep going, you bastard!' he screamed to himself. 'Keep going! You're free! You're free!'

He bounded forward, his long legs propelling him with the abandon of a colt on the loose. The burden was slipping from his shoulders. He longed to scream with the exuberance of his relief. His heart raced as fast as his legs. His mind could barely keep up.

Where would he go? What would he do? He'd detour around Nordhausen and stay in open country. Find an old farmer and his wife. Talk them into giving him some food and maybe a place to sleep in a hayloft. He could pull it off. He knew he could. His German wasn't Harz Mountain vernacular but ...

His legs turned to rubber. He slowed down and stumbled to a halt, the canvas bag slapping his thigh.

He'd forgotten the colour of his skin.

The elation leaked from his body like a man bleeding to death. He shuffled to the shoulder of the road and slumped down in the gorse. How long could a black man lie low in a white man's country? About as long as a white hiding out in Haiti.

Besides, he rationalized, escape hadn't been on his agenda when he left the dispensary; his goal had been to prove to himself that he wasn't afraid of Master Sergeant Brauny, and to revenge himself for the kick in the balls.

The canvas bag reminded him of what he planned to do inside Kohnstein to avenge himself.

Chapter Fourteen

The memory of the evening he'd sailed from Port-au-Prince filtered into his mind. Their tears and fears. His hopes. The overpowering feeling that the world had something great in store for him. But here he was, six years later, in southern Germany, masquerading as a downed American pilot, trying to hitch a ride back into hell.

His mother would never believe it. Neither would Carmen. Nor Vildebart. As for Uncle Fortune: he'd grin and accuse him of putting away too much rum.

Haiti had been so provincial. So suffocatingly dull after the Marines had left. Guadeloupe even worse.

He was staying with his mother's brother, Uncle Gabrielle, in Guadeloupe, until the French naval vessel arrived on its six-monthly recruiting tour of the Caribbean. The old man held him on a tight leash. Where are you going, Jean? Who are you going with, Jean? When will you be back, Jean?

Of course, the solicitous old fogey was only doing it at his mother's request.

It was ridiculous: he wasn't a child any more; it made him mad as hell. Uncle Gabrielle was a kind-hearted soul, though, and it was hard for Jean to deliberately flaunt his authority. So he forced himself to stay in line, killing time exploring the town and hiking around the island.

But how much of that could you take? A couple of months on the little island and he was climbing the walls. There was nothing to do. No gangster movies at the ramshackle little movie house. Practically the only diversion was hanging around the dock, ogling the daughters of the white French tourists. Or trying to see how far he could push the gendarmes.

Soon he was going out of his mind. The boredom – and the prodding of Uncle Gabrielle – forced him into a part-time job at the hospital in Fort-de-France and into some biology courses there.

Late in the fall of 1938 word came that the French naval vessel had finally docked at the island of Martinique. He grabbed his bags and hopped aboard the inter-island ferry for the 100-mile trip.

As he climbed the French ship's gangplank it was the high-point of his life: at the age of twenty he was free at last.

A few weeks later he was aboard the training ship *Courbet*. Later he was transferred to the *Ocean*, totally challenged and excited by the life of a sea cadet. Out on the briny. The Mediterranean and the Atlantic. The salt spray astringing his face. The thrill of standing on the deck, looking up at the glory of a ship in full sail.

Aloft in the rigging of the *Ocean* one cold, blustery day that winter, he lost his footing and crashed to the deck...

Slowly he recovered from his injuries and became insanely anxious to go back to sea. The navy thought otherwise. In March of 1939 they handed him a Certificate of Good Conduct. On the back of it they made the notation that his injuries rendered him unfit for further service.

After his discharge he returned to Paris and closeted himself at 97 Boulevard Diderot in the 12th Arrondisement, humiliated and disappointed. What a time to be in Paris! What a time to be rejected for military service! The talk of impending war with Germany was everywhere. While he was stowing away the uniform he had worn so proudly, millions of French reservists – including his brother Vildebart – were dusting off theirs in expectation of mobilization orders. It killed him to feel so worthless. A terrible new experience. He had lived his life with the dream of all French citizens born outside La Belle France of beholding Paris with their own eyes. The storeyed Eiffel Tower. The awesome Arc de Triomphe. The majestic Champs Élysées. All of it now shattered by the failure glutting his belly. A bottomless depression. Worse than the boarding-school homesickness a decade earlier at St. Nazaire.

Weeks later he abruptly decided the wake had lasted long enough. He snatched the allowance his mother had lodged in the bank for him, gave the glories of Paris the back of his hand and plunged into the life of a pleasure-seeker on the Riviera. Refusing to let his misery quench him, he turned his personality on high beam and drove a course through Nice, Marseilles, Cannes, Toulon and Bordeaux. Jean Marcel Nicolas of Port-au-Prince had become 'Johnny Nicholas' of Boston, USA. He flashed his devastating grin around the cocktail bars, bought drinks 'on the house' and consecrated himself to lasting friendships on the strength of a single night-on-the-town. He gate-crashed the society parties in his velvet-glove style and got his foot in the door of the colony of screen-writers, producers and movie actors populating the exotic Mediterranean coastline.

They discovered their new-found 'medical student from Paris' an urbane host, a witty conversationalist and – for an American – unbelieveably facile among the international set with his command of French, German and Spanish.

Until his money began to run low.

Browsing through the paper one day on his hotel balcony in Nice, an advertisement caught his eye: a Paris motion-picture company shooting on location in the Riviera needed the consulting services of a freelance producer. All he knew about movies was what he had seen in the Rex theatre at home, but that didn't stop him. He answered the ad, fabricated his experience as a producer in broad, sweeping terms – then went off to the Nice library and took out every book he could find on motion-picture production.

For three days and nights he lived with the literature, hardly bothering to eat or sleep, prepared to bullshit his way through.

On the appointed day he dressed himself in his impeccable 'American' best, and conned the interviewer with his credentials. He got the job, and they paid him 500,000 francs for his services.

Sometimes, however, as he discovered in the auction at Nice, it was a liability to be American.

In a conventional-style auction the highest bidder is the only person to pay out any money. In some private auctions held in upper-crust circles in France to raise money for charity, it was the custom for *every* bidder to pay his bid into the 'kitty,' even though the highest bidder was the one to get the item auctioned. On this occasion he was low on funds and high on champagne; but that did not deter him from bidding. He kept upping the bid and got himself into competition with a French philanthropist, who did not want to be outdone by an American. Each time the philanthropist bid, he raised it. His last raise was nine and one half million francs, which the philanthropist topped with a bid of ten million francs, and the auctioneer banged his gavel.

The next day two husky men from the charitable organization came around to collect their $9\frac{1}{2}$ million francs from the wealthy American Negro. Nicholas told them he was sorry, that he wasn't really an American but a poor Haitian medical student unfamiliar with that type of auction.

The men from the charity were enraged that they had been tricked. When they threatened to strong-arm him, he calmly pointed out to them that the auction was illegal. Why all the fuss? At least they did have the philanthropist's ten million francs, he reminded them, pointing out that the bidding would never have gotten that high had he not encouraged it. In the end they commended him and withdrew, sheepishly apologizing for having bothered him.

To Nicholas, slumped by the road leading to Camp Dora, in the year 1944, it seemed a century ago that the war had begun in Europe. In reality it wasn't. Hitler had invaded Poland on 3 September 1939 ... the fall of Paris the following year in June ... the German motorized columns trundling over the Seine bridges. He imagined himself riding his bicycle as he once had, amid hundreds of thousands of Parisians fleeing along choked roads southwest toward Chartres ...

He gazed dumbly at the headlights' black-out slits, his brain still locked in the past. He shook his head and tried to bounce back into the present. The pitch of the engine told him the truck was moving slowly. It wouldn't be hard to climb aboard. His hand idly flipped the flap of the bag. The coarse feel of canvas touched his conscience: the bag was the thing! The bag had brought him to where he was! The bag – and Brauny!

The vision of Brauny fuelled his rage afresh. He sprang to his haunches. The engine pitch rose as the truck's silhouette bulked larger. He could see the black-out slits grow wider. He braced himself.

God! The bag! Where was the bag?

The truck was yards away, whining down on him.

He was useless without the bag! It had slipped off his shoulder. He groped in the darkness like an epileptic. Miraculously he scooped it up by the strap on one crooked finger and leaped into the road as the truck whined by.

The jerk on his big body almost dislocated his shoulder blades. They were still not healed from his months in the tunnels. His fingers were spastic talons hooked over the edge of the tailgate as he struggled to pull himself over. His legs dangled beneath, exploring frantically for a toehold.

The truck had a canvas top and a cargo of fifty-gallon oil drums. Safely inside, he got down on his knees and began to clear a place for himself among the barrels. He slid them aside gingerly, fearful of alerting the driver. He

239

could see the back of the man's head through the cab window.

The engine revved down as the truck pulled into the open field at the base of the Kohnstein and rolled in under Tunnel B's awning. It stopped. He could feel the idling engine's vibrations in his body. He heard the driver roll down the window and call out familiarly to the guards. Jackboots scuffed the gravelly tunnel floor. Equipment jangled. He could hear the men exchange good-natured pleasantries. Obviously they knew each other well. He mentally cursed them for spending too much time on small talk. He heard one guard ask the driver what his cargo was. The driver said more alcohol and radio parts. So Nicholas knew what was in the drums. And in the cardboard boxes: radio components. 'Could be the last shipment of radio parts for awhile,' said the driver.

'Why's that?' asked one of the guards.

'Didn't you hear?' laughed the driver. 'They bombed the Mibau August 24. The whole damned thing went up in smoke.'

'*Kommandant* Fourschner wouldn't think that was very funny,' said the guard in mock reproval.

'*Mein Gott*! Didn't you hear about it? It's stupid telling all us drivers to keep our mouths shut. As if the damned Americans didn't know about it already. They're the ones who did it.'

Flattened against the floor of the truck, holding his breath, Nicholas listened ecstatically.

'All thirteen Mibau sheds?' asked another guard incredulously.

'*Ja*,' said the driver. '*Alles*.'

The truck, jerking as the driver changed gear, rolled into the tunnel and the engine's sound boomed deafeningly off the rock walls, mixing with the din of the tunnelling operations of the night shift, more than a mile away at the blind end of the tunnel.

Nicholas slipped from behind the barrels and edged toward the tailgate. He watched the ceiling: he remembered the lights were spaced every 50 or 75 yards. Very yellow. Very dim. He girded himself to hop over the tailgate. It would be most difficult for the S.S. guards to detect him if he made his break when the truck was halfway between the bulbs, where the lighting was worst. But he'd better jump soon; he didn't want to get too close to the blind end, where dozens of S.S. guards loitered. Between the mouth and the blind end the tunnel was almost deserted.

Somewhere in between would be ideal. As the truck moved on he watched the S.S. guard shack grow smaller, the illumination dimmer . . .

He hopped over the tailgate and hit the concrete floor. The canvas bag slapped audibly against his rump as he flitted to a tiny orifice in Tunnel B that opened up into a cross tunnel – one of the four – used as dormitory tunnels.

In the blackness of the four dormitory tunnels, which had been drilled off Tunnel A, the 5,000 slaves of the day shift roused from their tortured slumber. They were utterly stunned. 'Johnny's here!' someone croaked. 'The American's here! Dr. Johnny's arrived!'

Their voices were strained with awe. He had committed the forbidden act. If caught, he would be executed.

He asked them to point out those too far gone to report to sick call or too terrified by Maischein, the drunken S.S. medic. Down the rocky aisle between the four-tiered bunks he groped his way. Their hands clutched at him. Their voices cracked with emotion. He dipped into his bag and handed out the sulpha, the charcoal tablets, salves and paper dressings. Some gripped him so intensely that he had to pry their fingers loose. The stench was asphyxiating. He fought it by assuring himself that he was Brauny's superior; if their situations had been reversed, he told himself, Brauny would have been too cowardly to risk it. He forced his shoulders back a notch. He pushed his chest out an inch. He tried to think of Brauny seeing it all. He imagined the expression on the S.S. sergeant's smug face.

And in the darkness he smiled. Yes, they had their gibbets and their gas chambers, their *Bocks* and their bludgeons. Yet there were things that they couldn't hang, gas or beat out of a man.

It aggrandized his ego as whisky gives courage to the timid.

He had completely lost track of time as he handed out his remedies and whispered the news of the bombing of the Mibau ... Paris liberated ... the Americans and British rolling toward the German frontier ... Berlin smashed by thousand-bomber raids ... the Russian armies driving toward the Polish border.

'Keep your spirits up!' he told them. 'The end is in sight! Hold on! We will all return to our homelands!'

In the silence, wooden bunks creaked. Men sobbed. They called down on him the blessings of Jesus, Mary and Joseph and the saints. Or Abba, Father! And in the blackness the weeping slaves embraced their memories.

But there was more to come.

A small group, following him like a Pied Piper, moved out of the fourth dormitory tunnel to Cross Tunnel 42, where Pomaranski had been almost beaten to death. No. 42 was the site of four huge, metal reservoirs filled with water for mixing the hundreds of thousands of cubic feet of cement used to pave the floor. Prisoners so crazed with thirst that they would gulp down their own urine had tried to steal the water and been summarily hanged or shot. The same fate was suffered by those who simply held rusty tins under the pipes to catch drops of condensation.

'Where you going, Johnny?'

'For a swim,' he told them.

Pressing himself into the shadows of Tunnel A's rocky walls and drunk from the thrill of his ordeal, Nicholas turned the corner into Tunnel 42. He stood in the shadows, watching the S.S. guard walk the 130-yard length of the tunnel, back and forth, back and forth.

Holy Jesus! What was he up to now?

He peeled off his sweat-soaked stripes and stealthily

242

followed the guard along the tunnel. When Nicholas reached the first reservoir he silently climbed up and over the side and gently lowered himself into the water.

His disciples, crouching in the shadows, froze. They watched as in a trance as he thumbed his nose at the guard's back, cavorted in the water, pretended to scrub his back and shampoo his hair.

He was out and back in the shadows, shivering, before the unsuspecting guard had turned around on his beat.

Yes, he congratulated himself, he had shown them who were the masters and who the slaves. Most of all he had shown himself.[1]

No more Jews will be admitted to the *Revier*!

It was Commandant Fourschner's solution to the overcrowding in the prisoner hospital.

Even the calloused *Lagerschutz* turned a blind eye to the order. 'No Jews!' they shouted from the dispensary door each morning. 'All Jews will step out of line and return to their blocks!' But they wouldn't venture too far into the deep snow to ferret out those wearing the yellow Star of David.

Stars could be ripped off. For that reason Jews were still getting into the dispensary after the order was issued. Only when an S.S. was nearby did the *Lagerschutz* make a rigorous check.

Corporal Maischein lurched up the dispensary steps one dark, frigid morning after the no-Jews order. He was drunk as usual.

All in sick call stood rigidly at attention.

Maischein stared at several of the prisoners, slowly moving from one to the other. 'You!' he shouted, pointing to a feeble old man. 'You with the big nose! You are a Jew!'

The dispensary door opened and Nicholas appeared on

[1]'He was crazy,' Boruch Siedel, a Jewish prisoner, testified at the Nordhausen trials three years later. 'He was completely crazy.'

243

the porch. 'Prisoner No. 44451, Dispensary *Kapo*, reporting, *Herr Rottenfuehrer*!'

Maischein squinted in the dim light of the naked bulb over the door. 'This one's a Jew!' he screamed, pointing.

Nicholas looked down at the prisoner, who was trembling.

'Did you ask him if he was a Jew?' shouted Maischein.

'*Nein, Herr Rottenfuehrer*. He has not been admitted to the dispensary yet.'

'Ask him if he is a Jew,' screamed Maischein. 'Ask him!'

'The prisoner appears to be a very sick man, *Herr Rottenfuehrer.*'

Maischein stumbled up the steps and grabbed Nicholas by the lapels. 'You black bastard! I told you to ask him if he is a Jewish bastard!'

'Are you a Jew?' Nicholas asked the prisoner.

The terrified man's face contorted. His head jerked as he looked up at Nicholas, at Maischein, then back at Nicholas. '*Ja*, I am a Jew,' he wheezed.

Maischein squealed with delight. 'Beat him, you black bastard!' he commanded Nicholas. 'Show him what happens when a dirty Jew doesn't follow orders!'

A hundred times Nicholas had seen other prisoners in the same dilemma: beat or be beaten. He swung at the old Jew, and Maischein joined in.

In sick-call that morning was Valentin Kovalj, a 35-year-old Ukrainian prisoner of war. He would testify in the Nordhausen trials:

'I myself witnessed once when Maischein and a great, big Negro were beating a man like a log... He was dragged away by the legs... We knew already when anybody is dragged away by the legs he finally comes to the gas chamber... First they beat him in front of the door, then they beat him in the dispensary...'[2]

Corp. Paul Maischein, whose official job was in the hospital for the S.S., liked to consider the *Revier* his private practice, and he moonlighted there voluntarily. He epitomized the mentality of the S.S. enlisted man assigned to concentration-camp duty. Small in stature, he was the essence of the bully. He revelled in commiting the most bestial atrocities on prisoners. His 'gold tooth raids' kept even the bravest prisoners terrified of provoking him. It was said that in checking prisoners at the *Revier* his only examination consisted of inserting a tongue depressor into their mouths, asking them to 'open wide' while he scrutinized their throats to discover possible infections. But that was merely a ruse. His true purpose was to locate gold fillings. Should a prisoner later turn up in the corpse pile, Maischein could reach for his surgical pliers and quickly collect his prize.

A baker's helper in civilian life, Maischein was thirty-two when his path crossed that of Johnny Nicholas in 1944. Yet Maischein could sense that the American despised him and nothing pleased the S.S. man more than to intimidate Nicholas and try to make him squirm whenever he could.

Nicholas had studied Maischein's idiosyncrasies, piecing together snippets he had picked up from prisoner officials and others who knew him. He wasn't at all surprised to learn that Maischein was an unabashed transvestite who delighted in getting uproariously drunk and appearing with wig, painted face, falsies and bar girl's dress to pretend he was 'available' to his suitors in the S.S. barracks. But Nicholas was stymied by Maischein's lethal unpredictability and his total lack of rationality. If he was ever to manipulate the deranged S.S. medic, he figured he'd have to forge some dramatic demonstration of his

[2]Ibid. 12–481 Vol. 1, Book 8

faithfulness to Maischein's commands to throw him forever off guard. The Jewish prisoner, unfortunately, was Nicholas' ploy.

'Kick the Juden in the nuts!' Maischein bellowed.

By now the Jew was unconscious, thanks to the humanely levelled right uppercut Nicholas had laid on him when ordered to do so. After that, it became a scene from one of the Westerns or gangster movies Nicholas had watched hour after hour in Port-au-Prince, Paris and elsewhere. He made it look good. Occasionally the maniacally intoxicated Maischein flung a harmless blow to the Jew's arm or chest and Nicholas feigned approval with a toothy grin. Maischein urged Nicholas to give the Jew another kick and Nicholas appeared to comply.

When he felt that Maischein was satisfied, Nicholas reached down and checked the Jew's pulse. 'He's through, *Herr Rottenfuehrer*,' Nicholas pronounced, 'I will call for the death detail.'

Maischein was not convinced. 'Are you sure? If he is still alive you will be next.'

Cooly Nicholas replied: 'See for yourself, *Herr Rottenfuehrer*. Not a twitch.'

Maischein reached down and clumsily thumbed back the Jew's left eyelid. The eye stared innocently up at him. He let the lid drop, then opened the Jew's mouth and plunged a tongue depressor into it. '*Herr Rottenfuehrer*,' said Nicholas helpfully, 'you will not find any gold.' He reached dextrously into the Jew's mouth and whisked out the upper and lower dentures ...

Maischein screamed with laughter. His shrieks pierced the hushed silence of the prisoners who had witnessed the 'beating' and subsequent 'gold tooth raid.' When he regained control, he shuffled off muttering to Nicholas: 'Take the son-of-a-bitch to the pile ...'

Nicholas motioned to two prisoners whom he knew well to help him cart the body away. At first they refused, enraged at what they had seen. When Maischein was out of earshot, Nicholas whispered to them: Hurry up before

246

that imbecile comes back. This guy's okay . . . Just a little stunned. Let's get him inside and I'll work on him.' Flashing knowing looks at each other, the two men fetched the death cart and gently laid the Jew on it.

News of the Jew's 'brutal' beating and 'death' spread quickly among the prisoners. They were dismayed. Johnny? It couldn't be. Not the Johnny who took such chances to go into the tunnels that night with the medicines; not 'Saint Nicholas,' as they'd nicknamed him afterwards.

Gradually the truth filtered down the prisoner grapevine. Some were relieved. Others, despite their infirmities, could not help but stifle a giggle. Christ, what gall. He'd really put it over this time on Maischein. Even the most depressed, down-at-the-mouth prisoner found his spirits buoyed by the tale. They'd tell and re-tell it tirelessly, each time more fully embellishing the scenario for good measure until Nicholas not only had been confirmed in sainthood but was preparing, it seemed, to sit on the left hand of God.

Nicholas celebrated in his new role. Not only had he elevated the morale of his fellow prisoners, he also had won new – and important – trust from the addle-brained S.S. medic. Now, perhaps, he could enjoy the latitude he'd angled for: with Maischein off guard, his movements were less restricted; he could now work his way into the tunnels and find out exactly what they were making. He'd toiled there during the tunnel-boring stage, but except for his brief escapade in the reservoir, he hadn't been inside since manufacturing had begun.

What were they building? Casual chit-chat with his patients had produced pieces of the puzzle. Did anyone outside the S.S. know the full picture? A prisoner spent all his time trying to get enough to eat. He worked twenty-four hours a day just to stay alive. He had no time to worry about such things.

247

Was it a naval torpedo as the Norwegian figured it was? Or a new aircraft? In silhouette there wasn't much difference.

It was *verboten* for a prisoner to talk about his job. The S.S. kept the various blocks apart to prevent prisoners from comparing notes and experiences. Keeping them isolated from each other also kept them ignorant. To ask too many questions was to apply for a one-way ticket to the crematorium.

If anybody knew, Nicholas told himself, the Communists knew. They were so impeccably organized. So disciplined. When they made up their minds to do anything, they did it. If they wanted to find out what the S.S. was building in the tunnels, nothing could stop them. Maybe they already knew: it was paradoxical, but there it was: Moscow might already know more about what was going on in the Kohnstein than he did – and he was hardly a quarter mile away!

The challenge of trying to find out teased him. The more he thought about it, the more it fascinated him. Forever extravagant in his notions, he vaulted from the germ of the idea to the vision of getting the information to the Allies. He remembered a Yugoslav with dysentary talking about sheetmetal cylinders he was welding in the tunnels. Some kind of tank or container obviously.

A French patient he had treated for an eye injury mentioned adjustments he made to gyroscopic compasses. That would be for steering something. The Pole had gotten his burn welding long, metal tubes in an arrangement that resembled a huge waste basket. What could that be for? The Belgian who'd come off the *Bock* was a chemist in civilian life. He said he was working in a newly built tunnel complex off Tunnel A where they added chemicals to coal to make fuel.

While the huge new drafts of slave labour pouring into Dora ravaged food supplies, they brought up-to-date news of the outside world. Nicholas' new patients reported Hitler's broadcasts in which the German leader claimed he had a secret weapon. Several whispered about reading German newspapers' accounts of devastating raids on England by pilotless airplanes loaded with high explosives.

Jesus! That could be it! Not a torpedo. Not a regular airplane. But a pilotless airplane! That's what they were making in the Kohnstein?

It was too simple! Why hadn't he figured it out before?

A new supply of adrenalin surged in his veins.

Who else might have figured it out? The *Revier* Commies?

That's why they'd never let him in on news of the flying bomb raids! If the Nazis were boasting about it on radio and in newspapers, the BBC newscasts must have picked it up. The Red prisoner-doctors knew flying bombs were being built in the Kohnstein. But they didn't want non-Communists in on the discovery. They wanted to make absolutely sure only Moscow knew about Dora.

It made sense. The Reds had the opportunity to milk their patients as he had. They'd probably been doing so for months!

He pounded his fist in his hand when he thought of the weeks and weeks he'd wasted.

But how was it launched? How fast did it fly? How powerful was the warhead?

Thousands tramped in and out of his dispensary every week. Without any prompting they'd innocently volunteered scraps of information to him. But from now on he'd make it a practice to pump them for every last detail. It was up to him to grab the pieces and put the jigsaw puzzle together.

But he couldn't risk putting anything on paper. Too dangerous. He'd have to memorize it. He could do it. Nothing to it. His memory had made him 500,000 francs with the motion-picture company that time in Nice, hadn't it?

Once he'd made the decision, his wild imagination

pushed logic aside and took over. He is on a postwar parade ground. His name is called. The bugles are blaring. Flags flying. He can hear bunting snapping in the breeze. He steps forward from the ranks, shakes the general's hand and accepts the thanks of a grateful government. The medal is pinned on his chest. The band strikes up. In Paris the photographers crowd him. In London reporters mob him for interviews. And he is on the front page of *Le Nouvelliste* in Port-au-Prince, family and friends gathered proudly around him . . .

It was too easy. The scraps of bread, the withered carrots, the cigarette butts and the convalescent slips – these especially – worked like truth serum. But he had to be extremely careful: Gestapo stool pigeons roosted all over. He had to handle himself in such a way that if caught, they could never accuse him of asking specific questions. His approach had to be made circuitously until he could trust his sources.

His decision to record nothing on paper placed him under tremendous pressure, forcing him to pack his brain with facts and figures during the day. At night he had to unclog his mind, sift and assemble. He twisted and turned in his bunk, wondering if it really was a flying bomb.

A long, tubular-steel cylinder . . . A metal cone . . . Large, triangular slices of fin-like sheetmetal . . . Assembled in his imagination they did appear as a bomb-like object. But more than forty feet long – if his calculations were right. What bomb could be that long? Could it be slung *under* a plane for launching? Maybe it was a mammoth version of the little pilotless bomb the new patients talked about.

The Kohnstein's special underground caverns with the 100-foot-high ceilings: where did they fit in? Some said only German civilians and engineers were allowed into them. One hundred feet was more than three times the height of the two main tunnels. It was twice the size of the weapon that he'd figured out from the patchwork piecer supplied by his patients.

Was it a huge new artillery piece – an updated version of the Big Bertha of the First World War he'd read about as a boy? Maybe. The metal cones they talked about could be the shell cases. But if the cylinders constituted segments of a 100-foot barrel, the gun itself had to be 150 feet long, which was ridiculous. So big it would have to be on a huge platform to move it around. Maybe a railroad flatcar just like the Big Bertha?

They weren't planning on firing a monster like that from the inside of the Kohnstein, were they? But why not? It could disappear and be invulnerable to air attack? Maybe *that* was the meaning of the 100-foot-high caverns.

If it was an artillery piece, where did a compass controlled by a gyroscope fit in? A gyrocompass made more sense on a submarine or a torpedo. A hundred-foot-long torpedo? Never. Maybe a hundred-foot-long submarine. But what kind of sub. would have a radio with just one frequency? The Mibau radios had only one frequency. Maybe a remote-controlled submarine! A small submarine packed with explosives and guided toward the target by radio. And the liquid oxygen and alcohol? The fuel mix for the sub, of course.

It sounded plausible. But his theory had holes that were obvious to him: if the reports he was getting were reliable, the crisis for Germany wasn't at sea. It was in the air! If Hitler had a secret punch for turning defeat into victory, he'd use it against the massive Allied bomber fleets that the new arrivals at sick call talked about endlessly.

So a torpedo or a sub. wasn't logical. Unless it was an aerial torpedo! Maybe something fired from the ground into the middle of a skyful of bombers!

Once he had loathed the long, sleepless nights. Now he lived for them and the solitude where he could put together the pieces of the puzzle extracted that day. Sometimes he was punchdrunk with too much information. Often, just before dozing off, he was morbidly depressed that nothing made sense. Other times, when the pieces fell into place, he simply couldn't sleep because he was too excited. He would be awake until the shrill whistle blasts at 5:30 in the morning.

During the day he'd be dopey with the urge to sleep. The faces began to look the same. He was getting the names jumbled. He was continually on edge that, in his blurry state, he would slip up in his dispensary interrogations and fail to recognize a Gestapo plant when he saw one. Mixed with his fear, however, was the excitement of conspiracy, the thrill of each new piece that fitted. It was like strong rum on an empty stomach. When Maischein or Brauny came in, his heady new sense of power almost drove him to give in to his emotions and strangle them. Sometimes it took minutes for him to regain control. And when he did, he would appease himself with the promise that the longer he held off, the sweeter his revenge would be.

He was getting closer!

The trembling French engineer snatched the convalescent slip and told him that the ethyl alcohol and the liquid oxygen were mixed in a ratio of 17 to 21. A Pole working on the north slope whispered that at night he'd seen German civilians rolling huge, fifty-foot-long, finned cylindrical objects out the north end of Tunnel A. That information was worth a hunk of mouldy bread.

Each morning Nicholas found himself staring out in the sickly light of the single electric bulb, searching the sick-call faces, praying like a narcotic for a fix that his best sources had come back and help confirm his deductions.

His hand, remembering the Morse Code learned on the *Corbet* and the *Ocean*, was already tapping out the message. He could see the operator in London clamping his earphones to his head as the dramatic dots and dashes beeped in his ears changed the course of history . . .

Enemy . . . in . . . possible . . . production . . . mammoth

252

... rocket ... stop ... liquid ... oxygen ... fuel ... stop ... gyroscope ... control ... stop ... homes ... on ... radio ... beam ... stop ... approximate ... length ... fifty feet ... stop ... approximate ... diameter ... five ... feet ... stop ... underground ... factory ... located ... Harz ... Mountains ... stop ... five ... miles ... north ... Nordhausen ... stop.

He would tingle with excitement...

But how was he to get the message out?

Coicou and Pape? They would get information into the right hands. But after he'd been picked up that November, nearly a year earlier, they'd scattered. Changed their addresses, and routines. He didn't know where they were.

Wait! Those French civilians working at the Mibau plant in Buchenwald. They'd volunteered to work in Germany not because they were disloyal to France or loved the Germans; they needed the money because their families were starving. They were allowed to return home twice a year. Surely one of them had to be willing and able to place a message in the right hands!

But the Mibau had been heavily bombed. The Frenchmen might be dead. Yet why even bother with them when there was Block 43 at Buchenwald, the block where captured Allied agents were held. The S.S. lavished the most extreme secrecy on Block 43, but Buchenwald's Reds knew plenty about who was held there. The Reds liked to remind themselves of how superior they were; knowing the identity of Block 43's tenants was a measure of that. They often boasted about it to Nicholas. One Communist prisoner-doctor had informed Nicholas that the Englishman in Block 43, the so-called Captain Dodkins, was actually the top Allied agent in France.[3]

[3]He was in reality Wing Commander Yeo-Thomas, RAF, the elusive 'White Rabbit,' who was finally captured but protected his true identity under the pseudonym of Dodkins.

What fantastic luck! thought Nicholas. Dodkins obviously was his man!

But Buchenwald, only sixty-five miles away, might as well have been Boston: how could he get to the Britisher?

Night after night Nicholas' mind churned over the possibilities restlessly. His frustration festered. Insane as it seemed, the only one who suggested even a remote hope for getting his fantastic theory to the outside world was Dr. Kahr.

Yes, it was insane to think so. But Kahr was an Austrian. Major Gardemann had told him years ago in Haiti that an Austrian was a different breed of German; Austrians tended to be humanitarians. Kahr fitted that description. Nicholas was sure that the doctor's S.S. uniform was a façade; that he hated everything Dora stood for.

The Red prisoner-doctors often boasted how they'd been able to 'cultivate' an S.S. doctor up at Buchenwald. He was Dr. Ding-Schuler. Little by little they'd inveigled him into making 'illegal' concessions to the prisoners. Then they had blackmailed him into giving into their bolder requests. Ding-Schuler, they bragged, had been blackmailed to the point where he was risking his own life to save Buchenwald's prisoners.

Nicholas pondered whether Kahr could be manoeuvered along the same lines.

How would Dodkins in Block 43 react when an S.S. lieutenant he'd never set eyes on arrived with a message about secret weapons and an underground factory? Would the Englishman read it as a Gestapo trick and tell Kahr to bugger off?

The blizzards of November 1944 blew into December. The sky had the same drab, pendulous underbelly of grey. The lines of the sick stretched from the dispensary down the snow-covered slope to infinity. The *Revier* had become a merry-go-round that never stopped. More and more got on. No one ever seemed to get off.

Nicholas was now obsessed with the single task of getting his information to Buchenwald. But he was deathly afraid of approaching Kahr. The dilemma kept him in a kind of trance. His patients were becoming a blur of bones and shaven skulls. His awareness of himself was ebbing – except when he began coughing. When the spasms had passed, they were forgotten – but not Kahr. He'd prefer to go up against Maischein or Brauny any time. He tried to convince himself that Kahr was just another bastard in a black S.S. uniform. He tried to ridicule himself: since when was Johnny Nicholas scared of anyone? What was he afraid of? That Kahr would say no and turn him in to Fourschner as a spy? Sure; that was part of it. And the other part?

He was scared that Kahr *would* go along with the scheme and get caught by the Gestapo.

One morning in the dispensary he rehearsed his approach until his brain was numb, for he had solemnly promised himself that the bout with Kahr could no longer be postponed.

He planned to begin with the usual small talk. The rising numbers of sick and injured. The terrible weather. The short supply of medicines. Then he'd get more specific. 'They are collapsing where they stand, *Herr Doktor*. They are working sixteen and eighteen hours without relief while German civilians alongside them work eight and ten hours and get adequate diets and rest.'

He could predict what the doctor would say: '*Ja*, Major Nicholas. I am aware of the situation.'

But he could press on: 'They are hanged every day, *Herr Doktor*, because they are accused of sabotage when they take an old cement bag and wrap it around their feet with odds and ends of electrical cable to keep out the cold. What's to become of them, *Herr Doktor*?'

Dr. Kahr would be sure to give his standard reply: 'I am

trying to get more supplies from Berlin. But the real problem, Major, is their lack of resistance. Their diet is bad. They don't have the ability to resist infection.'

And then he would begin his move: '*Ja, Herr Doktor*. All the prisoner-doctors know what you have done and what you are doing. But what will happen when our food is gone? I have observed the many things you have done for the prisoners – things, *Herr Doktor*, which *Kommandant* Fourschner could not possibly understand because they were not permitted by his rules and regulations.'

That, of course, would break down Kahr's guard. He'd be curious. Even provoked. He'd demand to know what Nicholas was talking about. Nicholas would risk a faint smile – the smile exchanged between co-conspirator – and then pretend to make light of it: 'Nothing, *Herr Doktor*. Nothing that should be recalled. And I would make the same statement to *Kommandant* Fourschner if he were to ask me about those things.'

By this time, Nicholas was calculating, Dr. Kahr would have to be worried. 'If you have something to say, say it, Major.'

And he'd reply: 'Merely, *Herr Doktor*, that a humanitarian is bound by the laws of humanity. He is not bound by the laws of a factory manager worried about production rates. He must try to save life. All life at all times. Even lives he judges not worthy of saving.'

Because he was two years younger than the doctor, he knew he had to be careful not to sound intellectually superior. He was sure that if he could strike the right note, he could use Kahr's honesty, decency and compassion in his own cause. But he would have to watch the doctor closely. If it looked as if Kahr would hear him out, he would press on: 'But the question is: must we humanitarians patch up men today so that tomorrow they can kill each other?'

What would the doctor reply? He'd probably spar around a bit, giving himself time to think. 'What can one do with the Russian prisoners? They drink the ethyl alcohol and they die. They fight among themselves with knives and they die.'

'*Nein, Herr Doktor*,' he'd parry. 'I am not talking about that.'

The doctor would ask what he *was* talking about, and that would give him the opening to throw his punch. 'Do you know, *Herr Doktor*, what they are making in the tunnels?'

How would the doctor respond? He knew the Teutonic mind so well by now, he told himself, that he could almost write the script. 'Major, you are an intelligent man. Surely you realize you could be executed for asking that question?'

It was so predictable: the doctor would want to protect him. And that would be the time to start manoeuvring him against the ropes. He'd say: '*Ja, Herr Doktor*. You also are an intelligent man. You realize for that to happen, someone other than *Herr Doktor* Kahr would have to report to *Kommandant* Fourschner that I had asked such a question. In the same way that I would have to tell the *Herr Kommandant* that you had stretched his rules and regulations – for the cause of humanity, *natürlich*.'

The doctor would ponder that one. While he did, he'd probably try to cover up his anxiety. 'Major, you are a humanitarian, too. I knew I had chosen wisely. Your record has been excellent.'

But he had to remind himself the mild-mannered Austrian would be no push-over. He knew how he'd worked around Fourschner to get his way; he was clever, a good judge of human behavior. He would have to be ready for something like: '*Ja*, Major Nicholas, an excellent record.'

'They are making weapons in there for the destruction of human life, *Herr Doktor*,' he would state matter-of-factly.

'I don't want to hear anything about weapons, Major. I am a physician.'

Would he snap back the line that would leap to the tip

of his tongue? 'Physician! Heal thyself!' Would he cite the latest information bought with a convalescent slip from a Czechoslovakian skeleton?

'They are making a huge rocket, *Herr Doktor*. Fifty feet long. A warhead that may make a hole thirty feet deep when it explodes. There is probably no defence against such a weapon because it may travel faster than the speed of sound. It will kill women and children and they will never know what happened because there is no warning of its approach.'

'Stop! I don't want to hear any more about it. I am a physician. I don't know what you're talking about. We must stay out of things that don't concern us,' Dr. Kahr would respond.

'*Herr Doktor*, on the contrary. I know very well what I am talking about.'

'Stop it! You're signing your own execution papers!'

'The automatic pilot and radio are located directly behind the warhead section – '

'You are mad!'

'A madness we can halt, *Herr Doktor*, if you will take some information to the Englishman, Captain Dodkins, in Barracks 43 at Buchenwald!'

'Shut up! You're insane! Already I've had to intercede for you with the Kommandant three times because of the excessive number of convalescent slips you've issued. Hospital *Kapo* Schneider is just waiting for another chance to pounce on you. Brauny is ready to finish you off the moment my back is turned. Custody Camp Leader Moeser will joyfully order you hanged and administer the *coup de grace* the moment I am transferred! Major, I can protect you against them, but not against yourself. I'm going to have you transferred before you kill yourself and wreck everything we've managed to build here at the *Revier*.'

As Nicholas stood in the dispensary, steeling himself for the doctor's arrival, his heart fluttering wildly from the vividness of his day-dream, the public-address system blared: '*Achtung! Achtung!* All work will cease immediately! All detail leaders will assemble their formations. *Kapos* will march them immediately to the tunnels! All NCOs will report to the gatehouse! On the double!'

Inside the Kohnstein thousands of prisoners were converging from all over the camp. S.S. guards were herding them into the southern end of Tunnel B. The whirr of machinery had died down. All that could be heard was the shuffling of thousands of footsteps on the concrete amplified a million times by the echoing. The production lines had stopped moving. All manufacturing work had halted.

At the intersection of Tunnel B and Cross-Tunnel No. 41 thousands of prisoners were assembled.

Nicholas, hemmed in by the masses, could barely move but his height enabled him to see over their heads.

In the centre he saw a company of S.S. soldiers positioned in a large circle. Above the centre of the circle there was a gantry crane. From it hung a long, wooden plank in a horizontal position; and from the plank dangled ten nooses.

The wait was silent and interminable.

The sight of the nooses sickened Nicholas. They twirled innocently in the tunnel's air currents. He had the chilling certainty that he had been incredibly clumsy at milking the information and that the Gestapo was on his trail. A terrible premonition swept over him that the very next time the loudspeakers boomed, it would be a summons to his own execution.

An S.S. NCO appeared in the circle of guards followed by a long line or prisoners. The prisoners halted. The overhead crane moved into position. The two planks with the nooses silently moved lower.

'The following prisoners have been found guilty of criminal acts resulting in the reduction of production quotas of the Mittelwerk. Their crimes come under three specifications: the deliberate introduction of foreign objects into components and assemblies so as to cause them to malfunction ... unlawful acquisition and possession of property and materials belonging to the German government; to wit, cement bags and electrical cable ... and repeated and incorrigible malingering through the fraudulent acquisition of convalescent slips from the *Revier* ... '

The NCO began to call out the names.

The sounds reverberated off the tunnel walls. Piling one on top of the other, they were garbled and difficult for Nicholas to recognize.

' ... All the accused have admitted their guilt and have been sentenced to death under the general charge of sabotage. Signed by Heinrich Himmler, *Reichfuehrer* of the *Schutzstaffel*. Proceed with the execution!'

As Nicholas shuffled past the stiff, slowly twirling corpses, he stared at their features. He recognized many who had given him information in return for his favours.

An aged, half-blind prisoner with thick lenses in his glasses was on his hands and knees scrubbing the bare wooden floor in the S.S. Headquarters barracks at Dora. Nearby the teletype machine clattered. The busy office staff jostled past his mops and buckets. Occasionally they tripped, swore explosively and kicked him angrily in the backside. Other than that they tolerated him: it was the price of an immaculate-looking floor when he was finished.

If the headquarters S.S. had been more observant, they might have noticed that the prisoner was always scrubbing or mopping right by the teletype when the monthly execution list came in the first of every month from Gestapo Headquarters in Berlin.

This list was entirely separate from the routine shootings, hangings and beatings-to-death arbitrarily carried on each day by the local camp administration. These monthly orders covered civilian N-Ns and captured Allied secret agents assigned the N-N classification.

The decrepit old Green was more than a janitor. He was a key link in the prisoner government's intelligence chain. It functioned so well that often the Lagereldtester knew what Fourschner's new orders were before Fourschner did. As the teletype clacked out the November list, the janitor kept shuffling back and forth from the machine to a closet in the hall. He carried away pails of dirty water – and as much of the list as he could memorize at one time. Inside the closet he scribbled nervously with pencil stub on a grubby piece of paper. He hobbled back with pails of clean water to copy the next portion of the list.

When the floor was spotless, the old man made a final check, then gathered up his buckets and mops and cloths and carried them to the barracks porch. There he loaded them onto a handcart and as fast as his stick-thin old legs could take him, trundled off across the S.S. compound . . .

In less than forty-five minutes the list was in the hands of the president of the prisoner government.

There were few times in the politically and nationality divided concentration-camp society when prisoners acted as a single unit. The execution-list arrival was one of those times. Greens helped Reds. Politicals of the right helped those of the left. Germans aided Frenchmen; Frenchmen helped Germans. Nationality was forgotten for twenty-four hours as the men of twenty-six nations combined to defeat the execution order.

The *Lagereldtester*, conceding that it was impossible to save everyone on the list, had the awesome responsibility for determining who would live and who would die. Immediately the word was flashed to all *kapos* in the camp to alert the chosen ones.

Often the labour allocation *kapo*, by an administrative sleight-of-hand, instantly transfered a doomed man to a distant subcamp and arranged to have him 'lost.' If that wasn't possible, the man might be hidden in the space above the rafters in the barracks. When the S.S. came to take him away, the block leader would report him missing and the assumption would be that he had escaped. When the S.S. searched for him, the prisoners smuggled him from one barracks rafters to another.

When all else failed and the prisoner government wanted to save a highly valuable prisoner, they would try a body switch.

It was an extremely dangerous caper: the *Revier kapo* was charged with finding a corpse whose physical features closely resembled those of the doomed man, who was then stowed away in the rafters. When the S.S. arrived to haul him off, the hospital *kapo* produced his 'corpse' for them.

Or at least he tried.

If he failed, Fourschner arbitrarily added many more names – starting with his – to the Gestapo execution list.

Nicholas' name clacked over the teletype in November.

Recalling the events of more than thirty years ago, Dr. Kahr says that Nicholas 'had a good relationship with the prisoners. They liked him. He was a very good man. He was very friendly and always full of good humour. He always had a smile. In him the other prisoners had a friend in the *Revier*.'

For Nicholas, the investment of a grin and a good word reaped a fantastic dividend: the *Lagereldtester* chose him as one whose life should be saved. He informed Dr. Kahr, who immediately transferred Nicholas to the *Revier* at Subcamp Rottleberode.[4]

---

[4]Dr. Kahr had saved several prisoners in this way. Nicholas was probably the last: Labour Allocation Leader Simon denounced the doctor to S.S. headquarters in Berlin for 'sabotaging' V-2 production by his over-solicitousness of the prisoners. Shortly afterwards he was punished by being transferred back to the Russian front. Later he was re-assigned to the Western Front. He was captured by the Americans and was in a POW camp until 1948. In 1947 he testified at the Nordhausen War Crimes trials.

Chapter Fifteen

Underneath a thick layer of snow the road to Rottleberode was a mirror of ice. The driver eased his skidding, groaning truck cautiously along its twists and turns.

In the back Nicholas and the other prisoners froze. They stamped their feet. Thumped their bare hands. The blood just wouldn't flow.

Their S.S. guards rubbed their gloved hands vigorously and shivered under their heavy greatcoats and frigid steel helmets. They muttered in monotones, expelling their comments in plumes of frozen breath.

The prisoners had been ordered to keep absolutely quiet. They huddled with their fears.

Nicholas was an N-N and knew well what the designation implied, but he was still stunned from the shock of hearing that his name was on the list.

He kept staring out at the winding road receding behind, every moment expecting a big, black car filled with Gestapo to come careening down upon them. His stomach quivered. It was the same old mixture of fear and excitement. The thrill of the chase – of being chased. If the car appeared, what then? He should have a plan. He couldn't just sit there and let them take him without a fight. He thought of jumping over the tailgate. Making a break for it. And then he thought of his footprints in the soft, beautiful snow, leading them directly to him. The coughing started again. He tongued a gob of phlegm over the tailgate and idly watched it arc into the snow, where it stained red when it hit.

Up ahead subcamp Rottleberode was coming into view. Nicholas could see the peaceful little steep-roofed village houses mantled with snow. In a few minutes the truck left the tiny farming community behind and now he saw an ugly, brick building with a tall chimney silhouetted against the blue of the sky. A factory.

As the truck moved closer he could make out the coils and strands of barbed wire. He saw the hundreds of tiny, square windows with missing and broken window panes. Scraps of wood and cardboard nailed across the openings. The pudding-bowl helmets. The zebra-striped sentry boxes. The pungent smell of carbolic.

The news that 'Dr. Johnny,' Dora's American doctor, had arrived in Rottleberode caused a stir. When he made his rounds on each of the three floors of the old factory, where 1,200 men were crammed like bananas in a crate, he was bombarded with questions. How did an American POW get into Dora? How was the war going? How soon before the Americans would liberate Rottleberode?

He was just as curious about them: how was the food? Who was the custody camp leader? Who ran the prisoner government? The Reds or the Greens.

The non-Communist politicals, they told him.

What kind of a camp was it? Bad – but probably better than any of the other subcamps.

What did they do in Rottleberode?

They worked in the Kohnstein. Marched there every morning. Marched home at night. They toiled in the northern section of tunnels, in a group that made airplane parts for the Junkers company.

It was like his first day at the Aristide Briand boarding school. Starting at the bottom. He would have to learn the ropes all over again – if he were not to wind up as one of the twenty-five to thirty corpses that they carried out of the *Revier*[1] every day.

---

[1] The hospital's inventory showed one sunlamp, one sweat box, one closet with medical equipment, one sick ward with twenty beds, and three prisoner-doctors.

How could you have thirty corpses in a twenty-bed *Revier*? By putting two patients in some of the beds, the two prisoner-doctors told him.

One of them, Fernand Maistriaux, was a qualified physician from Belgium.[2] Robert Gandar, the other, had been a University of Strasbourg medical student. They briefed him in detail.

With 1,200 prisoners, they told him, Rottleberode had reached capacity. If it stayed at that level, they could manage the daily sick-call and the long-term patients in the ward. In the dormitories the wooden, two-tier bunks had hardly any space between them. In some cases bunks touched so that three men were jammed into the space of two. There were no tables. They had to eat sitting in their bunks. No indoor latrines. Anybody found outside after lights-out – even to use the latrine – risked being shot, so they scrounged rusty cans and jam pots to piss in. They were always brimming over by morning, when the dormitories reeked of warm, steaming urine.

Conditions, said the Belgian and the Frenchman, begged for an epidemic; and it was only the grace of God that had spared them so far.

Early each morning, they continued, the 120 guards watched over them during roll call, then bullied them into formation and herded them off *einhocken*[3] to the Kohnstein.

It was a routine 6½ days a week with Sunday evenings off.

They returned long after dark, numb with fatigue, to an hour-long roll call, a slice of sausage and cup of soup that was little better than Dora's. They had no plates. No knives. They scavenged for old tins for their soup. Anything solid was eaten out of their caps.

[2]Dr. Maistriaux was a Belgian resistance leader and was branded 'Nach und Nabel' by the Gestapo as was Johnny Nicholas.
[3]Each man in a rank interlocked his elbows with the men on both sides of him.

The *Revier* was a section of the third floor partitioned off from the dormitory with scraps of cardboard. Its beds were always full of malnutrition, typhus, dysentery and tuberculosis cases. Medical supplies, they told him, were limited to a few sulphur and aspirin, iodine and some bandages improvised from cement bags.

They answered his questions about the *Revier* candidly. But beyond that, they volunteered little: any newcomer had to break through a solid wall of suspicion. And he, behind his big high-wattage smile, was sizing *them* up.

Maistriaux, the Belgian from Beauriang, had been in charge of the *Revier*, but he was flat on his back in one of the bunks with pleurisy.

He was finding out first hand how terrible the facilities were.

Gandar, the skinny Frenchman – he was as tall as Nicholas – had joined the underground and been captured at a town in south-central France renowned for its resistance – Clermont-Ferrand. His credentials looked good, but Nicholas knew that in a concentration camp nothing was what it seemed.

Also, Gandar spoke fluent German. The S.S. trusted him sufficiently to let him make occasional trips to Dora for medical supplies.

It seemed to Nicholas an exorbitant degree of freedom to give to a French underground fighter! Was Gandar what he said he was? Could he be trusted?

Gandar had his doubts about Nicholas, too.[4]

A few weeks after Nicholas arrived Subcamp Rottle-

---

[4] "Some of my friends told me that he was a Martiniquean who had been arrested for dealing in the black market in Paris,' says Gandar, who is now a professor of gynaecology at the University of Strasbourg. Even so, he found himself impressed by the big black man and drawn to him. He finally decided to confront him with the rumours and ask for an explanation. 'He told me on his honour as a naval officer,' continues Dr. Gandar, 'that he was indeed an American citizen, that he was on a secret mission for the Allies and that for security reasons he could not tell me about it.'

berode got the worst possible news: it was getting a new camp commander – a master sergeant from Dora: Brauny.

Although Brauny had only been a roll-call leader at Dora, he'd had the authority to kill prisoners with his bare hands. As commander of an entire camp he would have the final say over life and death for every prisoner and S.S. man in Rottleberode!

There was a special formation of prisoners and guards the day the handsome little sergeant took over. When the roll-call leader finally dismissed them with the customary '*Mutzen auf!* . . . *Mutzen ab!*' Nicholas walked back to the factory, feeling Brauny's eyes boring into the back of his neck.

That night he couldn't sleep. His bunk was in the *Revier*. It wasn't the rasping and moaning of the patients that was keeping him awake. It was Brauny.

Nicholas felt naked without Dr. Kahr on the premises. There was the terrifying possibility that any night he'd feel somebody grab him, wake and find Brauny standing over him, gloating. He knew he had to keep hating him or he would start fearing him. And he began to dwell on the kick between the legs . . . the pain spreading out to his throat . . . warming his anger, melting his fear and ramrodding him with an uncontrollable thirst for revenge.

Weeks passed. Brauny still hadn't exploded upon him. He hadn't seen the commandant.

Was it possible that Brauny had gone soft?

It looked that way: a notice appeared in the bulletin board in the Prisoner Orderly Room that Brauny wanted volunteers for a camp symphony orchestra! Christmas was coming, said the notice, and Kommandant Brauny wished to encourage the prisoners to put on a programme for the holy season! Volunteers would be excused regular duties for rehearsals!

Could this be the same Brauny? The sadist who'd lashed

men on the *Bock* until he was exhausted? Who'd beaten prisoners to death with a piece of cable?

What a goddam laugh! Did Brauny think a few Christmas carols were going to make anybody forget? No, not that. The end of the war was near. Even diehards like Brauny knew the Third Reich was *kaput*. The sly bastard was taking out insurance – trying to come across as an artist, an intellectual and a humanitarian now that the Americans and Russians were about to close in.

The official German broadcasts were piped full blast over the public-address system at Rottleberode. All day long they kept boasting of massive Allied defeats and the skillful, strategic withdrawals by the German armies.

All day long Nicholas lanced carbuncles the size of small melons. In went the lance's blade, spurting pus three feet across the ward. When he squeezed out the contents there were holes large enough to put a baby's fist in.

Many had arm and leg bones laid bare by oedemas.

Few instruments were sterilized because water was almost unobtainable. There was one pair of scissors. No cotton batten. The tiny supply of clorethyl had to be kept for major surgeries. This meant that lancing carbuncles and scraping oedemas had to be done without anaesthetics.

They held the suffering patients down forcibly while the crude work was done.

At night men dying of dysentery, tuberculosis and pneumonia had risked everything to go outside the factory into extreme cold to use the latrine. Nicholas scrounged empty oil drums and located them at the far end of the ward. Many of the wretches were so feeble that they fell in. They had to be fished out and cleaned off. The job couldn't be done properly. There wasn't enough soap and water, and even if they recovered from one disease, they stank like shit and were treated as if they had leprosy.

A small hut outside the barbed wire was used as a morgue.

With the *Revier* continuously packed beyond capacity,

there were always seriously ill men out in the crowded dormitories, where Nicholas, Maistriaux – often sick himself – and Gandar worked exhausting hours taking temperatures, checking respiration and pulses and carting away the dead.

Just the sight of Nicholas, stiff-backed and formidable, in his white jacket and pants – they were always clean – and the 'Helf Arzt' red brassard on his upper arm, recharged the prisoners' ebbing hopes. And on the long, chilling Sunday nights that winter he ambled through the packed factory building shaking hands, bantering in several languages, performing like a politician up for re-election.

It was almost as if he was determined to live up to the larger-than-life reputation which had preceded him to Rottleberode.

The Rottleberode Symphony Orchestra[5] performed its Christmas concert. It was impossible for Nicholas to comprehend, yet there it was. The bunks on one of the floors were pushed into the corners and a space cleared for the musicians and a Christmas tree. The candles were margarine threaded with string. The presents: cigarettes and pieces of bread wrapped in chalk-covered paper.

With tears in their eyes the prisoners sang their songs of love and hope.

From beyond the barbed wire came the sounds of the S.S. guards, singing the hymn which all over the world symbolizes the hope of mankind, 'Silent Night.'

Stille Nacht! Heilige Nacht! Alles schlaft. Niemand wacht. Nur das traute hochselige Paar – Holder Knabe in lockigem Haar Schlaft in Himmlicher Ruh, Schlaft in Himmlicher Ruh...

---

[5] It was formed and conducted by a prisoner related to Chopin's mother, a Pole named Marian Krzyzanowski.

Rottleberode's share of the prisoner hordes being evacuated from Auschwitz and Gross-Rosen was 500 seriously ill prisoners, raising the camp's prisoner population to 1,700. They avalanched into the *Revier*, swamping it.

With them came their S.S. guards. Calloused, incredibly brutal. They bruised, flogged and beat, adding to the swamped sick-call lines.

And the second tragedy that January of 1945: Corp. Maischein, Dora's S.S. medic, was assigned to Subcamp Rottleberode as 'camp physician!'

He immediately posted the order he'd become infamous for at Dora: no Jews admitted to sick call or to the hospital!

Almost immediately after Maischein assumed his duties, he began charging healthy, gold-toothed prisoners with defying sanitary regulations. He then ordered the Lagerschutz to take them to the *Revier* for an injection 'to prevent them from catching disease.' Minutes later they were dead and Maischein was carefully inscribing a false cause of death on their death certificates.

The tiny stove glowed in the centre of the *Revier* floor.

It was after midnight. From his bunk among the sick Nicholas stared at the stove. The dull pain in his chest was keeping him awake at night. He was coughing more and tasting blood in his phlegm.

In a few days March would be gone. Almost all the briquets for the stove had been burned up; spring was still a long way off. How long would the sixty dying men jammed into the little cardboard-walled cubicle last? Within a week most would be in the mortuary – and their beds would be loaded with replacements.

He thought about his wild scheme to let his friends in Paris know about what was going in the tunnels; how for months it had consumed his life. Moved to Rottleberode, he was even further from the British agent at Buchenwald. And now Kahr, his one and only possibility, he'd learned through the grapevine, had been sentenced to the Russian front as punishment for pampering prisoners at Dora.

He saw again the twisted faces at the ends of the nooses – and the convalescent slips that had hanged them fluttered through his insomnia.

Why hadn't the Gestapo come for him? It had been four months. He'd seen *Kommandant* Brauny a few times, but always at a distance. What had happened with the execution list? Why hadn't they put the finger on him? Was it administrative blundering? Or his mother's prayers?

One of the bunks began to creak and shake. It was Janek, the Pole with a temperature of 104 degrees and an awful skin eruption on his face. Open sores with a liquid draining from them. It was erysiphelas. Highly contagious.

The Janek incident is still remembered by former inmates of the Rottleberode concentration camp. If Nicholas himself had penned the last act of his career as a prisoner-doctor in the final, incredible weeks of World War II, when Nazi Germany was crumbling, even he might have shrunk from such a self-aggrandizing tale.

Janek, oozing the virulent serum from his sores, became so delirious that he went berserk in the *Revier*, savagely attacking the other patients. It happened in the middle of the night. Nicholas had to subdue him with a punch to the jaw because he knew Janek would endanger the others if he weren't isolated. He slung the unconscious Janek over his shoulder, talked his way out of the building by telling the S.S. guards that the man had died from the dreaded typhus, and put him in the morgue temporarily.

Next morning the story going around was that Janek was dead. When the drunken Maischein heard that two prisoners had left the *Revier* without his permission, he erupted like a volcano. He ordered Nicholas to bring the body back to the *Revier*, and told him he would be shot for what he had done.

In the morgue overnight, Janek's fever had subsided.

271

When the other prisoners saw Nicholas carry Janek from the morgue and return him to his cot in the Revier, the word flashed around that the black American had brought a man back from the dead.

During the final days of March and the first few days of April the sick-call line wound all the way from the second floor of the factory out into the roll-call area. The *Revier* was jammed with sick two and three to a bunk until its cardboard walls bulged. Sick men stumbled off to their dormitory bunks to die in their own filth. Those less seriously ill huddled on the floor, poking their thin fingers into stinking vegetables, indifferent to an indescribable odour of decaying human and vegetable life.

On the afternoon of April 4 a squad of S.S. stamped into the *Revier*. '*Alles aus!*' they shouted. 'All out!' They went from bunk to bunk, hammering the sick with their rifle butts and prying them out on to the floor. '*Mach schnell!*'

'Prisoner No. 44451, Hospital *Kapo*,' said Nicholas, reporting to the S.S. squad leader. 'What's happening?'

'Never mind, *schwartze!*' snapped the soldier. 'Everybody out! You, too! Move!'

His throat went dry. He remembered Maischein's threat to have him shot. All the strength drained from his legs.

He and Gandar and some other prisoners helped carry the sick down the stairs and out on to the parade ground.

When he got there, he saw that the one hundred or so prisoners who normally worked in the camp were already assembled. It was close to evening roll-call time; he knew that at any moment he would hear the distant shuffling of the 1,700 slaves returning from the Kohnstein.

On the far side of the roll-call area he saw *Kommandant* Brauny dressed as if for a parade, with several officers and NCOs around him.

One of them was Maischein.

272

This is it! thought Nicholas. They're finally going to do it! They're going to make an example of me!

Chapter Sixteen

It was cold and drizzling rain.

Nicholas had waited a half hour and nothing had happened – except that he had exhausted all the possibilities of escape. If the sons-of-bitches thought he would simply stand there while they drilled a hole in his head or slipped a rope around his neck, they didn't know Johnny Nicholas. He had no weapon – only his bare hands – but he'd take a bunch of them with him. Brauny first. Then Maischein. Then whoever else got in his way.

But nothing was happening and it was getting dark.

He heard the clop-clop of wooden shoes in the distance! The prisoners returning from the Kohnstein. Finally he could see the first prisoner contingent wheel at the gate and march into the parade ground. The wind carried the revolting smell of their exhausted bodies.

The guards barked out orders. The prisoners assembled in formation around Nicholas, Gandar and the sick.

Nicholas braced himself as Brauny, flanked by a roll-call leader, emerged from the huddle of black uniforms and approached the formation.

It was now raining steadily, soaking their thin, tattered clothes. In fifteen minutes it would be dark.

'*Achtung*! *Achtung*! *Achtung*!' barked the roll-call leader through the slanting rain.

Brauny, the rain drumming on his long, leather great-coat, stepped forward. 'This camp is being evacuated!' he barked imperiously. 'It will form into four columns and

273

depart for Camp Dora immediately. Anyone who falls out will be shot. That is all!'

In the eerie stillness that followed Brauny's announcement, Nicholas could feel the coil of tension unwind. His confrontation with Brauny had once again failed to materialize. He swallowed and felt weak. The hearts of the 1,700 prisoners around him fluttered with fear. Evacuation? To where? To what?

On the sheet-size situation maps in Berlin at the headquarters of the S.S. junior officers reluctantly slid crimson arrows representing the U.S. First Division closer and closer to the Harz Mountains. To *Sturmbannfuehrer* Ludwig Wiegel, who was entrusted with security for slave-labour camps in that area, the time had come to implement the order of Deputy *Reichfuehrer* and Chief of the S.S. Heinrich Himmler that no prisoner be permitted to fall into the hands of the Allied armies alive.

Wiegel telephoned Major Fourschner at Dora and ordered him to send 'Commando 99' in action.

Commando 99 was a specially recruited detail of hardened Greens who had been promised their freedom if they would herd the Camp Dora complex's 40,000 inmates into the Kohnstein tunnel maze – then seal off the ends and leave them to die.

On the evening of Wednesday, 4 April 1945 the inhabitants of Dora and its thirty-one subcamps began to trudge by foot, horse-drawn wagon and truck toward the hill like innocent children returning home from school. The closer they got, the denser the traffic became until a colossal jam developed. Silvery American fighter-bombers, lured to the area by the dense concentration of men and machines, divebombed the roads and rail junctions, accidentally spraying the prisoner masses with machine-gun bullets. *Sturmbannfuehrer* Wiegel's grand plan for having Dora's victims converge in an orderly manner from the rim to the hub of the complex was crumbling into chaos.

274

The phone line between Dora and Berlin hummed. The air attacks were becoming increasingly heavy, Fourschner warned Wiegel, and lack of bulldozers and a shortage of explosives made it doubtful if the underground chambers could be sealed off as scheduled.

Wiegel switched plans: convey the *Haeftlinge* by all possible routes to central Germany for extermination at the camps of Bergen-Belsen, Neungamme, Ravensbrueck and Sachsenhausen.

All evening and into the night the 350 men in Nicholas' group, each hoarding his hunk of stale bread, marched toward Dora. Leading them was an old World War I retread with a limp, S.S. Sgt. Friedrich Teply. Riding herd on the flanks were armed S.S. Nicholas was with the sick in the rear of the column. They rode in hospital wagons pulled by fellow prisoners.

The night was full of droning Allied bombers and creaking wagons. The horizon flashed and the cannonade of exploding bombs rumbled through the darkness. Teply had ordered silence but the prisoners whispered excitedly: the end is near. The Americans can't be far away. Freedom's just around the corner.

After years of animal-like captivity the thought that they would soon be free made them slightly tipsy with excitement.

But they were sobered by the realization that they knew too much: the S.S. would murder them rather than risk letting the secret of the Kohnstein fall into enemy hands.

Teply's old injury began to slow him down. Every few miles he halted the column for a rest. When he did, the prisoners sank into the thick grass and heavy bushes by the roadside and escape conspiracies broke out like a rash. The Poles began plotting their escape. The Russians theirs. The Hungarians theirs.

Nicholas crouched in the darkness by the hospital

wagons and pondered the moral question of escaping. How could he? Who'd look after the sick?

For the time being he decided to stay with the column.

But others could wait no longer for their freedom. The sound of bodies brushing rapidly through the thick gorse. The guards' hoarse shouts. The type-writer clatter of the machine pistols and the crack of rifles. Then the ragged weeping of men leaking their lifeblood away somewhere in the dark.

Teply's pain got worse as he detoured the column off the road and through the rain-soaked woods and fields. If the pace was hard on the elderly S.S. sergeant, it was devastating to the feeble men pulling the wagonloads of sick.

By dawn the following day, Thursday, 5 April they stumbled into the little village of Niedersachswerfen, barely two miles northeast of Dora. It was a railroad junction which Fourschner had designated as a marshalling point for the massive exodus. Hardly had the sun risen above the horizon when the guards screamed: 'Achtung! Achtung! Air raid! Air raid!'

Nicholas glimpsed two aircraft streaking along at tree-top level. They had sneaked in unobserved by flying below the hills bosoming up on all sides. The main street of Niedersachswerfen was choked with thousands of prisoners being herded toward the village's railroad station. At the sight of the planes they halted and gaped. When the bombs erupted and bullets began zinging off the cobblestones, they dove headlong into the scanty cover of store doorways or threw themselves flat on the railroad platform, hoping its corrugated-steel roof would shield them.

Nicholas huddled in a doorway as bullets ploughed a furrow up the centre of the street past guards and prisoners alike pressed into the gutters. He thought fast; now was the best time to make a break: the guards had

276

their stupid faces against the ground. The bullets were still richocheting as he raised himself like a sprinter, waiting for the starter's pistol. In the utter confusion his instinct for survival overpowered his allegiance to the sick and dying.

Suddenly he was off and running.

He charged down the centre of the street, his body bent forward. He could hear an S.S. man screaming: shoot him! Don't let him get away!' His legs worked like pistons as he threshed along. A huge explosion ripped a crater in the street and blew him against the side of a building.

When he regained consciousness, the aeroplanes had gone and the S.S. were bullying and prodding the prisoners to their feet. Teply was hobbling around, trying to separate his column from the multitude of prisoners thronging the station.

The S.S. put the entire army of prisoners to work clearing the debris from the tracks.

'Hi, Johnny!'

Nicholas turned to see a prisoner he recognized from his days at Dora. He returned the greeting.

'Hey,' the prisoner called to a group of distant comrades. 'It's Dr. Johnny!'

The prisoners grinned widely, waved and called out: 'How've you been, Johnny? We didn't expect to see *you* here! Hey, Johnny, your pilots really gave it to the bastards, didn't they? How far away are your tanks?

The guards moved in with their rifle butts and broke up the impromptu reunion, forcing them back to work. Nicholas kept his head bowed, looking around when he had the chance to see if any other friends had arrived: maybe he could organize some of the old crowd into making a mass break before they were packed aboard the trains awaiting them.

He wondered what had happened to Gandar and

Maistriaux. He hadn't seen them since leaving Rottle-berode.[1]

He worked with the rest of Teply's contingent until mid-morning when more columns of Rottleberode prisoners shuffled into Niedersachswerfen. By that time the prisoners had cleared the tracks and the station platform, and a train pulling fifteen freight cars clanked slowly into the station. It came to a halt with the screech of steel on steel and the hiss of steam. Several of the cars were packed with prisoners. Voices called out from one of the cars: 'Johnny! Johnny! Hey, big Johnny!'

He recognized more faces from Dora but he couldn't call or wave back: The guards had herded his column into formation again and Teply and Brauny were standing too close. But his cronies in the freight cars got the message when he flashed the don't-give-a-damn grin for which he'd become famous.

Teply bellowed an order for his column to climb aboard. The guards badgered them to move faster. It was obvious they were anxious to leave Niedersachswerfen before the American planes returned. The prisoners, packed 120 to a car, found it impossible to sit down.

Without Gandar and Maistriaux, Nicholas had to look after the sick himself. Teply assigned him a detail to help transfer the sick from the wagons into two canvas-covered freight cars at the end of the train.

Brauny climbed into the cab of the locomotive with the engineer and the fireman, and the train slowly puffed out of Niedersachswerfen.

---

[1]Gandar and Maistriaux took charge of hospital cars on another train during the mass evacuation. Gandar recalls seeing S.S. Medic Maischein at Niedersachswerfen, but not Nicholas. When his train halted in Osterode, not far from Niedersachswerfen, Gandar escaped with two Russian prisoners during a P-38 strafing attack, and wound up in a worker's camp where he was fed some soup. A few days later he was liberated by U.S. troops. Maistriaux's movements can't be pinpointed. Gandar says the Belgian remained on the same train from which Gandar had fled. Maistriaux died some years ago.

For four days it chugged due north across the rolling Harz landscape, coming continuously under air attack.

Time and again it halted screechingly to avoid careening into bomb craters pocking the tracks. Each time the engineer was forced to back up for miles until he reached a railroad junction. Then he'd take off in another direction, hoping that the tracks would be clear. In the open cars, the tightly packed prisoners stood freezing in the chill night air of early spring. Without food or water many became so weak that they fainted and slipped down between the packed bodies in the shit-covered floor. There the remaining life was unavoidably tramped out of them by the feet of their compatriots.

It was an obscene way to die – and woefully ironic – when freedom was so close at hand. A bullet in the back was cleaner, and when the target-hungry Americans zoomed down with cannons belching and Brauny commanded the train to halt, many leaped over the sides and scrambled stiff-legged for the cover of the woods, the S.S. firing after them. It was hard for the S.S. and the Americans to miss at such close range, and when the planes had streaked off again, there were always zebra-striped bodies littering the embankment, oozing blood in the vapid sun.

The guards didn't take time to bury the dead. They'd roll a body over with the toe of a boot to make sure it was dead. If they saw an eye blink or a limb twitch, they'd stitch the body up and down with a row of bullets for good measure. Meanwhile the mass of prisoners, who'd been too terror-stricken to run and were huddled in the embankment, wondered when their turn would come. When the sound and smoke of the attack had dissipated, they'd docilely trudge back and board the freight cars like obedient sheep under the nervous barking of the guards.

Back in the two hospital cars, many broke into hysteria when the airplanes thundered down for the attack. They thrashed around on the straw-covered floor in their own shit like beetles wiggling to escape a foot. At night they

279

were frozen into immobility. By day the weak April sun bathed the cars' canvas covering, magnifying the heat inside and making the stench unbearable.

When they died, Nicholas could do little more than slide them to a temporary resting place in the rear of the car where he stacked them so as to make more room for the living.

There hadn't been an air attack in three hours and the train chugged along valiantly. Then Nicholas could feel it slowing down.

Another crater, he thought.

The steam hissed as brakes were applied. The wheels skidded on the tracks. '*Alles aus! Alles aus!* All out! All out!' shouted the guards.

Nicholas heard the pins snap back on the hinged doors of the hospital cars. He jumped out, sucking in great draughts of fresh air to purge his lungs of the diseased atmosphere inside.

They were in open country. The guards barked and the prisoners, stiff and wretched, painfully climbed over the sides and arithritically eased themselves onto the grassy embankment.

Nicholas glimpsed a familiar, stocky figure coming toward him. Maischein! He'd prayed that they had left the drunken bastard behind. Probably he'd arrived at Niedersachswerfen with the second, third or fourth column from Rottleberode.

'How are the sick prisoners,' Maischein grunted.

Nicholas gasped. Maischein worried about prisoners? Talking in a civil tone? 'Worse than yesterday, *Herr Rottenfuehrer*,' he responded, trying to conceal his shock.

'Your goddam American *Luft* gangsters,' growled Maischein. 'If it hadn't been for them we'd have been there days ago.'

He noticed that Maischein's eyes were heavily bloodshot and that he reeked of liquor: the swine was running yellow; changing his colour now that the American ground troops were closing in. Nicholas decided to risk it: 'Where are we headed, *Herr* Corporal?'

Maischein stared at him with the lugubrious expression of a bereaved St. Bernard. 'Are your pilots blind, for Christ's sake? Can't they see that this isn't a troop train?'

Unbelievable: the sadistic corporal turning humanitarian!

Maischein climbed into one of the hospital cars, his hands clutching his mouth and nose against the smell. He came out in a few seconds, ready to vomit.

'How long are we stopping, *Herr Rottenfuehrer*?' asked Nicholas.

'Minor track repairs,' muttered Maischein grudgingly.

'Long enough to make them some soup?' asked Nicholas, nodding toward the hospital cars.

Maischein stared at him. '*Ja*,' he finally muttered, 'but you'd better be ready when we pull out.' He turned around and shuffled back toward the head of the train.

Nicholas sent some of the walking wounded into the nearby fields to scrounge for potatoes while he lit a small fire.

'Herr Rottenfuehrer!' he called out.

Maischein stopped and turned.

'How about some hot water from the boiler?'

Maischein waved him forward to the engine where the fireman bled off some scalding water into a discarded meat can. Nicholas took the water back and sloshed it in and out of several other empty meat cans to give it some flavor.

He took the rusty cans into the hospital cars and tried to coax the steaming liquid into the dying men. Their stubbled jaws, hollow as the back side of a billowing sail, creaked as they tried to swallow. 'The Americans aren't far away now,' he whispered to them. 'You can hang on for a few more hours; you can make it ...'

Nicholas couldn't get over the change in Maischein. He knew it could only mean one thing: the Germans realized

281

that the day of reckoning wasn't far off. Maybe in the next village. Maybe over the next hill. He joked with the sick about Maischein's conversion to boost their will to live.

He watched the pencil rays of sunlight coming through the bullet holes in the tarpaulin. He wondered how he could warn off the American pilots if they returned. The hospital cars had no Red Cross markings. What a lousy shame: the poor bastards, lying in their own filth, could make it with just a little help.

He fumed at his helplessness.

Up ahead Brauny had pressed into service a huge gang to pull a section of displaced track back onto the railroad ties. They mobbed the bomb-cratered embankment like ants while the former Rottleberode commandant pranced nervously, squinting at the sky and demanding greater efforts.

Suddenly the fighter-bombers came roaring back again. Diving. Blasting. Zooming up. Barrel-rolling over and in again.

The prisoners scattered for the fields.

Nicholas peered from his cover to see bullets rip into the vacated wooden freight cars. The planes dived parallel to the length of the train. He saw the bullets kick up gravel between the tracks and heard them ping off the locomotive's steel hull.

The hospital cars were still full; there'd been no time to unload them. What a way to go, Nicholas thought. Killed by the bullets of your liberators. My God! Don't they know what they're doing? Don't the stupid bastards realize they're attacking a trainload of helpless prisoners? What had become of the much-vaunted efficiency of the American military – the well-oiled machine he'd seen perform so flawlessly when the U.S. Marines ruled Haiti?

Prisoners and S.S. alike pushed their bellies flatter into the damp soil. The planes' awesome, full-throated roar scared the breath from their bodies. The ground quivered under them . . . The engines whined higher in pitch as the pilots pulled up, jammed their throttles forward for the arcing climb into the blue.

'Sons-of-bitches!' screamed Nicholas. He wanted to stand up and wave something. His filthy old jacket, maybe. But the S.S. were all around him.

Again the Americans bored in, engines thrumming like the Mormon Tabernacle Choir holding a chord.

He slipped off his jacket . . .

The amphitheater of blue sky swelled with the roar.

He waved it cautiously. He got on his feet and waved. He squinted into the sun and saw the whirling sheen of propellers rush indifferently toward him.

He dropped his jacket and dived headlong into the embankment as the machine guns raked the ground around him, showering him with clods of sod and bursts of gravel.

To the Ninth Tactical Air Force pilots all trains looked alike, whether they were fleeing away from the traffic congestion around Dora or scurrying toward Nordhausen – the gateway to the fastness of the Harz – crammed with haggard troops and battered equipment: this craggy, mountainous area had been designated by Hitler as the storeyed 'Redoubt.' Here his threadbare legions were to reform around him as the 12th Army Group and hold out indefinitely.

Intelligence had passed the word to the briefing rooms of the Ninth Air Force fighter-bomber groups that in the area west of Nordhausen they'd find action.[2] For the

[2]The U.S. Air Force had 27 twin-hulled Lockheed Lightning P-38 fighter groups during World War II. The Ninth Air Force had three such groups, including the 474th – the only P-38 group to remain operational until the end of the war. The 474th took part in D-Day and in August, 1944, moved from England to the continent where it provided ground support for advancing troops. The group was in on the ill-fated invasion of Holland, the Battle of the Bulge, and the crossing of the Rhine. Because the Ninth's other P-38 groups converted to P-51 Mustangs and P-47 Thunderbolts prior to the war's end, it's virtually certain that the P-38s which raked the Dora evacuation trains were manned by pilots of the 474th Fighter Group.

283

hyperactive young pilots, many of them replacements fresh from the States and ravenous for their first taste of combat, the war was winding down. It could end any day. Any train was better than none at all, and it was so easy: the *Luftwaffe* had been swept from the skies.

At forward airstrips, many of them hastily evacuated by the retreating Germans only hours earlier, the Americans impatiently gunned their P-38s down the metal grid over soggy runways, climbed and vectored on Nordhausen with the throttles wide open. At 1,500 feet their targets resembled HO-scale models on a tabletop diarama. But at twenty-five feet, the recommended altitude for 'train-bustin,' there was something defective about a pilot's vision if he thought that Brauny's train was crammed with troops.

It was open season on trains; if there was fog on a pilot's goggles, it was the thrill of a kill before the final whistle.

Mieste is a small farming village and railroad junction about 100 miles north of Camp Dora. In normal times the train trip takes a morning or an afternoon. But because the American pilots had raked the tracks so thoroughly, Brauny's train took four days.

The fifteen freight cars rattled into Mieste station around ten o'clock on Sunday morning, 8 April. Inquisitive townspeople on the platform stared disbelievingly at the wasted, shrunken hulks in their filthy prisoner uniforms. The stench made them pinch their noses and keep their distance. They weren't hostile; some even waved – a little uncertainly. They said the Americans were reported to be eight miles away. Brauny passed the word among the *kapos* that there'd probably be a big battle with the Americans if they stayed at Mieste.

After four days virtually without food or water, the prisoners were near collapse. Packed solidly shoulder to shoulder, immune to the curiosity-seekers, they had become human logs. Yet escape was the fantasy that bedevilled their bovine resignation: Mieste had been bombed. Through glazed eyes they could see how close

284

the homes and stores were to the platform. A man could bound over the side of a freightcar onto the platform and disappear among the buildings in a flash – if he had the strength.

All day Sunday and Monday, Brauny's train waited in Mieste station – behind a long ammunition train. The little Rottleberode commandant, obviously compromised by the townspeople on the platform, was forced to relax enforcement of inhuman conditions. He ordered the prisoners out of their freight cars – a car at a time – to stretch their limbs. Meanwhile he dispatched guards to forage in town for provisions. They returned with small cans of meat, bread, some potatoes and vegetables, which they handed out to the prisoners.

But Brauny was taking no chances: he set up machine guns and spaced guards all along the length of the train.

During the loading at Niedersachswerfen the S.S. had intentionally mixed the nationalities in each freight car. It was the principle of divide and conquer. But during the ceaseless air attacks, with the frantic flights and returns to the train, the Poles had concentrated themselves in several adjacent cars.

They represented the largest single ethnic group among the approximately 2,000 prisoners who had survived the trip so far. During the two days in Mieste the Poles hatched an escape plan.

Nicholas, wearing his '*Helf Arzt*' armband, had Maischein's permission to move freely among the prisoners. While organizing details to collect the sick and dead from each freight car and carry them back to the hospital cars, he eavesdropped on the whispered conspiracies. Under a Polish naval officer[3] they were organizing themselves into three-man escape teams, hiding potato peelings in their clothes, bending empty food cans into pointed weapons, whispering encouragement to one another.

[3]His name was Wladyslaw Opiala; eighty-one Poles had agreed to escape under his leadership.

'Come with us, Johnny!' they pleaded. 'We can use a big fellow like you. Besides, you'd be handy when we run into your countrymen, the Americans!'

When he got back to the hospital car he thought: Goddamn Poles! There were three or four hundred of them. If they took off in a herd like that, Brauny's sharp-shooters would pick them off like ducks in a shooting gallery. No, if Nicholas was to make a break, he'd go it alone. It was cleaner, neater that way. Besides, who among them would be strong enough to keep up with him?

It was hard for him to distinguish the living from the dead in the hospital car. They were all matted with the same shit and straw. Motionless. Arms and legs poking out at bizarre angles. Pumpkin heads on stalk-thin necks. An occasional groan, a cough, a wheeze, a feeble fart that told him some still lived.

He was sure they were beyond help; it made no difference whether they got to the Americans or not. He could do nothing more for them. So why should he stay? Why didn't he tell the Poles he was coming along? And he still had all that incredible information about the rocket weapon. Wasn't it his duty to channel that into the right hands?

About noon another flight of P-38s zoomed down out of the Sunday sky and began ripping the Mieste railroad station apart with rockets, machine guns and the dreaded napalm. Guards and guarded stampeded from the platform, scurrying into streets, alleys and doorways. Moments later the ammunition train in front of Brauny's train took a direct hit. For an instant the entire village seemed to be engulfed in one gigantic explosion, punctuated by hundreds of smaller explosions as individual shells, mortars and rifle rounds went off.

Nicholas ripped off his conspicuous armband and bolted. He was plunging down an alley when the shock wave hit. It slammed him face first into the side of a building. He folded to the pavement, the wind knocked out of him. Pain stabbed his eardrums. His legs and arms had no feeling.

In the silence following the explosions he lay motionless.

He could hear groaning. Crying. Guards bellowing 'Halt! Halt!' The ripping sound of Schmeisser machine pistols. He struggled to his feet as the dense, black clouds began to infiltrate the streets of Mieste. He began running. His heart pounded wildly. His chest ached from the exertion. He was running clumsily, as if his arms and legs were tied to his torso with rubber bands. The numbness faded as the frantic exertion pumped blood to his extremities. He gradually regained control of himself. His head was now bent forward, his arms chopping rhythmically to the beat of his feet. His breathing had been fast and shallow; now he forced himself to take deep, regular lungfulls of air. He was on his way. He'd waited a long time for this. Nothing was going to get in his way.

He concentrated on pistoning his long legs faster and further . . .

He could feel the inactivity of captivity catching up on him. His muscles protested and his lungs began to hurt. He tried not to pay attention to them. The feeling of freedom was intoxicating. He was dizzy. The shop windows and store entrances of Mieste swept past him in a blur. He couldn't believe he was free. It was a dream surely – like those cruel delusions he'd had back in the dispensary at Dora; dreams of food, of women, of Paris, of sunswept beaches. The breath rattling in his windpipe convinced him it was no dream. Was the sound real? Or was it just a flash of lucidity in the hallucinations of the months and months of imprisonment? But dream or no dream, he wasn't taking any chances as he pushed his coltish limbs to their utmost.

He choked down the regurgitations of logic: how in the name of God was a black man to escape? The question had stopped him once before – but not this time. Keep

287

running! Which way? Who knows? Who gives a damn? Just run!

His body ached as he pushed himself faster and faster. It was paradoxical: the pain of exertion; the ecstacy of escape.

But he couldn't play games with himself much longer. He had to have a plan.

The cobblestones below him turned to grass: he was on the outskirts. As he raised his head up to get his bearings a huge explosion blasted his eardrums.

He felt a searing pain in his right leg, which suddenly went numb. Then he buckled, slamming full-length on the ground . . .

When he opened his eyes, he saw an overweight German farmer in knickerbockers standing over him. The man wore a Volkssturm armband and held a big blunderbuss with smoke curling from its barrel.

Nicholas explored his calf cautiously, then looked at his hand. It was covered with blood.

Limping heavily, he was escorted back by a posse of S.S.

Mieste station was in a shambles. Brauny bestrode the rubbled platform, raging like a tyrant: the smoking hulk of the ammunition train blocked the forward movement of his train. Huge, ragged chunks of locomotive and box cars lay all over the railroad yard. There was no way Brauny's train could detour around it. Back-tracking was also impossible: a second train of Dora prisoners had pulled in behind Brauny's train during the two-day stopover. He was boxed in.

Rottleberode's former commandant was now in charge of both trains – more than 3,000 prisoners – less five prisoners and seven guards killed in the raid and countless numbers of prisoners who had escaped.

Brauny wasted no time. He ordered Teply to line up the prisoners on the debris-strewn platform. Teply limped off, bawling commands. Meanwhile Maischein bustled down to the end of the train, clambering over fallen roof trusses and piles of rubble, and stopped at the hospital cars. He poked his head inside and saw Nicholas nursing his blood-smeared calf. 'Everybody out who can walk!' he shouted. 'Move!' He snapped the pins and the sides of the car slammed open.

Some of the sick couldn't move. Others, with agonizing slowness, raised themselves up and inched across the floor onto the platform. Maischein watched, saying nothing. He didn't rant and rave at the delay. He waited until all the walking sick had left the two hospital cars, then ordered them to join the main body of prisoners at the head of the train.

About two o'clock on Wednesday afternoon, 11 April, Teply marched out of Mieste at the head of approximately 3,000 evacuees from the Dora camps. The column was flanked by 150 S.S. guards; but Brauny, their commander, was absent. The column, inexplicably, was heading east – away from the Americans and toward the Russians! To make his work easier, Teply ordered them to march *einhocken*, and the prisoners locked arms.

They hadn't shuffled far when they heard several long, stuttering bursts of machine-gun fire coming from the train station to their rear.

The S.S. had executed the occupants of Nicholas' two hospital cars and all others too weak to march. When the smoke cleared over the orgy, some 200 lay dead, soaking in their own blood.

All day and night Teply drove the column eastward. He led it through woods and forests during daylight to avoid the predatory American pilots. At night he shunted them back onto the country roads. The prisoners were so exhausted that when Teply stopped to rest, many dropped off into a dead sleep and the guards had to batter them to get them on their feet again. Some escaped; most who tried were caught in a hail of bullets and left to die. The main body of prisoners, submissive from hunger and fear, lay sheep-like in the damp woods, listening to their racing heart-beats, the dying's feeble pleas for help, the boom of artillery to the west.

Would the Americans arrive in time? Where were the S.S. taking them?

Throughout Wednesday night they staggered and stumbled. And when the sun came up glaring in their faces Thursday morning, they prayed they'd be greeted by the brash young Americans Nicholas had told them so much about. But fate had something else in store for them. It had selected them for roles in a horrendous drama. It would be so macabre and so repugnant to the norms of civilized society today that the young German boys and elderly men who participated in it thirty-five years ago have managed to keep it out of the history books until now.

Brauny was anxious about the Americans too – but for the opposite reason. He'd spun out of Mieste on a motorcycle Wednesday afternoon shortly before the sick had been murdered. He'd been gone for hours; then he'd come roaring back to the column where he, Teply and Maischein had whispered by the roadside with heads bowed. Then he'd roared off again.

It was obvious to Nicholas that Brauny was scouting ahead for Teply and Maischein to avoid the infiltrating Americans.

He felt weak. His leg was badly swollen. He had lost blood continuously. His wound had become infected. But he knew the Americans were coming closer; that gave him strength.

The guards were growing panicky. Some were deserting in twos and threes; others were becoming trigger-happy, shooting prisoners on the spot for the slightest tendency to straggle.

By first light Thursday the artillery boomed closer and the guard force had shrunk to less than 100. As the webs of fog lifted and the sun turned the damp countryside to steam, the column slogged through soggy farmland. En route it wound past several large mounds under which local farmers had stored last year's beet crop. A dozen

Russian prisoners, insane with hunger, flung themselves from the column onto the mounds and scrabbled for beets like hogs hoking for truffles.

The guards sprayed them until beet juice and Russian blood had mingled indistinguishably.

The sun was high in the sky. The shuffling column was repeatedly crowded off the narrow country road by German military traffic streaking in both directions. At first the trucks, troops and equipment were nothing more than a blur to Nicholas. Gradually it dawned on him that some of the convoys he'd seen roar west toward the American lines fifteen minutes earlier were now barrelling back the way they'd come. Brauny's movements, too, he noticed, had also become more frantic and illogical: he was shuttling up to the column, then speeding off mysteriously every fifteen minutes.

To Nicholas it meant only one thing: the Americans were extremely close and the Germans were trapped. This was the word he passed around.

'They're through,' he croaked exultantly. 'I told you we'd make it!' Then, despite the pain hobbling him, he snapped his shoulders back further than they'd ever been. For a moment he was one of those uniformed figures in the Boy Scout hats striding down the Champs de Mar in Port-au-Prince. He smiled through his tears. It had taken years of charade, but in that instant he discovered what it really meant to be an American.

His surging spirits infected the others. Good old Johnny. He was their American. Somehow – if they stuck close to him – he would deliver them safe and sound into the hands of his countrymen.

It was close to midnight and the prisoners straggled eastwards. The horizon lit up behind them with the lethal illuminations of war. Thundering up out of the night came a truck convoy that almost ploughed into the front of the column. A thousand tyres squealed in a chain reaction as the lead truck's driver desperately manoeuvred to avoid crashing into the prisoners. A German officer in a motorcycle sidecar roared up to the head of the column.

'Who's in command here?' the officer demanded angrily.

Brauny saluted, stepped forward and identified himself.

'Who are these people and what are your orders?'

'Approximately 2,500 protective-custody *Haeftlinge* from Camp Dora being conducted to Gardelegen, *mein Kapitan*.'

'To Gardelegen? American patrols are in that area! Turn back! Or find yourself another route!'

The captain snapped a command to his driver, and the convoy rumbled off into the darkness.

The news crackled among the prisoners like fire in a hayfield: the Americans were in front and behind.

Would the S.S. bastards desert *en masse*? Nicholas wondered. Or would Brauny repeat the solution used with the hospital-car passengers back at Mieste?

The crackle of Brauny's motorcycle ripped the silence as he revved its engine impatiently, then again tore off into the darkness.

What now? Nicholas thought.

Teply ordered the column off the road and into the fields where they were to spend the night. Neither side slept for fear of the other.

Friday's dawn seeped in, blotching the night with pink, scrambled-egg clouds. Nicholas was completely worn out. He hadn't slept. His leg had pulsed painfully throughout the night. It had continued to swell, and his knee and ankle were frozen stiff. He struggled to his feet and gingerly put his full weight on the leg. His gasp of pain erupted into a deep, subterranean fit of coughing that ended in a slobber of bloody spittle.

He looked around, shivering, staring hump-backed at the human wrecks littered all around him.

Then he noticed something. No, he was just imagining things. He looked again, slowly, deliberately. He whispered to the look-outs. They couldn't really be sure until the sun rose a little further, but it certainly looked like it . . .

'The guards have gone!' screeched one of the look-outs, unable to restrain himself any longer. 'The bastards have taken off!'

Heavy heads slowly raised on stiff bodies. Was it a cry in their dreams? Cautiously they crouched, scanning the trees, bushes and shadows for the loathsome black uniforms and the pudding-bowl helmets.

'We're free, comrades!' screamed a Pole. 'We're free!'

The meaning slowly percolated through their shaven skulls. Many had been in concentration camps for eight years and the word freedom had lost meaning for them.

The hoarse command of one of the Polish leaders shattered their trance: 'Get back from the road! Quickly! They could come back at any moment! Hurry! Hurry!'

Like a colony of clumsy beetles they crawled off into the thick woods behind them.

The 405th Regimental Combat Team of the U.S. 102nd Infantry Division was 7½ miles away, saddling up for the attack on Gardelegen, an ancient town surrounded by a moat. From all the intelligence that division G-2 could gather, it promised to be a bloody battle.

Gardelegen, with its 14,000 population and its rustic life-style, was like many other farming towns in the Altmark region. The burghers worked hard from dawn to dusk. They esteemed the Biblical injunctions of thrift, frugality and charity and went to church on Sunday. But there the resemblance ended.

Almost ninety percent of Gardelegen's adults were registered in the Nazi Party. Most of the still-not-drafted fathers, husbands and sons were in the S.S. reserve forces – to be called up only in special emergency. There was scarcely a teen-ager who didn't belong to the Hitler *Jugend*, an organization of armed youth; and it was rare to find a male over sixty-five not proudly wearing the

293

armband of the *Volkssturm* – the German Home Guard – and toting an old shotgun or fowling piece in the crook of his arm.

For a town so devoted to Hitler, Gerhardt Thiele, thirty-five, was an ideal mayor. He looked cast for the part by a Hollywood studio. With his duelling scars on both cheeks, he was a university product with a refined arrogance and a messianic sense of mission in the Thousand-Year Reich. He was the Nazi incarnate, an archetype.

Thiele was far from being the common or garden variety of German backwoods *Burgomeister*, and his town bore little resemblance to the typically somnolent, politically apathetic burgs abounding in the province of Altmark.

Gardelegen also was a military town: the seat of a distinguished cavalry-training school for young cadets; a *Luftwaffe* field on the outskirts of town: and also a base where crack but surplus-to-requirements German paratroopers were re-mustered in assignments less glamorous than jumping into combat out of aeroplanes. Bursting at the moat with uniforms, the sentiments of its wives, children, parents and girlfriends, Gardelegen was a bastion of Nazism.

During 5½ years of war, when Gardelegen had been a training base far from the front lines and its fields planted and harvested without interruption, soldiers and civilians had worked well together. But with war rumbling on the horizon, enemy airplanes buzzing overhead with frightening regularity, and the eighty-eight-millimetre anti-aircraft pieces at the airfield blasting off for real and not in practice, the solidarity was magnificent. It was the real thing now, Mayor Thiele grimly told them. All Germans were soldiers. The prayer which every devout German offered nightly during the war had been answered: he was getting the opportunity of defending the Fatherland on the field of battle.

As the first rays of the weak April sun warmed the town's rooftops, the citizens were literally trembling in their boots, for a horrendous incident had been reported from the nearby village of Kakerbeck: about ten days earlier escaped slave labourers had ravaged the beet and potato dumps of local farmers, murdered them, then raped and killed their womenfolk. And now Commandant Brauny had arrived with the paralyzing news that 3,000 of the *Haeftlinge* animals were just $7\frac{1}{2}$ miles away from their town!

Burgomiester Thiele's most inflammable nightmare had been ignited. He lunged for the phone to alert city, county and party officials. Also the commandant of the cavalry school and the commanding officer of the airfield's infantry and anti-aircraft units.

Gardelegen was on red alert within an hour.

On Wednesday, April 11, the senior officer in the Gardelegen sector, *Luftwaffe* Gen. von Einem, had ordered that the threatening slave army on the horizon be brought to Gardelegen – one way or another.

In the woods the prisoners argued about what to do. Four hours earlier they had awakened to find the S.S. gone. Some wanted to move on, fearing that the Germans would come looking for them. Others wanted to stay put and wait out the end of the war. But most, paralysed by the sudden responsibility for their own lives, didn't know what to do.

It was a sound they had never heard in their lives. A high-pitched wail . . . up and down . . . up and down . . . and the hum of a light vehicle approaching along the nearby road.

The braver ones wiggled to the edge of the trees and peered apprehensively. Soon they could make out a small car. It was olive-drab in colour and bore a white star. From the front bumper flew a white flag. As the vehicle came nearer, they could make out four passengers in uniforms of the same olive-drab colour. They wore round helmets like Russians. The prisoners looked at one another and shook their heads.[4]

Sometime later prisoner lookouts shouted an alarm: German farmers were coming along the road! Now they were approaching the woods!

What should they do if the Germans tried to enter the woods?

Kill 'em!

No, counselled the older prisoners. Let's see what they have to say first.

The farmers, plumpish and elderly, ambled along as if they had nothing on their minds except a bracing constitutional on a splendid spring day. It was about eleven o'clock as they neared the woods and began calling: 'Are there any of you foreigners in there? Hello! Hello! We are friends! Hello! Hello! We understand there are some of you foreign gentlemen in our woods! Listen! You can all come out! The war is over! We are enemies no longer!'

In the woods were men who had entered the German system of mass brutality in 1937 with the establishment of Buchenwald; some who had been in it since the founding of Dachau in 1933. A decade of experience had taught them a knee-jerk reflex of disbelief to German offers of civility and kindness.

'It's a trap! Kill 'em! Kill 'em!' they shouted.

'Wait!' said the others. 'They have no guns. They are old men. As long as we have our knives, we have them at our mercy. At least let's hear what they have to say!'

Several prisoners were appointed to go forward and speak with the German farmers.

[4]Later they would learn that it was a jeep of the 405th Regimental Combat Team, its siren going full blast like a police car racing to the scene of a crime. Inside were staff officers en route from a forward combat post to Gardelegen to parley over surrender terms.

They identified themselves as members of the *Volkssturm* from the village of Wiepke. The war was as good as over, they said, and the Americans would be in the area within twenty-four hours. They asked if the prisoners had heard the siren: it was the American commander on his way to Gardelegen to arrange surrender terms. 'So, it is all over, gentlemen, and there is no need for us to be enemies any more. Please come with us. We will give you food and water, and you will be safe. There are many diehard S.S. wandering around. They are liable to shoot you on sight. You will be safer with us.'

Some prisoners couldn't believe it could be so easy.

The German farmers waited patiently as the newly freed men argued among themselves. 'How do we know you're telling the truth?' they demanded. 'How do we know it's not a trap?'

The *Volkssturm* farmers shrugged. They said they had come by themselves. They had no weapons with them. They would provide them with food and water if the 'foreign gentlemen' would accompany them to Wiepke. They would also provide horse-drawn wagons to transport the sick and injured.

The prisoners wrangled among themselves, fear tugging them one way, hunger and thirst pulling them another.

'Don't waste time. There are many S.S. in the area who haven't heard that it's all over. They're still hunting people like you and shooting them.'

As Nicholas and the army of prisoners hobbled into the picturesque hamlet of Wiepke, apple-cheeked farm girls tossed words of welcome and early-spring flowers at them. In the narrow street they found several horse-drawn wagons drawn up for the sick.

On the remaining trek to Gardelegen the morning was radiant with sunshine but strangely calm. The boom of artillery had stilled; it had been replaced by the peaceful chirping of birds, the shuffling of 3,000 pairs of feet, the creaking of the wagons and the clopping of the hooves.

297

Already some of the prisoners had shed their wariness and were laughing and chattering excitedly. But the bulk of them hunched along mutely behind the farmers, ready to grab them as hostages and flee to the woods at the slightest sign of danger.

Nicholas loathed his useless leg. If he hadn't been shot at Mieste he'd never have gone along with the *Volkssturmers*; he'd have taken off on his own long ago. He wasn't buying their hospitality no matter what: you couldn't trust a German.

The Dora contingent stretched in a column-of-fives for almost three-quarters of a mile along the narrow, country road from Wiepke to Gardelegen. About noon on Friday they began arriving at the high fence surrounding the airfield on the outskirts of Gardelegen. They were tense, alert in their exhaustion, suspicious: for years their reflexes had been conditioned to fear, brutality, scheming and lies. Freedom was too rich a meal. Their minds couldn't digest it. On the other side of the fence German parachute troops in mottled-green smocks and black-garbed S.S. lazed and laughed in the sun, totally disinterested in their arrival. Yet the prisoners knew they were still the enemy. With the buxom farm daughters and wives clustered at the airfield gate, however, it was palpably different. They smiled widely and cooed welcome as if being paid by the word while they loaded the famished men with food and drink. Gradually the black bread bulked in their shrivelled bellies. The hot coffee swilled down their gullets, melting their tongues and thawing their profoundest reservations.

'Anyone see Wradke?' called out a Pole who was wolfing down a chunk of Braunschweiger sausage.

'I saw him just after the Americans plastered us a Niedersachswerfen,' another prisoner muttered, his bearded cheeks ballooned with bread.

The Pole elbowed his way through the pack of filthy, stinking bodies toward the man who had responded. 'Was Wradke okay?' he asked anxiously.

298

The man shook his head. 'He got it in the chest. It didn't look good.'

Conversation hummed as the prisoners' sense of security increased. They exchanged experiences, inquired about missing comrades. Some collapsed in the noonday sun, stunned by the fact that they were free again, wondering about their wives, their children, their parents. Some wept. A few prayed.

Nicholas sat hunched by the fence, hugging his injured leg. He had never felt so weak. The hot food threatened to seduce his self-discipline. It tempted him with sleep. But an animal instinct told him to keep his leaden eyelids from shutting.

Suddenly he noticed Brauny[5] on the other side of the fence! He tensed. The little bastard who had kicked him in the balls. He felt anger pump through him.

It didn't look like the same Brauny! This version was lounging against an airport building. His tunic was open at the neck. A cigarette dangled from his lips. He wasn't wearing the high-peaked hat that made him look three inches taller.

Nicholas forgot his pain as he rolled around in his pleasure centres the fantasy of smashing the life out of Brauny.

He also noticed Ripka, a well-known Polish prisoner from Rottleberode. What was *he* doing among the Germans on the other side of the fence? And why was he wearing a German Army jacket?

He wondered about Ripka: the Pole hadn't left with the first of the four Rottleberode columns. So how had Ripka gotten to Gardelegen *ahead* of the first column? There were more than 40,000 prisoners in the Dora camps.

[5]During the Nordhausen trials, Brauny was asked by Lt. Col. Berman whether he had ever ordered Johnny Nicholas killed. 'No, I did not give the order,' the Nazi replied. Berman continued: 'You say you last saw him alive at Gardelegen?' Brauny replied: 'Yes.' (File 000-50-37, Volume 34, U.S. vs. Kurt Andrae et. al., Federal Records Center, National Archives, Suitland, Maryland.)

During the evacuation, with the P-38 attacks and the chaos, they had become separated. Maybe Ripka's column had run into fewer problems than Nicholas' column. That had to be it. And the jacket? Well, some German soldier had shucked it to avoid being shot at by the Americans and Ripka had grabbed it to keep himself warm.

But a rifle didn't keep a man warm. Ripka had a rifle!

'Hey, Ripka!' someone called over the fence. 'Ripka!'

The Pole, who'd been Rottleberode's resident clown, recognized the caller but seemed reluctant to come over and renew acquaintances.

'Hey, Ripka! What the hell are they going to do with us?'

Ripka unshouldered his rifle and held it in both hands low by his side, as if to shoot from the hip. He wiggled his trigger finger suggestively.

The banter at the fence froze. Then someone snickered nervously, reminding them what a wag Ripka had been. Sure, that was it: the big Polack's crude sense of humour.

Nicholas was suspicious; something definitely wasn't right: nobody in his right mind would give an idiot like Ripka a weapon!

He stared through the fence. He saw many buildings clustered around the airport. There were barracks, administrative brick buildings, large warehouses, corrugated steel hangars. Military vehicles were parked here and there and German military personnel loitered untidily in little groups.

For the organization-happy Germans, he reflected, it looked out of character.

He now noticed more figures in German tunics. A very tall one looked as if he could be the twin brother of another Rottleberode inmate, Wladyslaw Musielewiez. Holy Christ! It *was* Musielewiez!

Somebody hailed Musielewiez and he came over to the

fence. He was asked what was going on. Musielewiez explained his column had arrived in Gardelegen the day before (Thursday). Because his mother was German, he said, they'd put him in a special detail and tossed him some surplus German Army clothing to replace his filthy rags.

'They're being pretty nice to us,' he told his comrades. 'They gave me an old suitcase to put my stuff in. They fed us and put us up in a barracks with a bunch of young army paratroopers.'

What barracks?

'Not here,' replied Musielewiez. 'In town. About fifteen minutes walk from here. An old cavalry school barracks. Yes, they're nice to us. There wasn't enough room for us all in the barracks, so they put the rest of the fellows in there.' They looked where he was pointing and saw a large, brick warehouse about a half mile away on the top of a small knoll, all by itself.

'And you know something?' continued Musielewiez enthusiastically. 'That bastard Brauny! He even gave me his cigarette butt. And he told me he's going to turn us all over to the Americans tomorrow morning.'

'Did you check the butt for rat poison,' growled one prisoner.

'Oh God! We'll be really free tomorrow!' sighed a less cynical prisoner, making the sign of the cross.

About two o'clock in the afternoon Brauny ambled up to the fence. He was very casual, still bare-headed and smoking. He began chatting as if nothing had ever happened between him and the prisoners. He told them he'd been asked to break the column up into manageable groups. He asked them to pass the word around for all *Reichsdeutsch*, or German-born, prisoners to fall out and form into a separate formation.

The German-born prisoners meekly complied.

'*Volksdeutsch!*' said Brauny, now addressing himself to all prisoners born outside Germany of German parents. When the *Volksdeutsch* group had formed, he called for an *Eindeutsch* formation; that is, prisoners with one

301

German parent. Finally it was the turn of the *Stamm-deutsch*, those who could claim some German ancestors. Throughout the proceedings, Nicholas noticed, the diminutive sergeant's manner was conspicuously lacking in its old, strident authority. Did it mean that Brauny had been chastened by the thought of the Americans on the outskirts of town? Or was it a big act?

When the four 'German' groups were culled from the column, Brauny swung open the gate, admitted them to the airfield and they were marched away. Nicholas remained outside the fence with the chaff – Russians, Poles, French, Belgians, Hungarians, Czechs, Norwegians, Greeks and other nationalities.

A thought curled his guts: if they were free, why were they still taking orders from Brauny? Why did they meekly jump when he spoke – as if they were still behind barbed wire?

About fifteen minutes before twilight Brauny appeared again at the gate. He swung it open and pointed to the building atop the knoll that Musielewiez had indicated a few hours earlier. 'Some of you will have to spend the night up there,' he said expressionlessly. 'The rest will be going into town.'

None of the non-Germans wanted to be first through the gate.

'We'd like to get you bedded down before night,' said Brauny persuasively.

Finally one prisoner stepped forward, then another and another.

Brauny and some other S.S. began counting them as they came through the gate.

When approximately a thousand had entered the airfield, Brauny swung the gate shut.

He led them slowly along a narrow, worn path up the gentle, half-mile incline to the desolate warehouse. Once there, he slid back two massive doors and beckoned for them to enter. They hesitated, just as they had at the airport gate, peering nervously into the dark, cavernous

302

interior. Brauny pointed to the floor. It was covered with a thick layer of straw.

'Get a good night's sleep,' he said. 'Then you can join the Americans in the morning.'

Still they clumped hesitantly around the threshold.

In the deepening dusk an airplane engine droned in the distance.

The mass of men fidgeted on the shoulder of the knoll.

The aircraft came nearer. When it was overhead, its engines thundering, there was a burst of machine gun fire: an impatient S.S. man, who had materialized seemingly out of nowhere, had fired a few rounds into the ground behind the prisoners to hurry them up. Some of the men screamed. Others flung themselves to the ground.

'Take it easy,' shouted one prisoner.[6] 'Don't panic. They're firing at the American plane. Not at us!'

While the sound of plane's engine faded, the prisoners sluggishly collected their thoughts. At the same time shadowy figures began to ascend the knoll behind them. Some were paratroopers. Some S.S. troops. Many were young Hitler *Jugend* and elderly *Volkssturm*. All were armed – including Ripka and twenty-four other former prisoners wearing German Army tunics over their concentration-camp stripes.

'The war is over for you,' coaxed Brauny, waiting patiently for his Judas goat.

First one prisoner, then another, shuffled into the warehouse . . .

Brauny slid the big double doors shut, slammed home the bolt and signalled to the armed men slowly advancing up the knoll. Silently they trod, fanning out around the warehouse, setting up heavy machine guns at its four corners.

It was Friday the Thirteenth.

---

[6]He was Zbyszek Waltz, one of the Polish leaders among the prisoners.

Chapter Seventeen

From roof chinks and spaces around the doors a dim light suffused the musty gloom of the warehouse, known locally as the Isenschnibbe barn. Otherwise it was almost completely dark inside. There was little room for the thousand prisoners to move around. The farmsweet smell of straw gradually surrendered to the pungent stench of unwashed bodies. In the close atmosphere the temperature rose, incubating the rancidity. The ragged men grew drowsy and in twos and threes they sank into the soft, two-feet-deep straw.

The race of events of the past nine days since they'd left Dora had made their minds reel. The days and chilling nights of being packed into the freight cars. The terrorizing air attacks. The endless night-time marching. The full-busted maidens and the roses. The plump farm wives with the food and drink. It was too much.

They fought sleep.

After years of concentration-camp life each man had developed his own early-warning system. It could not be switched off merely because the war was over and was no longer needed.

The sweating men began to remove their caps and jackets, uncovering their ugly bodies. The glut of Gardelegen cuisine had bloated their shrunken bellies. Combined with the heat and the soft straw it created an irresistible narcosis. Their eyeballs rolled leadenly. The drug of long-forgotten comforts numbed their animal wariness, and twenty minutes after they'd entered the barn most were asleep . . .

They heard the scraping sound of a bolt sliding back. A door screeched open to create a large rectangle of subdued, evening light. Some of the prisoners stirred and looked up to see a youthful S.S. sergeant step into the rectangle. He held something in his hand – and he smiled. He tossed the object into the barn, struck a match and jumped back through the opening, slamming the door shut. It was approximately seven p.m. Twilight time. A curtain of flame erupted from the straw. The smell of gasoline wafted backward through the barn. Several voices shrilled the alarm. Instantly the thousand men exploded to their feet, screaming and shouting.

Many of the prisoners closest to the flames were Russians. They assaulted the fire with old blankets, shirts and jackets, shouting '*Urra! Urra! Urra!*'

When the flames were beaten out, they stood dazed, coughing from the acrid smell of burned straw and gasoline fumes.

'They're going to kill us!' shrieked one man.

'No,' protested another, 'it must've been an accident!'

A third man swore violently. 'I saw the bastard strike the match!'

'Let's get the hell out of here!' screamed a demented prisoner.

'The war's over!' persisted another man. 'The Americans will be here tomorrow!'

While the argument raged, one half of the sliding door moved back a second time. Like moths drawn to the candle's flame all eyes fixed on the rectangle of fading light. Something round, shiny and flaming sailed through and smashed on the ground with the sound of splintering glass. Instantaneously the front half of the barn was engulfed in flame.

'*Urra! Urra! Urra!*' shrieked the Russians, wading into the flames again, blankets and jackets flailing, feet

305

stamping the curling tongues of fire illuminating the terror on their wizened faces.

'They're trying to kill us!' came the screams. 'They're going to murder us all!'

The mass of Russians, now joined by other nationalities, gradually beat back the flames. With the final tuft of burning straw stamped out, any lingering doubts about what *Burgomeister* Thiele had in mind for them had gone up in smoke.

The Isenschnibbe warehouse was 146 feet long and 65 feet wide. It had brick walls and a tile roof. Along the walls on the inside were thick vertical logs supporting the rafters. There were four exits – all sealed off by fourteen-foot-high, sliding oak doors.

How were they to get out?

A thousand men had a thousand suggestions: Climb the vertical logs and break through the roof? Charge one of the doors *en masse* and smash it down? Wait until the Germans open the door again, then stampede through and attack them with messkit knives and forks?

The silence was suffocating. Occasionally it was broken by prisoners coughing from the thick, black smoke. In the deepening gloom they huddled in panic. Minutes ago they were delirious about being free; now they were back in the nightmare of their years of slavery. Or worse – imminent death by fire.

Was this to be the end that they had staved off so long? How many times before had they stood on the precipice only to snatch themselves back – by cheating, by conspiracy, by any means that had insured they would breathe another breath, see another tomorrow?

Outside, *Burgomeister* Thiele stood by his large, black staff car in the rutted field. In his additional capacity as *Kreislieter* of Gardelegen County he had circled the barn with more than one hundred uniformed men and civilians.[1] He and his various troop commanders gathered around the car some distance from the barn with S.S. police dogs yelping and snarling on short leashes.

Inside, the silence dragged on. The prisoners crouched, their fists spastically clutching knives and forks and rocks. Far away artillery rumbled. If only the Americans would hurry! Where are they, Johnny? Where are they? They strained to listen. An order shouted. A cough. A footstep. The jingle of equipment. Anything that might help them guess the enemy's intentions.

Even if they could overcome the teen-age boys in men's uniform and bowl over the old men, there were still the diehard S.S. out there. And yet even if they did break out, what then? The Isenschnibbe barn was set down in the starkly flat Altmark meadowland. There'd be nowhere to hide. The nearest woods were hundreds of yards away: the machine guns would cut them down before they took more than half-a-dozen long strides.

Unless it was dark.

Now it was nearly eight o'clock and almost dark. The European twilight was already growing faint through the cracks in the roof tiles . . .

The bolt rattled again.

The mass of men poised like a single muscle reflexing, clutching their crude weapons, ready to rush through.

[1]The troops surrounding the barn came under the nominal command of a *Luftwaffe* general named von Einem, who was made responsible for the defence of Gardelegen. He had approximately 1,200 troops under his command. In addition he controlled the 101st Airport Maintenance Co., the 73rd Panzer Grenadier Replacement and Training Battalion, *Wehrmacht* military police units at the airport and the Cavalry Remount School. On April 11 an unidentified German general was ordered to Gardelegen. Allegedly he announced to his staff that the prisoners were to be assembled in the Cavalry Remount School and shot, but because the school was in the centre of the town and their execution would be too public, it was decided to kill them in the barn. The contingent of troops around the barn seems to have been token units from von Einem's command, plus those from Master Sgt. Brauny's S.S. guard force, Thiele's *Volkssturmers* and Hitler *Jugend*, and twenty-five prisoners who agreed to don German uniforms and participate in the massacre.

The door slid back and a heavy black object flew through the opening.

'Grenade!'

They dove into the straw. The grenade exploded with a deafening blast, scattering white phosphorous throughout the barn. Men caught in the blizzard of light screamed as the sticky globs of molten chemical melted through their flesh. A hundred tiny straw fires broke out instantly, expanding rapidly into a single island of flame.

The snapping sound of blankets and jackets flailing and the screams of horror were joined by the chatter of machine guns and the crack of rifles. The bullets ripped through the oak doors and tore into their bodies. Droves of them keeled over and fell face first into the flames. Discipline collapsed. Courage melted.

The Isenschnibbe barn was an *Inferno* beyond Dante's imagination.

Inside, the flames feasted on the gasoline-saturated atmosphere. Groups threw themselves uselessly against the massive doors, ripping their nails to blood on the tough German oak. They slapped themselves and wriggled as if ravaged by an itch as the fire licked their bodies and melted their hair. They milled around in epileptic ferocity in a thousand different directions. Their wailing and keening was from the abyss of hell. It was matched in intensity only by the guffaws of Thiele's troops outside. Men with flames dancing on their backs clawed up the vertical logs for the refuge of the rafters. Instantly knots of them fought one another to be next. Where the straw was thinly spread the fire was weakest. A mad rush to these sections bowled over the weak and sick, who were trampled into early, merciful death.

For an incredible instant the frenzied helter-skelter of bodies became a stampede in a single direction that rammed a door and dislodged the bottom of it from its metal track. Sweet country air was sucked in through the opening and the insane men exploded out of the barn with their clothes and hair aflame. The machine guns and rifles hosed them. The blue-and-white-striped bodies fell heavy-headed like wheat before the scythe. But still they came, for those in front couldn't push back against the crazed forward momentum of those in back, and layer after layer was cut down on the threshold until they were piled six bodies high.

Crouched behind the mound of corpses the terrified prisoners peered out into the darkness and sobbed. Freedom was so near but yet so far . . .

During the lull Thiele's troops crawled up to the dislodged door, flicked meathooks into the piled-up bodies and dragged them off into a nearby slit trench fifty feet long.

For almost three hours the conflagration raged. Bullets ripped through the smoke-choked air. Grenades thundered in the confined space, smashing eardrums. *Panzerfaust* (bazooka) rounds tore through the doors. And still the fear-crazed, life-hungry wretches lunged through the gap left by the detracked door – only to be mowed down in their tracks.

On the opposite side of the barn a clutch of prisoners had cleared the straw away from behind a doorway and were attacking the earth floor with messkit knives and forks, trying like frenzied animals to burrow a hole. Their ribby torsos expanded and contracted wildly as they competed with the hungry flames for oxygen. Dozens surrendered to their frantic exertion and lay down and died gasping. They slipped to the floor as if the intense heat had melted their minds and bodies. Their cries and groans, once a vehement chorus of protest and prayer, became weaker and weaker, and the screams of anguish were now like the plaintive keening of lonely seagulls on a dark, wintry night.

One of the few survivors, Romuald Bak,[2] a Polish

[2]Bak now owns a motel in Brampton, Ontario, Canada.

prisoner from Rottleberode remembers that horrific night:

'It was awful. Many people went crazy. They were screaming, praying, swearing, doing everything you can imagine. It was like hell... I lay down by a door because there were some holes between the bottom of the door and the ground and I could get fresh air. I had a knife and I started to make a bigger hole... It was easy inside because the floor was dirt, and I was thinking that I could dig a hole and get down below the level of the machine-gun fire. I raised myself up momentarily and I felt as if somebody had punched me.' (Ed. Note: A bullet had gone through his jacket and shirt without touching him.) 'Then a body fell on top of me. Then another body... I realize I can get out under this door, but outside the pavement is ashphalt. So I cut piece after piece. Finally I broke my knife and I thought everything is over for me. So I called out in the Polish language: "Is anybody still living? Has anybody got a knife?" There were still some people living and they gave me two knives. The first one broke – on the hard asphalt – so I was really careful with the last one while I'm making the hole bigger and bigger. Finally I came to the point where the hole is big enough for my head to go through – but not my ears. And I was thinking: ears are nothing. You can live without ears. At that very moment some grenades exploded close to me, blowing everything in my eyes and I was thinking: this is the end of the road. But after a few second I was still living...'

'I'd got this hole under the door large enough for my head to go through. After the grenade was thrown, I couldn't get my head through.' (Ed. Note: the blast had dislodged the door so that its bottom edge was now resting on the ground *inside* the barn.) 'I gave up. I was very tired. But a few minutes later a grenade exploded in the same place. Again I was stunned, as if someone

310

had hit me. But I regained consciousness and I noticed that the door was completely loose on the bottom and still hinged in the metal track on the top. I saw that if I catch the door and pull back, I can crawl under and get out without any trouble. But I waited for some time because it's hard to make a decision to go now or not. It was almost dark and I observed that the clouds were very low. There was no moon, no stars and there was a lot of smoke. I was getting a picture of the situation. I could see the Germans immediately outside. About ten of them, maybe fifteen feet apart. I called out in Polish: "Is anyone still living. If there is, come here. I have a hole here. Maybe we can get through." Three guys came. We waited for a while, then we decided to go.'

'I pulled back the door and the first one got out very smoothly. The second one got out very smoothly. I told the third one to hold the door so that I could go. He said no and got very excited. So I told *him* to go next, so I held the door and he got out. But it was bad for me: if I had to hold the door for myself, and if it slid back while I was going under it, it would pin me and they'd catch me. I needed someone to hold the door and there was no one. I'd have to do the whole job myself but I couldn't make a sound because they were very close, maybe fifteen and thirty feet away. But somehow I got out. When I did, I bumped into the body of the third man out. He was dead. I crawled a little bit further and bumped into another guy. I whispered in his ear: "You got a knife?" There was still lots of noise – grenades and guns. The massacre was in full swing . . .'

I started to roll along the ground, metre after metre, and I went through the line. I got dizzy, so I stopped for a rest and I turned and looked back at the barn. The shooting and all was beginning again, and the barn looked bad. There were many holes in the roof and the doors. There was a lot of light inside. It was just like hell, and I started to run away . . .'

311

On Saturday morning, April fourteen, *Burgomeister* Thiele's car wheeled into the area followed by a truck loaded with elderly *Volkssturmers*. He and several S.S. jumped out and approached the barn, cans of gasoline in their hands. The previous evening, close to midnight, when all sign of life had vanished from inside, he had inspected the corpses. Several were not completely burned and he ordered them doused with gasoline and re-burned. This time, however, the gasoline wasn't necessary. The sickly sweet smell of roasted human flesh, imprisoned by the low clouds, hung in the air. It seared their nostrils when they entered the barn.

The inside was thick with smoke and soot. The massive logs were deeply charred. Some still glowed red; others had gone out and were powdered with thick, grey ash. Patches of straw still smouldered. The floor was littered with a thousand flame-swollen bodies in bizarre positions, arms and legs grotesquely intertwined. The glowing phosphorous had eaten through clothes and flesh, laying bare bone. The flames had licked the skin off exposed surfaces and men who'd clutched their faces in protection had pulled their hands away, shedding panes of skin that stuck to their fingers like the web in a duck's foot. Some of the bodies were piled high in mounds: those on the outside were charred beyond recognition. Those on the inside were less badly burned. Here and there men had died alone, the terror on their faces frozen in rigor mortis. And by the open door the machine-gunned bodies lay stacked like human sandbags. Under the bodies the straw was matted with heat-blackened blood and stiff with excrement squeezed from their terrified bodies.

Thiele nodded to one of the S.S. NCOs.

The NCO shouted: 'If any of you are still alive, you will be taken to hospital and given food!'

A few clods of charcoal groaned in response.

The S.S. man beckoned to a *Volkssturmer* with a machine-pistol who walked around riddling the still-alive bodies . . .

Thiele barked orders. The elderly farmer-soldiers broke into two groups. One group began enlarging the fifty-foot-long burial trench prepared the day before; the other started dragging the bodies outside and laying them in neat rows by the western wall.

In the distance cannon and artillery explosions of the advancing Americans rumbled a descant to the macabre funeral rites. '*Mach schnell*!' barked Thiele nervously. '*Mach schnell*!' He watched his men perform their grisly task for a few minutes, then walked briskly to his car and drove off.

They dug and dragged until 5:50 p.m. when the crackle of American M-1 rifles and the thrum of Sherman tank engines panicked them into flight.

At seven o'clock on Saturday evening, exactly twenty-four hours after the massacre had begun, the 462nd Regimental Combat Team of the U.S. 102nd Infantry Division moved cautiously through the narrow streets of Gardelegen. From alleys and doorways uniformed Germans appeared, their hands in the air and were shunted off to 102nd's POW cages. On Sunday morning, April 15, the 2nd Battalion of the division's 405th Regimental Combat Team was engaged in a routine search of the area surrounding the Gardelegen airfield. Company F trudged up the long, gentle hill to the knoll which overlooked the town. Remaining wisps of smoke led them to the blackened, brick warehouse standing alone on the expanse of meadowland. There was little cover and they moved cautiously from bush to bush and tree to tree. F. Company's point man made it to the barn's northwest corner. He was joined by another. And another. The squad peered around the corner and saw a trench, three feet deep and stretched to 180 feet by the *Volkssturm*. It was full of loose, freshly dug earth bristling with scrawny arms and legs. Close to the wall was the neat formation of bodies – blackened, blistered, shrivelled, bowed, bullet-ridden – staring up at the dusk with empty eye sockets. It was too much for the 102nd's combat-toughened veterans: most turned pale with rage; some wept openly.

Divisional commander Maj.-Gen. Frank Keating still had a war to win. Speeding across Altmark at thirty-five or forty kilometers a day, his objective was the Elbe River, many miles to the east of Gardelegen, and he couldn't afford to spend much time or manpower on the town. Like the dozens of towns he'd captured, Gardelegen would have to be held by small token forces until the rear-echelon troops moved in to secure the area.

But on that Saturday morning he and the assistant division commander Brig.-Gen. Alonzo P. Fox, had noticed a mysterious cloud of black smoke on the horizon and idly wondered what was burning. On Sunday morning the report came back that F. Company had found something which demanded the attention of the division's intelligence officer, Lt.-Col. Charles Parsons. He, in turn, ordered Capt. Horace Sutton, a 25-year-old, red-headed New Yorker, to investigate.

'When we saw the column of smoke,' says Sutton, who commanded the division's Counter Intelligence Corps detachment, 'we didn't know what it was. So I took part of my group into town.'

'Nobody was there – no troops of any kind, but plenty of civilians.'

Arriving with special agents of his CIC detachment, Sutton got the word that a German force of so-called Werewolves[3] was going to try retaking the town. That meant that the investigation of the smoking barn would have to wait.

Before the Werewolves' attack materialized, however, Sutton got a response to his frantic radio call to division for help. The 462nd Regimental Combat Team detached a force to scout the Gardelegen area and left Sutton with

[3]Roving groups of armed teen-agers stiffened with tough S.S. combat troops and used as guerillas behind Allied lines.

314

some heavy-duty protection until the full division had moved up.

'They were three hairy hours in the afternoon,' he says, 'when we didn't know what was going to go on. Then these (U.S.) troops came in, and I would judge it to have been ... seven o'clock at night. Then, when the rest of my own CIC detachment came in, we set up command post in a hotel in downtown Gardelegen, sort of like a *gasthaus*, as I remember it. A *bierstube* downstairs and a few rooms upstairs. Just a little country hotel ...

'We went out to this area and saw a large barn. It was still smoking.'

'Inside there were black, charred bodies everywhere, including one that I remember vividly. It kind of reminded me of Rodin's "Thinker," with chin on hand and absolutely frozen – if that's the right word – burned to a crisp. Immolated in that position.'

Capt. Sutton and his CIC detachment had two immediate objectives: to find the perpetrators and to dispose of the remains of the barn victims. Working through the Gardelegen civilian police chief, he issued an all-points bulletin for *Burgomeister* Thiele and two other county officials believed to have been the ringleaders and began questioning other townspeople.

While the interrogations were going on, Sutton's men organized all the local civilians and marched them to the barn. The reason for the object lesson, he explains, was that 'when you went through Germany at that time and you were looking for Nazis,[4] you found no one. No one had ever belonged to the Nazi Party. There was complete disavowal of everything. So when you asked about (the barn-burning) incident, nobody knew anything about it.'

For six days following the grisly discovery troops under the New York captain's command marched apprehensive groups of men, women and children out of town along the dusty half-mile to the barn. As they stood there, weeping

[4]Sutton carried with him a list of more than 150,000 'wanted' Nazis.

hysterically and covering their eyes, they heard a grim-faced German-speaking American officer tell them: 'You supported and encouraged the regime responsible for this hideous scene.' 'We didn't know! We didn't know!' they protested tearfully. But the officer pointed to the houses of Gardelegen only 300 yards away. It would have been impossible, he told them, for their occupants not to have heard the screams of the dying.

On April 19 Sutton[5] posted a proclamation in the town square ordering fifty of Gardelegen's wealthiest Nazi Party members to report with shovels to his HQ the following morning at 0800 hours. When the appointed hour arrived, more than 200 stood self-consciously in the street. Flanked by seven tight-lipped GIs from the 327th Engineer Combat Battalion with M-1 rifles, they were escorted to the barn. Twenty minutes later they were exhuming the bodies from the shallow graves and digging new deeper graves.

At the sight of the grisly remains many wept hysterically. The tears may have been from sorrow or compassion. But they may also have come from fear that the enraged Americans would do the same to them. To a man they turned their heads away, blaming others for the slaughter. A GI guard asked one of the gravediggers, a Nazi Party member since 1934, if he'd known about the mass murder. Yes, he had, the man sobbed, but he'd been powerless to interfere.

The infuriated American guards worked the townspeople until they were sweating. Sutton had assigned affluent Party members to unearth the bodies and lower-level Nazis to dig fresh graves. When they saw the grotesque expressions and twisted positions of the dead, practically every man dropped his shovel and protested that he was too ill to go on. One of the guards, Corporal Steve Bonham from Wytheville, Va., cursed them

[5]Today he is an associate editor and noted travel writer with the Saturday Review of Literature in New York City.

roundly and lashed them with the only word German he knew. '*Arbeiten!*' he shouted, pointing toward the trenches with his rifle. 'Work!'

They exhumed 574 bodies and carried 442 from inside the barn. Of the total of 1,016, only four could be identified by appearance. American grave-registration officers were able to identify 305 by matching still-legible tattooed prisoner numbers with a partly burned prisoner list that was found. But 711 of the corpses couldn't be identified.

When the Gardelegen gravediggers quit that night, they brought home with them a smell of death that has lingered in their town more than thirty years.

Among the cameras snapping off the dreadful record that day was that of U.S. Army Signal Corps Sergeant P. R. Marks of Swayzee, Ind. Like the others, Marks was lured by the fascination of revulsion. He'd gotten there as the bodies were being removed from the barn. His camera scanned the cavernous, blackened interior, the remnants of mess gear, the caps and clogs, the precious soup cans – the pathetic personal items hoarded by desperate men through years of hell.

His shutter also clicked on a lone, charred figure lying by itself on the straw-littered ground. The corpse was on its back. The heat had grossly charred it. It looked as if, in the final agony of death, the victim had grabbed a handful of shirt-tail in the front and had been trying to rip off his clothes when death overtook him. There were bullet holes in the head, chest and stomach.

But it was the corpse's facial features that arrested Marks' attention. They were those of a Negro. That was impossible, of course, except that it tied in with reports Sutton had received from townspeople that they had seen a Negro among the hapless slave labourers.

317

Chapter Eighteen

Although Concentration Camp Dachau had been liberated more than two years earlier, the stench of death still clung in the air. By the time World War II ground to an end, it had become synonymous with brutality and death. An estimated 70,000 of the 206,000 prisoners who had passed through the camp, eleven miles northwest of Munich, had been eliminated.

Now, on the hot, sunny morning of 7 August 1947 the black uniforms of the S.S. were gone, replaced by the olive drab of the U.S. Army. The proceedings were officially labelled Case No. 000-50-37. Through the *Jourhaus*, or arched entrance building, to Camp Dachau passed the American prosecutors and former Dora inmates and S.S. men who would play key roles in the drama about to unfold.

Chosen as the courtroom was the former S.S. sessions hall. It was a low-beam-ceilinged room with floor-to-ceiling windows, heavy dark drapes, globed lamps, and Kleig lights strategically spotted to aid in filming the proceedings for posterity.

A large American flag was tacked to the rear wall. Beneath it was a raised platform built to seat the seven-man tribunal. They were all senior U.S. Army officers. Directly beneath the tribunal table sat court reporters. A table at the tribunal's right was reserved for the chief prosecutor and his three assistants. Behind them on a riser were the earphoned interpreters. The prisoners were seated at the left of the tribunal on a four-tiered grandstand, and in front of them was a table for their U.S. Army and German civilian attorneys.

Witnesses and observers occupied rows of seats directly facing the tribunal.

'Hear ye! Hear ye!' barked a U.S. Army staff sergeant. 'By authority of Allied Council Law No. 10, promulgated 20 December 1945 and signed by the Commanders of Occupation of the Republic of France, the Union of Soviet Socialist Republics, the United Kingdom of Great Britain and Northern Ireland, and the United States of America, this honourable tribunal is in session, Colonel Frank Silliman III[1] presiding. Please be seated!'

The scuffling of feet and creaking of wooden folding chairs quieted down in the once-dingy hall, refurbished and repainted to camouflage Dachau's bloody past.

An Army clerk read the opening statement: 'A special military court appointed by Special Order No. 144 Par. 17 dated 5 August 1947, Headquarters European Command, APO 207-1, met at Camp Dachau, Germany, on 7 August 1947 at 0915 hours as directed by the president thereof . . .'

Thus began the trial of the United States of America vs. Arthur Kurt Andrae et. al. Andrae and eighteen other Germans were 'each individually accused of murder' of inmates at Camp Dora and its sub-camps where – the indictment read – 15,000 prisoners perished between August 1943, when Dora was established, and April 1945, when it was liberated.

The accused, including four civilians and fifteen former S.S. officers and NCOs, each heard the charges lodged against him and impassively entered a 'not guilty' plea. Most were fresh from the hairclippers of vindictive U.S. Army barbers at the POW stockade and they represented a motley crew with their baggy cast-off GI clothing. None of them appeared the least bit remorseful. Former S.S.

---

[1] Col. Silliman was from Philadelphia, Pa. The other six members of the tribunal were Col. Joseph W. Benson of Los Angeles; Col. Claude O. Burch of Petersburg, Ind.; Lt. Col. David H. Thomas of East Palestine, Ohio; Lt. Col. Roy J. Herte of Floral Park, N.Y.; Lt. Col. Louis S. Tracy of Hartford, Conn.; and Maj. Warren M. Vanderburgh of Boston, Mass.

Master Sergeant Andrae, 47, and former S.S. Capt. Heinrich Schmidt, 35, even sported ridiculous-looking Hitler moustaches. Strings around the defendants' necks suspended six-inch-square cards bearing their numbers starting with '1' for Andrae and progressing alphabetically to number '19,' the civilian Willi Zwiener, a stern-faced man of 39 who parted his hair in the middle.

Appointed to defend the accused were Maj. Leon B. Poullada of Los Angeles and Capt. Paul D. Strader Jr. of Salem, Ohio, assisted by three German civilian lawyers.

Heading the opposition was a tough, overweight criminal lawyer from Boston and New York, Lt. Col. William Berman. His chief assistant was Capt. William F. McGarry of New York City.[2]

The trial preliminaries took slightly more than $2\frac{1}{2}$ hours, and court recessed at 1150 hours for lunch. Promptly at 1330 hours Berman bellowed: 'The prosecution calls its first witness, Cecil Jay.'

Jay, the short, wiry, 41-year-old carpenter who had built the bunks in Dora's tunnels, was a native of Plymouth, England. He had served in Germany with the British occupation forces after World War I, from 1925 until 1931, with the Third Battalion of the Royal Tank Corps. After his discharge he returned to England – only to return to Germany shortly afterwards to marry his German sweetheart in the town of Springe, near Hanover, where he settled down and raised a family.

Jay retained his British citizenship, and when the war broke out in 1939 he was interned in Buchenwald as an enemy alien.

When construction began at the Kohnstein in mid-1943 he was among the first prisoners to arrive from Buchenwald. During questioning by Berman he pointed a finger at

[2]The authors traced Berman to Westbrook, Me., where by the late 1960s he was a partner in a local law firm. It was this initial contact that was to trigger a chain reaction leading to other sources in the search for Nicholas. Berman died in 1973.

one of the nineteen defendants, Brauny, as one who took prisoners to the Dora quarry and shot them – or had them shot. Brauny, already suffering from Hodgkins Disease, of which he was to die in 1950 while in Landsburg prison, trembled more than usual as the cocky Briton relished his day in court.

An hour and forty-five minutes after taking the stand, Jay was describing his evacuation from Camp Weida, which was one of Dora's outlying subcamps, when Capt. McGarry – then heading the prosecution – interjected a question: 'Did you know a person named Johnny Nicholas?'

Jay: 'Yes.'

McGarry: 'What was his nationality?'

Jay: 'He was a nigger. He told me he was an American, sir. I spoke with this man almost every evening.'

Thus was Johnny Nicholas' name first mentioned in the Nordhausen trial. But over the next several months, scores of witnesses – Nazis and former prisoners alike – would recount their associations with him.

Among the key witnesses was a Pole, Wincenty Hein, a lawyer from Krakow.

Hein, then 38, was little more than a skeleton on 11 April 1945 when the U.S. Third Army armour clanked into the emotional ambush of Nordhausen. A walking encyclopedia on the subject of the Dora complex, he was a natural target for War Crimes Investigation Team No. 6822 when it jeeped into Nordhausen nine days after the end of the war.

The Pole had been recovering from a heart attack when team investigator Capt. Robert G. McCarty had arrived at the camp. Hein volunteered to show McCarty around. As they entered the barracks which the S.S. had used for a prisoner post office,[1] they discovered a large, wooden

---

[1]Lots of mail from home and food packages from the International Red Cross arrived at Dora for the prisoners but it was systematically plundered by the S.S. There was never any out-going mail.

filing cabinet containing five-by-seven-inch index cards. While thumbing through them, Hein came across one made out in the name of Nicholas, Johnny; Nationality American; Prisoner No. 44451.

Hein, a clerk for a time in Dora's *Revier*, had known Nicholas well. In a sworn statement that day (13 May 1945) Capt. McCarty questioned Hein as follows:

'Tell me all you know about Johnny Nicholas, who had Prisoner No. 44451 and whose card you have found.

'Johnny Nicholas, A Negro, appears from the card to have been born on 5 October 1918.[2] He was an acquaintance of mine at the camp. He was very conspicuous because he was the only Negro there. He was a tall man about six feet in height. I met him the first part of November 1944, although he had been present at the camp for a period of what he told me (was) one year prior thereto.

'At the time I became acquainted with him he was working as a doctor in the hospital (at Dora), and I worked for him. He told me that he had parachuted from a damaged American plane into France, where he had a secret-service assignment to perform in the nature of setting up a medical practice in Paris, communicating information to the Allies.

'He also told me that after landing he was arrested by the Germans but later released, and that he did establish in Paris a medical office which he operated for a period of time that he did not disclose to me.

'I did not ask Nicholas what sort of plane he was in at the time of parachuting into France or in what part of France he landed.[3] I never questioned his story, although he indicated to me that his original arrival in

[2]The date was in error: Nicholas was born on 20 October 1918.
[3]Nicholas confided to another inmate that he had landed by parachute near Orleans.

322

France was prior to the entry of the United States into the European war...

'From Dora he was transferred to Rottleberode on the first part of January (1945), and that is that last I saw of him...'[4]

It was two years before Hein's provocative deposition was used. It was 1947 and most of the combat troops had left Europe; but the legal soldiers and investigators of the 7708th were still in business at Camp Dachau, sifting through the stacks of Dora documents for the upcoming Nordhausen trials. Berman came upon the deposition and logically concluded that the American Negro could be an excellent witness for the prosecution – if he had survived the war and if he could be found. Had Nicholas, he wondered, been one of the lucky ones freed by the Third Armoured Division troopers who had liberated Camp Dora? If so, where was he now?

Even after two years of peace, hunting for him would be a monumental assignment. Europe was still littered with millions of refugees, displaced persons and homeless POWs. The survivors of Dora had long ago commingled with these masses. Granted he was black; but where would one start looking?

Berman handed the impossible job to William J. Aalmans, a Dutch civilian[5] hired as an investigator by the 7708th. By interrogating former prisoners arriving at Dachau to testify, Aalmans discovered that the Negro American had been something of a legend at Dora. A

[4] At war's end Hein began amassing his own personal archives on Camp Dora. In Volume 36 of them appears a Daily Report for Camp Dora; in this report Nicholas is identified as a doctor from Boston, USA. Hein is a practising attorney today in his native Krakow.
[5] Aalmans, whose home was in Kerkrade, the Netherlands, also worked in the Dutch Resistance. He prepared a booklet entitled 'The Dora-Nordhausen War Crimes Trial.' He was last reported as serving in the Dutch embassy in Madrid.

323

painstaking investigation traced Nicholas to a Rottle-berode evacuation group that had made it to Gardelegen. There the trail ended. Eventually Aalmans obtained enlargements of the thirty-five-millimetre shots taken by Sgt. Marks of the blackened corpse inside the Isensch-nibbe barn. He showed the pictures to former prisoners who had known Nicholas.

Some were doubtful: the lips were too thick; the features not fine enough. And the body was too short.

But most nodded. Yes, it was Johnny.

The heat had been tremendous, bloating his features and shrinking his body. Besides, it was a black man's corpse, they insisted, and Johnny had been the only Negro in Dora – or in any other concentration camp, as far as they knew.

On July 18 Chief Prosecutor Berman drew up the Charge Sheet for the Nordhausen War Crimes Trial. On August 7 the accused fifteen former S.S. men, a German civilian engineer in charge of the V-1 and V-2 production in the tunnels and three German Greens shuffled into the assembly hall at Camp Dachau and took their places.

Berman launched into his opening statement:

'May it please the court . . . The trial which has begun has brought to the power of justice some nineteen individuals who participated in various capacities in the operation of Concentration Camp Dora – officially called Mittelbau – and some thirty-one subcamps. The evidence will show that the accused, as part of a common plans with others, subjected Russians and Poles, Frenchmen, Dutchmen, Belgians, Italians and Jews to indignities, tortures and to enforced slave labour in Dora and its subcamps. The evidence will show that among these people subjected to these crimes were prisoners of war. Among these prisoners of war were Italians and Russians, Frenchmen – and even one American . . .'

Among the nineteen prisoners were two of Nicholas' mortal enemies – Master Sergeant Brauny and Dora's custody camp leader, First Lieutenant Moeser.

Brauny sat righteously on the bleachers. He looked bored by the stinging indictments of Berman's opening statement as it was translated into German.

Besides the Englishman, what other witnesses would they bring against him? Who among the hundreds of malingering bastards he'd punished would show up to whine their groundless allegations?

He would have little chance, he told himself, if the black American turned up in the witness box. What hope would any German have fingered by an American in a U.S. courtroom?

But then, it occurred to him, the *schwartze* had been led into the barn like the other *Stucke*, hadn't he?

Chapter Nineteen

Blood sausage. Black bread. Steaming coffee. Like the notion of being free, it was too much for Nicholas to digest.

And broad-hipped farm girls built for comfort.

Amazing how a bloated belly dulled one's reflexes.

The prisoners lolled in the broad, sunswept meadow below the Isenschnibbe Barn, almost mesmerized by the abrupt change in their fortunes.

But to Nicholas it smelled. Who did Brauny think he was kidding?

Nicholas lay near the fence amid a huddle of his followers, clutching his shattered leg. Several men indebted to him for convalescence slips and more clustered close to him and blandished him with reassurance that the Germans would soon look after his wound.

'You kidding?' he mocked. He was furious with himself for being temporarily immobilized at so critical a time.

'We're free, Johnny! They'll fix us up,' his comrades insisted.

'You bet they'll fix us up,' he chided.

Lying in the sun for four hours had stiffened his leg. He tried flexing it and the pain curled the corners of his mouth. Inwardly he cursed his festering leg for costing him his independence.

Yet he had to play out the charade which he knew was expected of him. He smiled and volleyed the banter as he slowly manoeuvered himself to his feet. They tried to help him but he waved them back with his characteristic grin. 'Don't worry about me! Who's the doctor anyway,' he quipped. 'It's you guys I'm worried about. Brauny's up to something. We all know what he's pulled before.'

The debate went on.

He sent several of them back to the airport gate, where Brauny stood, to see if they could learn anything new. 'I'd go myself if it weren't for this,' he said, looking down contemptuously at his blood-crusted leg.

They returned later, armed with optimistic accounts of prisoners who'd arrived the previous day in Gardelegen and had been billeted overnight in the Cavalry Remount School with German soldiers. If *Stucke* and Germans had slept and eaten together without incident, the war had to be over.

Nicholas shook his head. 'You believe it,' he insisted, 'because you *want* to believe it. That's exactly what they want.'

He slowly got to his feet.

'Where're you going, Johnny?'

'To see Brauny,' he muttered, biting down on the pain. Then he grinned like a circus pitchman. 'I'll tell the sonofabitch I'll order the Americans to go easier on him tomorrow if he quits lying to us.'

326

They howled.

Waves of nausea washed through him as the effort of standing exacted its toll. 'Okay,' he said, grinning falsely, 'lead me to the little shit.'

They pointed him along the fence toward the gate leading into the airfield.

Between him and the gate hundreds of prisoners basked in the soft sun. He hobbled painfully through the crowd. Occasionally prisoners suddenly recognized him, grabbed him and pummelled him excitedly. He was intermittently ambushed by strange prisoners asking him for help for sick comrades. With all of them he maintained the same facade of insouciance, making light of his own wound and fighting the urge to fall flat on his face.

He was some distance from the gate when he heard Brauny call out for the *Volksdeutsche, Reichsdeutsche* and others to form separate formations. He knew now beyond any doubt that it was a trick. A monstrous deceit. The reflexes conditioned during his seventeen months of captivity were giving their signal full strength like a radio homing in on a transmitting frequency. But the poisons in his shredded leg had spread, debilitating his will to respond to the warning.

He leaned against the fence and hung his head. His heart pounded irregularly. His mind was fuzzy. He knew it was early afternoon; it shouldn't be getting dark so soon, he told himself. But the light was fading, and he realized that the blood poisoning had finally affected his eyes and his mind.

He felt a pair of human scarecrows, one on either side, helping him along, supporting him. It was like a nightmare, where the real is unreal. Soft voices in his ears reassured him he'd feel better after a good night's sleep; that he'd be with the Americans in the morning.

He told them they were all going to be killed. They soothed him as if he were a baby having a bad dream. He could hear Brauny's voice far behind them, as reasonable as he'd never heard it before, coaxing, persuading.

He had to save himself. The others had become deaf to reason. He struggled feebly against the bodies packed around him. He felt the fear of suffocation. The more he struggled, the harder they pressed against him and the dizzier he became.

They whispered to him, trying to calm him, as they continued up the hill. He stiffened with all the strength left in him, broke from his supporting comrades, slipped to the grass and wriggled like a blinded animal through the forest of legs.

He was jerked back to consciousness by a string of explosions.

He was in pitch blackness. He felt spongy dampness beneath him and realized that he was on the ground. He reached out and touched tree branches around him.

His head had cleared in the cool night air. The pain still throbbed but the grogginess had gone. And he could see again.

More explosions. He pivoted to the source of the sound and saw the barn across an open stretch of meadow about a quarter of a mile away. He saw the flames shooting through the roof. He heard the chatter of machine guns and the screams of the dying.

His mind shrieked for him to flee but the fascination of revulsion paralyzed him . . .

He pulled himself to his feet and hobbled deeper into the woods. Emerging on the other side, he arrived in open meadowland. The ground was sodden in stretches and the mud sucked loudly on his wooden clogs as he limped along. There was no moon. The clouds were low and heavy and he had no sense of direction. He used the continuous explosions and machine-gun fire from the barn as his compass, keeping the sounds directly behind him. He moved as fast as his wound would allow, reasoning that if he'd gotten away, others had too. Armed patrols and dogs would surely be hunting them.

He heard voices ahead. He stopped and listened.

Ukrainian voices. Ukrainian S.S., he thought. He crouched and winced with the pain of the movement. He moved forward frog-style with agonizing caution, listening intently. They didn't sound like S.S.

They were civilian workers forcibly drafted from the Ukraine as farm labourers, huddling in one of the pits used by German farmers to store potatoes. He identified himself as an escaped slave labourer from the burning barn. They told him they'd seen the massacre. They pressed some raw potatoes on him and told him that the area was crawling with German Army and *Volkssturm* patrols. He'd be shot on sight, they warned.

He thanked them, asked for directions and hobbled off into the night. When daylight came, he knew, his black skin would make it impossible for him to bluff his way to safety. He realized he'd have to travel at night. He slopped and slipped in his ill-fitting wooden shoes across the muddy meadow, rapidly becoming exhausted. He no longer had the limitless stamina that had carried him so far. It meant he had to find a haystack before dawn.

The Ukrainians had pointed him toward the advancing Americans. He was holding steadily to that course when the click of a rifle bolt made him freeze. He contracted into a crouch, barely noticing the pain because of his intense concentration. Ahead he could see glowing cigarette butts.

For a long time he remained motionless in that position.

'Who goes there?' snapped a German voice. 'Come here!'

He wanted to flee but he knew they'd easily outrun him and gun him down. His only hope was to stay put. He longed to take the weight off his throbbing leg. He began to ease back the way he had come, slowly, gradually, a few inches at a time. Eventually he stood up, stretched and unlimbered his tortured body. He stood motionless in the dark for several minutes, then hearing no response from the direction of the trees, he hurried away.

When he felt he was well out of earshot, he circled around the trees until he was once again on a bearing toward the American lines.

He was cold. The bottom of his pants were soaked from the rain-sodden meadowland. He was shivering with pain and fatigue. He had lost all concept of time. It was still pitch black, but he didn't know if it was close to midnight or near dawn.

He lumbered along, panting heavily. His eyes had become accustomed to the dark and he was able to make out the bulk of some farm buildings. Where there was a farm, he thought, there'd be hay. Water too, he hoped, for he was desperately thirsty.

As he moved closer, he strained to catch any sign of life in the farmyard. The farmer and his family were apparently asleep, the animals in their barns. He figured he could easily slip into the hayloft and hide until dusk the following day.

As he was getting ready to move in, he heard a chain rattle.

His heart slammed against his chest wall. He listened acutely. It was a tethered animal moving around. Likely a dog. A watchdog. He winced. If the beast started yelping, the farmer would charge out with his shotgun. German patrols would hear the blast and come running.

He swore and reluctantly backed away.

The further he trudged, the more exhausted he became. If he collapsed somewhere, the Germans would find him at daylight and finish him off. Maybe it would be better to find a hiding place and stay put until the Americans came. One of the big potato pits would do. Or the woods.

No, he told himself; he had to get as far as he could from the barn. He had to keep moving.

As he slogged along, he heard far behind a sudden string of explosions and machine-gun bursts. He was puzzled. He was sure he'd left the barn many miles behind, for it seemed he'd been travelling for hours. A sickening

330

thought struck him: maybe he'd been walking around in circles. It could happen in his befuddled condition.

He didn't know where he was, but he could now make out details of the terrain. God! Was it getting light? And him still in open country!

About a half mile ahead was another clump of woods. He'd have to run to make it before the sun came up. He'd rest there and move on after dusk.

Twelve hours of flight on his blood-poisoned leg was now exacting its toll. He tried to go faster but nothing happened. It was like pressing on the gas pedal when you're out of fuel. Moving sluggishly up a long, shallow, wooded incline, he came upon a road in front of him. On it he saw the dark outlines of figures walking and riding bicycles. Some were civilians, some soldiers. He had to reach the woods on the other side before first light. He started to hobble faster downhill – and almost fell into a large pit with an antitank gun and two machine guns. He stumbled to a halt, barely missing a cunningly concealed defensive position and a squad of Germans huddled around their weapons. Terrified he'd been spotted, he dropped to the ground and backtracked. He crouched in some bushes, wasting precious minutes of darkness while he tried to unscramble his emotions. Finally he circled widely around the German position, and crawled awkwardly down the slope, hampered by his cumbersome leg. He huddled in a wooded culvert by the side of the road, waiting for the traffic to thin before racing to the woods on the other side. As he hoarded his strength for the high-speed sprint, he noticed a figure silhouetted at the top of the hill he had just descended.

It was a soldier, and from the position of the arms, he knew that the man was scanning with binoculars. He was sure that the German's field glasses were trained directly on him. But maybe, he hoped, it was still not light enough for him to be detected through the bushes' meagre spring foliage.

German civilians rushed along the road with their

331

belongings. Military vehicles zoomed back and forth. Platoons of bedraggled soldiers slogged along on the shoulder of the road above him, so close that he could see the hobnails in their boots and feel the vibrations of their step. He clutched the damp embankment and flattened himself against it, trying to become one with the earth. Finally the traffic thinned out. He cautiously raised his head and peered through the foliage at the gentle slope of woods whose summit was his destination. If he could get there without being seen, he'd be free: the Germans were retreating and the Americans were surely advancing along the road in vengeful pursuit. If only he could make the final effort. He could already visualize the eager American *blancs* swarming excitedly around their *noir* 'country-man.'

His spirits soared as the traffic thinned and the sun broke over the horizon behind him. His old cockiness flooded in as the sun's rays warmed his back. His leg continued to throb, but he knew he could take it for a while longer, now that the Americans were near. He could hardly contain himself as he began rehearsing his accounts of the barn, Brauny, the weapon being made in the tunnels and all the other stories that he'd pour out to them.

He shivered with anticipation: he would tell everything, right down to the minutest detail, and the S.S. would squirm. The satisfaction of it would be worth everything he'd suffered . . .

His reverie was shattered by the sound of marching feet. He rammed himself deeper into his hiding place, pulling the branches around his head. The footfalls grew louder; now they were passing directly above him.

'*Kommen sie hier*! Come out of there!'

He didn't move.

The rancorous voice repeated the order, and for emphasis a machine pistol's blast shredded the bushes concealing him, ripping his hopes apart.

He grudgingly emerged to find himself staring into the

spout of a Schmeisser held by a man who hated him enough to gleefully drill him where he stood: Dora's custody camp leader, Moeser.[1] He was enroute from Gardelegen to Sachsenhausen extermination camp, eighty miles to the northeast. With him were 150 prisoners whom *Burgomiester* Thiele hadn't been able to squeeze into the Isenschnibbe Barn.

If anyone could deliver the *haeftlinge* to Sachsenhausen, it was Moeser.

Yet there was more to his dedication than his sense of duty: many of the 150 he personally had beaten, kicked and whipped. How their tongues would wag if the Americans captured them alive.

The sporadic small-arms fire and the intermittent artillery salvoes made sweat beads pop on the brow of the 39-year-old first lieutenant who, after fourteen years in uniform, had yet to experience his first taste of combat. With the barrel of machine pistol hanging from a strap over his shoulder he prodded them forward. '*Mach schnell! Mach schnell!*' Through the mud-sticky ploughed fields and the woods he routed them. Coming out of a wood he'd bark them to a halt while he reconnoitred the open meadowland ahead. Once assured the way was clear, he would wave them on. The guards would move in on the panting prisoners and worry them forward like dogs herding balky sheep. Much of the time Moeser's neck was craned as he scanned the lead-belly sky for American fighter-bombers.

Six miles east of Gardelegen, at the hamlet of Javenitz, Moeser's patience with the stragglers wore out: Their continual staggering and falling slowed the column to a crawl. He halted the column for a moment, and as usual the prisoners spread out like grazing cattle. He beckoned

[1]Moeser once told a fellow S.S. man that he performed his chores 'with the same pleasure as you shoot a deer. That is how I shoot a human being. When I came to the S.S. and I had to shoot the first three persons, my food didn't taste right for three days. But today it is a pleasure. It is a joy for me.'

to his NCO, Staff Sergeant Emil Buehring, a 43-year-old ex-farmer.

Moeser anticipated no dissent when he whispered to Buehring to shoot the stragglers – now!

While Buehring talked quietly with his guards, Nicholas and the main body of prisoners huddled on the grass. Most were stretched out full length in a state of near-collapse, waiting for the laggards to catch up.

A line of S.S. moved in between the main body and the approaching stragglers. The weapons stuttered and the doomed men jumped as in a frenzy. Some dashed wildly through the trees, chased by a hail of S.S. lead.

Nicholas and the others clutched the ground as the bullets sprayed over their heads.

When Buehring cried 'Cease Fire!' thirty-five bodies littered the woods near Javenitz. Then, before the skinny heaps of bones could cool off, the survivors scurried over and scavenged their dead friends' clogs and clothes.

'Schnell!' bellowed Moeser, pointing his machine pistol toward the east. 'Schnell!'

For Nicholas each step was agony. The week-old wound had swollen his leg to double its normal size. It dragged like an anchor on his will to stay alive. Each stride pumped pain through him. Each step now meant one step less he might be able to take later.

Where was madman Moeser taking them?

Moeser snarled for more speed. Obviously he was terrified that he'd look over his shoulder and see jeeps of the 102nd U.S. Infantry Division's reconnaissance squadrons in hot pursuit.

Artillery growled and small arms crackled all around.

The prisoners threaded single file along beaten paths, with Moeser up ahead intermittently stopping the column, cupping his hands to his ears and rotating his head like a radar dish. The whine of an engine. The clatter of a tank track. The snick of a rifle bolt. They were enough to stampede Moeser and the guards back into the trees.

The S.S. hunkered down in the woods, munching on

their rations. Nicholas and the prisoners littered the ground with their bodies, vomiting on the spongy forest floor.

When they'd gotten their wind back and their bellies had stopped heaving, they cynically whispered their stark alternatives: die now – or later. Flee into woods and get stitched across the back before they got twenty feet away? Or stick with Moeser and get it in some gas chamber later?

Couldn't they drag the pace so perhaps the American patrols would catch up?

Only if *all* dragged their heels – not just a few, who'd be knocked off as stragglers, Nicholas muttered. But if everyone held back, Moeser might be panicked into slaughtering them all on the spot.

Nicholas concluded that his only hope was to make a break at the most unpredictable time, when the guards were at their greatest disadvantage. That would be when the fighter-bombers caught them in the open: Moeser and his entourage would be so busy trying to stay alive, and a solitary runaway might have a chance.

Yes, Nicholas told himself, he would have to do it alone.

He kept forgetting about his leg. How fast could he move? How far could a goddam cripple run?

The humiliation enraged him.

He'd ripped his pants leg to ease the pressure on his leg. Purplish threads of blood poisoning streaked toward his groin. He coughed deeply and realized that his wind was almost gone.

'*Aufstehen! Aufstehen! Aufstehen!*'

Buehring badgered them to their feet again. In the deepening dusk the guards, using their rifles like cattle prods, poked the doomed men out of their torpor. Some struggled to their feet unaided. Others were lifted by comrades. Some were too weak to walk. The column marched on without them for a short distance, then halted.

Buehring scurried back into the woods. Half a dozen shots ripped the silence, then he returned, rebuttoning the flap on his holster.

Again they staggered forward along the dark woodland trail. Soon they were out in the open fields again.

There was no moon but the horizon glowed like a miniature aurora borealis with the incandescence of battle. The prisoners, hemmed in tightly by the guards, struggled across the mushy, grassless terrain which sucked at their feet like a plunger in a stopped-up drain.

Again and again Nicholas teased himself with the idea of making a run for it. He kept replaying the fantasy until his high-flying spirit was shot down by reality. He'd be just a blink away from making his break when he'd remember his encumbrances – his rotting leg and his wasting lung. He had to violently force himself to even consider the possibility that the body in which he'd always taken such immense pride was now a burned-out hulk, as useless as the hobbling, disfigured beggars he'd so deeply loathed on the streets of Port-au-Prince.

Around midnight Moeser ordered the column to stop near the edge of the woods. He cupped his hands to his ears and listened raptly in the inky blackness. He growled for Buehring. They talked in low, querulous tones. Buehring then whispered to a nearby corporal. Unsnapping the safety catch on his machine pistol, the corporal disappeared into the darkness.

The prisoners sank leadenly to their knees, taking advantage of the respite. Some collapsed full length, the breath rasping in their throttles. The guards squatted, too, their weapons cradled in the crooks of their arms.

The corporal finally rustled back through the trees and consulted in a low voice with Moeser. The S.S. lieutenant then ordered the column to move out. The guards pummelled the slumped bodies to get them moving again.

Nicholas was jerked away from his thoughts of Haiti and home by the unmistakable sounds of traffic. My God!

336

The Americans? But as he strained to listen he discovered to his crushing disappointment that it was the screech of farm wagons. The clop of hooves. As the din intensified he picked up the shuffling of thousands of feet along a paved road. The occasional whine of engines. Slowly he perceived the silhouettes of men, women and children and horse-drawn carts piled high with household belongings.

The sombre procession passing before him stretched as far as his eyes could pierce the night.

He felt a stab of elation at the sight of fleeing Germans. Thousands of sullen, exhausted, beaten Germans – refugees in their own blood-soaked country!

Moeser halted the prisoners on the shoulder of the road while he scrutinized the refugees. He called out, demanding to know if there were any S.S. or *Wehrmacht* among them. An old farmer muttered that all the military men were at the head of the column. Moeser whispered the news to Buehring. The sergeant, masking his sadistic demeanor for the benefit of the civilians, quietly asked the prisoners to form a column-of-fives and march alongside the refugees.

Nicholas recoiled in agony as his engorged foot hit the hard surface of the road.

It was still some hours before dawn when the motley procession shuffled through the outskirts of Stendal, a village fortress bristling with machine-gun nests and hastily improvised barricades. Men and women sweated in the predawn chill as they feverishly excavated pits. Tank engines thrummed powerfully as the metal monsters clanked down ramps into the pits, where they would function as fixed artillery. Soldiers stripped to the waist sawed down trees and rolled them across the road. Small, tow-headed boys exuberantly lent a hand.

The imperious *Waffen* S.S. colonel presiding over the fortifications stared expressionlessly at the refugees as they staggled past. But a sneer curled his lips when he saw the filthy, hump-backed Dora survivors in their tattered prison stripes. His sneer blossomed into a scowl as

Moeser, Buehring and the S.S. guards pompously paraded into view. It was obvious that the colonel despised his S.S. cousins, who weren't combat soldiers and had fought the war in concentration camps against defenseless prisoners.

He bellowed a summons to Moeser, and they exchanged words.

The colonel demanded that Moeser's prisoners and the guards be drafted for the defence of Stendal. Moeser timidly replied that his orders came from the highest authority in Berlin – *Obersturmbannfuehrer* Wiegel: The prisoners were incorrigible terrorists, many of them in the *Nacht und Nebel* category, being escorted to Sachsenhausen for execution. If they were to remain in Stendal and escaped in the heat of battle, *Herr* Colonel, argued Moeser persuasively, they would be a dangerous threat to him.

The colonel grimaced, dismissed Moeser with a contemptuous wave of his hand and returned to supervising the town's defences.

The refugee column and Moeser's prisoners emerged gasping from the east edge of Stendal, where a bridge took them across the wide, deep waters of the River Elbe. Once on the other side they swarmed northward on a two-lane road.

Moeser, obsessed with the need for speed, steered the prisoners out of the turgidly moving column and into the outside lane against oncoming traffic. This meant they were marching in a column-of-fives parallel to the hapless civilians and continuously moving past them.

As the prisoners pulled ahead of the refugees Nicholas sneaked a few stitches of conversation with them.

It was his first real contact with the outside world in eighteen months.

In great anguish they wove a woeful tapestry of collapse. Cities burned to the ground by the British and American *Luft* gangsters. Hundreds of thousands of innocent men, women and children heaped to cinders on sidewalks. Russian maniacs screaming through Poland, buffeting the banks of the Oder River and flooding into the Fatherland to kill, rape and destroy.

The refugees told him they were marching north to join the *Fuehrer*: he had summoned all loyal Germans to rally around him. He had promised them a secret weapon so awesome that it would level London, New York and Moscow.

A secret weapon! It seemed a lifetime ago, Nicholas thought, that he had suffered those torturous nights in the dispensary, trying to piece together the incredible details of the monster rocket. How he had fantasized about getting his incredible intelligence into the hands of the Allies! It had softened the guilt he had felt over his good life in the *Revier* and it had been an unfailing massage for his irrepressible ego. But now, with the snout of Moeser's machine pistol never more than a few yards from his back, he suddenly realized how inconsequential it was compared to his rage to continue living.

He considered sneaking a ride in one of the horse-drawn wagons. But there'd probably be someone inside. They'd scream at the sight of a filthy, bearded black spectre with a sausage leg, and Moeser would come running.

Frequently the prisoners were forced off the road by convoys of tanks, self-propelled guns, half-tracks and truckloads of soldiers.

The refugees' column coiled through villages and hamlets and towns, flattening and lengthening as if it were a giant centipede with a million legs gorging itself on hobbling old men in felt hats and knee breeches, and wrinkled *hausfraus* with sobbing children tugging at their heavy, black skirts.

The pain had ballooned beyond Nicholas' tolerance. His teeth had been clenched so long that his face ached. He grasped for thoughts to divert his mind from his misery... What if rampaging Russian tanks drove right over them in the dark... If only he had some clue as to where they were... He tried to conjure up in his mind the picture of the last map of Germany he'd seen – the one on the wall of the Political Department at Dora. He tried to focus Berlin in the hazy vision. On Dora. On Gardelegen. Stendal.

A man could walk four miles an hour. How many hours – or days – had elapsed since he'd left Gardelegen?

The Elbe River wears a slanting, northwest course through northern Germany and slices it in half. If Moeser had only known it, he could have stopped worrying about the Americans once he crossed the river: by agreement with the Russians, the Elbe was the furthest east that the Anglo-American armies would advance. When they arrived at its west bank, they had orders to dig in there and wait for the Russians to reach the opposite bank.

The distance between the two armies was narrowing daily. About April 20, when Moeser herded his prisoners across the bridge at Stendal, the gap was a huge triangle of territory. By April 26 the base of that triangle had contracted to a hundred-mile width along the Baltic coast and an apex on the Elbe, ninety miles southeast of Stendal at a place called Torgau, where the Russians and the U.S. 69th Infantry Division reached across the water and shook hands.

The British, Americans and Russians had knotted the noose around the Third Reich's midsection at Torgau, sending millions of German soldiers and civilians scurrying northward in thousands of columns just like the one Nicholas was in.[2]

First Nicholas saw the dirty, black smoke funnels. Then the high stone wall and barbed wire. Then the rows and

[2]As it turned out, S.S. Lieutenant Moeser didn't have to drive them so ruthlessly: the U.S. 102nd Infantry Division, after discovering the Isenschnibbe barn massacre at Gardelegen and pressing on to the east, didn't reach the Elbe River until April 30. There it crushed all German resistance – except for a tiny, fanatic pocket on the east bank at Stendal, where the *Waffen* S.S. colonel continued to resist.

rows of ugly, one-storied huts of Sachsenhausen's extermination camp.

The sixty-mile trek from Stendal had just about finished him. Meekly he let himself he herded through the vast, muddy compound. He found thousands like himself sprawled at hut entrances, huddled inside on bare barrack floors, staring into space. He collapsed on the floor, his chin on his chest. Each time he coughed the haemorrhaging in his lungs pumped between his lips. His leg was pregnant with putrefaction. The pain of leg and chest fused and his mind and body became a single agony.

Was this how Jean Marcel Nicolas, son of the proud Hilderic and Lucie, was going to exit, he asked himself? Jean, who had exploded from little Haiti determined to see his name in lights? Who could fight or finagle his way into or out of any situation? Who had pledged to himself to set the world on its ear?

Would he strip meekly, shuffle into the tiled cubicle and whiff the Zyklon B vapours without a whimper? Or would he punch, kick, butt, scratch, gouge and scream until he stopped twitching?

Would he, as the end came, slump in mind and body as befits a slave? Or would he stand tall, with his shoulders back, as his mother had told him when he was a little boy, he must always stand?

But at Sachsenhausen concentration camp the commandant had run low on Zyklon B; the fumes were too weak and the lean mixture, instead of acting in fifteen minutes, took three hours. The S.S. took to machine-gunning prisoners in slit trenches where they sought refuge during the Russian bombing raids on the camp. But still the commandant could make little dent in the hundreds of thousands scheduled for extermination.

The overload would have to be shipped elsewhere.

Nicholas, who had managed to elude the showers and slit-trenches, was one of 40,000 Sachsenhausen inmates in two massive phalanxes that flowed out through the camp

341

gates on April 21 headed for Ravensbrueck concentration camp.

They had been rousted from their nightmares at three o'clock in the morning. It was now dawn and drizzling rain. Behind them pink clouds curdled in the acrid smoke above the blazing cauldron of Berlin, which was being systematically razed by 2.5 million Russian soldiers.

An eight-day growth of beard shadowed Moeser's face. His long greatcoat was soaked with rain and slapped against his jackboots. He leaned into the wind, clutching his pistol as a child hugs a favourite toy.

Buehring kept up a steady snarl of profanity, barking at the drenched prisoners to stay tightly together, constantly glancing at Moeser for reassurance.

In the rear of the Sachsenhausen evacuation were representatives of the International Red Cross. The IRC had appealed unsuccessfully to the German government for custody of the concentration camps and their inmates. Nevertheless they continued as shepherds of the exodus on the remote chance that the Germans might change their minds.

In the first four miles the IRC men counted twenty dead – all shot in the head.

Nicholas wondered who was going to be next. Even his extravagant arrogance, which had won friends and enemies throughout his life, was beginning to desert him. He reached down inside himself and all his fingers touched was the reality that he was dying.

Chapter Twenty

Even in the best of times the journey to Ravensbrueck is depressing.

From the East-West crossing point on Friedrichstrasse in Berlin the drive is forty-eight miles. The road weaves through grey hamlets, drab and uninviting. The terrain is flat and dotted with small farmhouses whose foundations have shifted, skewing roofs and walls. The wind whips down from the Baltic, ripples the grain and snaps the hardy scrub pine.

Above all there's a lunar quality to the desolation and silence. It's as if the land is ashamed of what it witnessed thirty-five years ago.

As the tourist's car speeds past the town of Oranienburg, on the Havel River, a sign points to the Sachsenhausen camp memorial.

The shaggy Brandenburg terrain subtly becomes the sand and swamp of Mecklenburg. The land is ridged and bumpy.

Furstenburg, the first sizable town, has stood frozen since Nicholas and his doomed comrades hobbled through it that fateful day in April of 1945. The main street, now asphalted, was cobbled then. The houses huddle under steep sod roofs like people pressed in by a crowd.

Ravensbrueck, just outside Furstenburg, is a one-street hamlet whose insignificance is out of all proportion to the infamy it earned during World War II. At the end of that street, which is actually Route 96 – the north-south highway from Berlin, narrow country roads angle off aimlessly in various directions.

Amid a cluster of signposts is a very special one pointing

east: National Memorial and Commemorative Site at Ravensbrueck – one kilometer.

Moeser's group staggered through Ravensbrueck's main gate as dawn was breaking and roll call was already in progress.

Nicholas gaped at their massed ranks – 20,000 of them, square after square, 20 women long by 20 women wide. Since 4:30 a.m. they had been standing rigidly upright in the chilly damp. They were bowed, gnarled, shrunken forms on tree-trunk legs bloated with the oedema characteristic of heart congestion.

He watched the camp commandant, *Sturmbannfuehrer* Fritz Suhrens, escorted by his two roll-call leaders, amble down the ranks, personally examining the wretched women.

As of April 22 Suhrens had begun evacuating Ravensbrueck concentration camp in groups of 400 at a time. He released only the healthiest; he could never allow the weak and diseased to be seen by the Anglo-Americans or the Russians; he tagged them for elimination.

Nicholas, almost at breaking point, shivered spastically in his rain-soaked uniform, and watched incredulously as Suhrens dropped to his haunches. The commandant poked his riding crop between the lumber legs and hiked the tattered skirts of the women, searching for the telltale symptoms of puffed flesh snaked with blood vessels.

This simple test determined who would live and who would die.

Nicholas and the other *Nacht und Nebel* prisoners were locked in the cells of the camp jail.

Each of the eighty cells in the stone, two-story structure was five feet wide, ten feet long with a tiny, barred square window near the ceiling. Each was furnished with an iron bed and a four-legged, wooden stool.

Nicholas eased his tortured hulk face down on the bunk. His wild imagination, once crackling with high-voltage

344

fantasy of escape, was becoming neutralized by his dying body. Remote in his consciousness he felt the hollow reverberations of the Russian artillery. Far away – near enough to resonate asceptically through the jail, amplifying the detonations as if inside a giant kettle drum.

He didn't know how long he'd been unconscious. Something had jolted him back to reality. He shielded his eyes against the shaft of sunlight stabbing the cell's gloom. He heard the shuffling of feet outside and the yapping of guards.

Was it morning? Which morning? The first since his arrival? The second? The third?

He was badly disorientated. His senses and reflexes were lazy. He strained to focus his mind as if it were a stubborn muscle. It was no good. He was totally exhausted.

How long had he been asleep? Or unconscious?

He tried to push himself up in the iron cot but pain stole his feeble strength. He gasped like a man dashed with ice water. He fell back on the cot, pinned to the mattress by a huge lead weight in his chest.

Outside the shuffling of feet continued.

He tried once more to get up. The pain held him rigid. He felt as if he had an anvil on his chest. Sweat soaked him. His heart pounded irregularly. The stench of his rancid body made him want to retch. His leg was an anchor clamped to this life. He felt a sudden impulse to cut it off. It had betrayed him. Reduced him to the level of some obese slug, squirming helplessly under a stone, fit only to be stepped on and put out of its misery.

He thought of what it would be like to be six feet under the earth. Or soot belched from a chimney, floating black particles somewhere in the stratosphere. Strange: in the months that had gone by since Florence had played her exit scene masterfully he'd repeatedly faced death, but he had always managed to spit in its face. The awful spectacle of the women had finished him. At Buchenwald and Dora he had seen men reduced to the level of animals; but to see women, like his mother, his sister Carmen – even like Florence, pillaged of their feminity; transformed into ogres in skirts . . .

He cursed himself for allowing them to grind his spirit down to the nub. Goddam sons-of-bitches!

There were tears in his eyes. Jesus Christ! He was only twenty-six years old! He'd barely begun to live!

The fear of death had always haunted him. Often he'd pondered it uneasily. It had been the compulsion for his foolhardiness, his bravado, his courage, his paranoid dalliances with danger. Picking fights with Marines. Diving recklessly into the Bois de Chêne. Coolly staring down the Nazi officer in the Metro. Blithely bathing in the reservoir at Dora. Flirting lasciviously with death. Fascinated by his fear of dying, by his fear of fear.

But there was still a dram of insufferable arrogance left. He ridiculed himself to his feet and now stood unsteadily on the bunk. His knees quivered as he raised himself on his toes and tried to peer through the tiny window. He shielded his weak eyes against the sun and tumesced with rage when they refused to focus. The pain made him dizzy, and rivulets of sweat dripped down his cheeks . . .

The cell door rattled. The S.S. was coming for him.

But so was a troop of American armoured cavalry. Would it get there in time?

The town of Ludwigslust was choked with bumper-to-bumper traffic of the U.S. Seventh Armoured Division and captured German prisoners. First Lieutenant William A. Knowlton, the slim, 24-year-old West Pointer commanding B Troop of the division's 87th Cavalry Reconnaissance Squadron, opened up the siren on his armoured car and flattened the gas pedal to the floor: the radio message had crackled that the colonel wanted him on the double. But Ludwigslust's clogged streets slowed him to a crawl.

'Knowlton,' the colonel told him at division headquarters, 'Ludwigslust is as far as we're allowed to go. Our troops are drawn up along a north-south line just outside the town.

'I want you to take your troops and contact the Russians. They are somewhere to the east – between 50 and 100 miles, according to rumour. Get someone from their staff and bring him here.

'The German 12th Army lies between you and the Russians. If you get in trouble, we can send you no help. Don't get too entangled. And let me know your progress. Good luck.'

Knowlton didn't realize what he'd been ordered to do until he'd gotten rolling: with six days left before the end of the war, there were millions of German soldiers scattered across northern Germany – all retreating before the Russians. In venturing eastward from Ludwigslust B Troop was charged with the awesome task of running the gauntlet between 200,000 troops of the German 21st Army.

Knowlton's entire force[1] was 95 men, 11 armoured cars and 20 jeeps. If a fight became unavoidable, it would be 95 against 200,000! Knowlton had nothing but speed and mobility on his side against such lopsided odds. But if he was to carry out the order, he would have to stab into the German rear – and out before they knew what had hit them.

B Troop saddled up and rumbled across the line-of-departure, heading along the main highway northeast.

Immediately they ran into mobs of German soldiers clamouring and clambering to surrender. Deeper into enemy territory the Germans' enthusiasm for surrender cooled. They hadn't yet made up their minds what to do, and Knowlton's column began running into clutches of sullen-faced soldiers loitering around heavily fortified strongpoints. At the sight of the ominous big German

[1] He had chosen to leave his assault artillery and half-tracks in Ludwigslust in order to travel light and gain more speed.

88-millimetre artillery pieces, the instantaneous reaction of Knowlton's men was to duck down and slam shut the hatches of their armoured cars. But they knew they'd be blasted across the Luneberger heathland if they did. Their only hope was to bluff it: make it look as if they were the spearhead of a massive American armoured thrust. So they stood tall in their turrets as if they were a conquering army that didn't give a damn.

The bewildered German gun crews continued to track them – but held their fire.

B Troop wheeled arrogantly through Neustadt, which was ten miles into the German rear. Still no sign of the Russians. But there were thousands of German soldiers and civilians thronged in the streets, believing Knowlton's force to be the tip of a U.S. armoured column rushing up to join them in fighting the Russians.

Traffic-snarled streets and hordes of surrendering troops slowed them by two valuable hours in Neustadt. Finally B Troop shifted once again into high gear and rolled eastward through a pine forest so dense that the trees formed towering walls on both sides of the road. It was excellent terrain for a German ambush.

The lead jeep's tyres squealed suddenly as it skidded to a halt to avoid smashing into a logjam of abandoned German trucks and half-tracks. Finding the road impassable, B Troop halted while Knowlton took stock of the situation. From the turret of his armoured car he saw stone-faced S.S. soldiers stripping the vehicles of food and equipment, then scurrying back into the trees.

He quickly sensed that he could be in serious trouble. His unit couldn't move and the woods thronged with hostile Germans. 'Don't get too entangled,' headquarters had admonished him. 'If you get in trouble we can give you no help!' Knowlton hesitated momentarily, then cupped his hands to his mouth. 'Come out and surrender!' he bellowed in German.

The S.S. men stopped, looked around indecisively – then raced deeper into the woods.

Knowlton and his platoon commanders were spoiling for action but their mission wasn't to fight; however, he had to live up to appearances, so he passed the word down to maintain the pose of nonchalance. The troopers continued to play their roles to the hilt, all the while dreading the possibility that a *panzerfaust* would start woofing...

Back in Ludwigslust headquarters radio operators stayed bolted to their headsets as division officers fidgeted nervously...

Knowlton's ploy paid off once again and the S.S. soldiers dropped their weapons and filtered out of the trees.

The ribbon of roadway finally emerged from the forest, and Knowlton's tension eased. He had a relatively clear field of vision across the sparse growth of the Mecklenberg countryside.

On the flank! About a thousand yards!

His eyes bulged. His heart kicked. Four huge 88-millimetre artillery pieces, their predatory shouts sniffing armoured steel!

He was the only one who'd seen them. He kept his mouth shut and his radio off. His throat dried up. B Troop could be thirteen blazing armoured hulks in as many seconds. Weakly he clung to the side of the turret in full view of the German gun crews. Out of the corner of his eye he could see the barrels pivoting as the Germans tracked them. Then he spotted their helmets popping up above the parapet like inquisitive squirrels. More helmets...

Finally forty-five soldiers shuffled out of the prepared position, flinging away their rifles and machine guns.

If the bastards only knew, Knowlton chuckled.

The S.S. guard at the cell door was strangely reserved. His voice was quiet – almost apologetic. He didn't point his weapon. He said that the Russians would arrive soon and that Commandant Suhrens was giving all prisoners their choice to go or stay behind.

The parade ground was a madhouse. Tears. Laughter. Embracing. Kissing. Hugging. Dancing. Incomprehension. Stupefaction...

Off to the sides, in between the ugly, green-painted barracks, the S.S. frantically ripped off their caps and insignia from the uniforms they'd worn so vaingloriously as if to say: well, so much for the Thousand Year Reich! Some were already pedalling furiously out through the main gate on bicycles; others were skulking off into the woods.

When the delirium of freedom had subsided on the parade ground, the women littered the area with their hastily snatched-together belongings which they crammed into old, torn blankets and bags. Then they surged like a human tidal wave through the main gate.

The Russian army, which liberated Ravensbrueck on April 30, paused there only long enough to post a holding force; then it continued its westward rush after the 20,000 fleeing inmates and their former guards.

By May 2 Nicholas and three comrades[2] were fifty miles from Ravensbrueck. All the way they'd looked nervously over their shoulders in dread of the Russian forward-reconnaissance patrols in their nut-brown uniforms and astride their shaggy ponies.

A man can endure the severest pain as long as he knows it won't last forever. Yet even a trifling agony becomes unbearable if there is no known end to it. Nicholas didn't know how much longer he could hang on. When he collapsed, he begged his comrades to pull him to his feet again and push him on. Each time he slumped to his knees it became easier to stay there, harder to go on. Did he really want to survive and live as a cripple? He had

[2]One is believed to have been Jean Haricourt, a Frenchman, now deceased.

revelled in his physical perfection; now he was repulsed by his deformity. He could never endure a lifetime of being loathed. Especially by beautiful women, who would point to him with pity. To rot away in some sanitarium, coughing out his life spit by spit . . .

The rumble of heavy vehicles vibrated the ground. He opened his eyes and stared up at the sky through the slender pines, elders and aspens of the copse in which he lay.

The Russians!

He tried to get up. Waves of weakness washed through him. He broke out in a fit of coughing so violent that it sounded as if he were ripping off chunks of his lungs. He wondered between paroxysms where his comrades were. He coughed out their names. There was no reply. He coughed them again and again . . .

They were gone. Had they left him? After all he'd done for them. At Dora. At Rottleberode. Never mind. Johnny Nicholas didn't need them. He didn't need anybody. He never had. He never would. He rolled off his back cautiously as if his belly were made of glass, gritting his teeth against the pain, his chin dripping with gobs of crimson phlegm. Digging his elbows into the spongy floor of the woods he began to inch his way forward.

The effort quickly melted any strength left in him. By the time he got to the treeline, his body was racked with another explosion of coughing. He slumped face down on the ground. About fifteen minutes later he had revived enough to stir slightly and to raise his head.

He looked down the side of a hill, but his vision was obscured by the long, spiny shafts of new grass on the heathland. He slowly pushed himself up on his elbows, fighting pain that was like a bayonet under his rib cage. He fought his eyes for refusing to focus. Yes, a town. Several roads radiating from it. Streets thick with traffic. Vehicles? Tanks? He could hear voices below. Commands.

Smell the tang of exhaust fumes. Feel the creaking of tank tracks.

His failing senses delivered a single message: the Russians were all over the place.

The shock squeezed a little more fuel into his wasted body. He squirmed back from the tree line and into the woods. He realized that if some of them wandered up the hill and found him, they wouldn't know who he was. His uniform was filthy. The stripes had faded long ago under the grime. So had the red triangle with the 'A'. The Russians would suspect he was a fleeing German and spray him where he lay.

He stopped the dialogue with his muddy brain and resigned himself to the Coke-bottle vision of his blurring eyes. He lacked the strength to cough away the maddening tickle deep in his lungs. The blood on the back of his hand where his mouth had been bubbled like a soft drink.

He was irretrievably spent.

The rumble of traffic waned. Birds chirped. He was strangely comfortable as the pallid May sun bathed his body, suffusing him with an ineffable calm.

Nothing in West Point's textbooks could possibly have prepared Lt. Knowlton for the preposterous charade.

Lubz was forty miles into the German 12th Army's midsection. The town was held by 5,000 Waffen S.S. infantry and the paratroopers of the crack Hermann Goering Parachute Division. B Troop was outmanned fifty to one and had lost radio contact with Seventh Armoured Division headquarters back at Ludwigslust.

What was he to do?

Since his orders were to make contact with a senior Soviet commander and there were no Russians in Lubz, he was justified in rolling on through the town. The problem was that it would be night soon and the Germans could easily ambush him in the dark. For this reason he decided it would be safer to spend the night in Lubz and masquerade as the victorious spearhead of a huge Allied

352

armoured division about to thunder into town at any moment.

But if B Troop muffed its lines and failed to convince the Germans in Lubz, the corpses of one U.S. first lieutenant and ninety-five of his countrymen would decorate the town square by morning.

That night, with their jeeps and armoured cars parked in the town square and the streets jammed with unarmed – but suspicious German military, Knowlton and his men went through the motions of the deep and comfortable sleep that is the privilege of the victors.

They hardly slept at all. The thought of having their throats slit or being riddled in their bunks was the cause of their insomnia.

B Troop breathed easier when the sun came up on May 3. The men were punchy with lack of sleep but elated that their bluff had survived the night.

With audacity bordering on foolhardiness Knowlton nonchalantly announced in the town square that two B Troop platoons would stay behind to remind the glowering German soldiers who was in control of Lubz. With his force dangerously depleted, he rolled out of town, grinning at the stone-faced S.S. and parachute troops lining the streets, praying that he'd soon encounter a senior Soviet commander.

His troopers' hearts began to beat a little slower as the impudent little column reached the outskirts. It was a splendid day; their spirits were rising. The sight of hundreds of freed POWs and concentration-camp inmates on the highway ahead and the joy on their faces made them feel that the risks they'd taken were worth it . . . The bedraggled escapees clambered around the armoured cars and jeeps, jubilantly acclaiming the GIs as liberators, hugging and pounding them.

'Wait!' called one of a trio of escapees who were huddled by the roadside over a still form. 'We've an American POW with us! He won't survive if he doesn't get help!'

Knowlton told his driver to pull the armored car onto the shoulder. The vehicle's powerful engine revved, impatient with the delay, as the young West Pointer looked down from his turret at the unconscious form.[3]

He knew that a dying man would slow them down, and he couldn't afford to lose any more time. Yet it was obvious that the poor bastard had come through hell for his liberation. It would be a damn shame if he checked out without knowing he'd made it.

Knowlton grabbed his microphone, radioed for one of the other vehicles to take the man back to safety, then roared off in search of the Russians.[4]

Chapter Twenty-One

'It will have been the emergence of good from evil,' says Dr. Robert Gander, Nicholas' friend and fellow prisoner-doctor at Rottleberode, 'to establish the exact identity of Johnny Nicholas.'

To his concentration-camp confidants such as Gandar, Hein and Jay he was an accomplished physician – even though they suspected that he hadn't finished medical

[3]Knowlton is currently a lieutenant general and Chief of Staff of the U.S. Army European Command in West Germany. Of the Lubz interlude he remembers 'a little southeast of Lubz having a very ill prisoner carted over to our column with a request that we get him back ... We put him on an armoured car until we got him back to Lubz and then may have evacuated him by jeep to a collecting station, where an ambulance was available ...'

According to the records of the National Federation of Deportees, Resistance Fighters and Patriots in Paris, Nicholas was found by an American 'tank' unit on 3 May 1945 near Lubz.

[4]Later that morning he made contact with them fifteen miles east of Lubz at the village of Reppentin. He delivered six bottles of Hennessey's cognac as a present to the senior Soviet commander from the U.S. Seventh Armoured Division commander.

school – and the mysterious Allied agent captured while on a highly secret mission.

To his patients at Dora and Rottleberode he was the grinning magician who distilled from the horror all around them the elixir of their survival.

To his close friends and associates in France and Haiti he was Jean Marcel Nicolas. Headstrong. Brilliant. Untamed and untamable. The youth with the big heart and the grand flair for theatricals whom they knew like a book – yet hardly knew at all.

To relatives and family he was the unreliable letter writer.

Madame Nicolas knew more about him second-hand from the correspondence of friends' and neighbours' sons studying in Paris than she learned directly from him. It was a poor substitute for a solicitous family craving to know if he was well or sick, happy or sad, where he was, what he was doing.

The little she knew of him, however, was fuzzy, impressionistic and mostly based on hearsay.

The last time she saw him was in 1937 when he left for Martinique to enlist in the French Navy. He was a strapping teenager; cocky, strutting, rebelliously impatient with the land that bore him; raging to remake the world in his own, private image. And impulsively, unpredictably affectionate.

Hers was the fretful lot of all mothers who conceive their children in countries umbilically tied to poverty and indulge them with liberal educations that foster in them deep discontent with the limitations of their homelands. And Haiti's slumbering, ancestral inertia dragged as an anchor on Jean's restless quest for adventure.

A frail woman of 84 when she died in 1974, Mme. Nicolas kept alive the memory of her son until the end. While she lived, he also lived in the thick, glossy-backed photo album of family portraits as stiff and formal as those of any Victorian-era family of substance. Within the pictures' scalloped frames he poses at various ages. In one

355

he's about ten years old, dutifully solemn in a dark suit with knee pants and long socks, an elbow resting on the curved arm of a studio's French Provincial drawing-room chair. In another he's perhaps thirteen, slightly overweight and with a chubbiness that excites the maternal instinct; a handsome boy with large, lustrous eyes and a pout that ominously portends strain on the parental leash.

During the war years the family's only news of him arrived via the post card he smuggled out of Buchenwald to Vildebart in Paris. Its mud-brown, *erzatz* paper has deteriorated within the heavy album covers over the years but the cancellation mark of the Hitler stamp is legible: 10 March 1944.

Written in cramped longhand and in German, the message is a pathetic request for food, tobacco and toiletries.

When Mme. Nicolas was confronted in 1972 with a photograph – taken in the late thirties – of a dapper Johnny in evening dress, lounging with cigarette in hand outside a high-class Paris emporium, she broke into a high-pitched keening sound reminiscent of an Irish wake. Her head bowed repeatedly as she kissed the eight-by-ten enlargement of the son she hadn't seen in thirty-five years.

At war's end many Haitians who'd been stranded in Paris during the German occupation finally returned home. Several brought news of him – particularly Drs. Pape and Coicou. The Nicholas family consumed their information ravenously, but to their chagrin the picture painted of Jean lacked cohesion. Instead the family got a shotgun blast of reports of bizarre activities that blurred their image of Jean, making him more mysterious and more remote than ever.

From Vildebart's letters they learned that he was admitted to the Hopital Lariboisiere in Paris on 26 June 1945 in serious condition.

There were few cases of tuberculosis in the U.S. Army in Europe – and apparently none in the Hopital

Lariboisiere, which the Americans had commandeered. When Vildebart and his wife, André, came to visit Jean they were conducted into a spacious ward that was empty except for a single bed. To isolate the bacillus the army doctors enclosed his bed in a transparent tent. From a nearby metal cylinder tubes piped oxygen up his nostrils.

The American physicians told Vildebart that they were having special drugs flown in from the U.S. for his brother, who was unconscious and delirious, talking incoherently as if in a dream.

Johnny Nicholas was not very different from anyone else in one respect. He yearned for a role in life that would let him express his unique individuality and a stage on which to play it.

In reality he was two distinct personalities, one the contradiction of the other.

The first was the lusty, dynamic, self-aggrandizing, egotistical Johnny that all who knew him well remember. The second, masked by the braggadocio, was a highly sensitive youth imprinted deeply with a mother's love, a father's sense of duty and the spiritual *noblesse oblige* seeded in him by his Catholic schooling as a son in an élite family.

If the first Johnny, in order to save his life, had not manoeuvered his way into the sanctuary of the Dora *Revier*, the second would never have had a chance to appear: both might have succumbed in the tunnels. But he had connived his way into the dispensary, and for weeks he laughed up his sleeve at how adroitly he'd outwitted the minions of the 'master race.' But gradually he grew aware that the sick inmates, whom he'd initially regarded as mere pawns in the lethal game of trying to stay alive, had slavishly come to depend on him; that he'd become victim to his own cunning.

All of his life, from Port-au-Prince to Dora, he'd been a loner. True, he had many glittering friends on the fringes of his life; yet he did not establish deep relationships. His glad hand, his bonhomie and his smile were a cosmetic behind which he could fend off intrusive associations and remain his polite, unaffiliated self. They befriended him; he enriched himself on the relationship, amused them but seldom revealed his true self. Yet he was driven to continue playing the role in the dispensary. However much he may have resented it in the beginning, he realized there was no one else who would do the work. Initially his obligation was not so much to the prisoners as individuals; it was more to an ideal, to a sense of mission. But gradually, seduced by his obsessive interest in the medical profession, his work grew to become an end in itself. Perhaps it was a legacy of his mother's life-long passion for herbs and healing; but whatever it was, being a prisoner-doctor in Dora became the most consuming role he had ever played in his life.

It was Vildebart who finally disclosed to the U.S. Army doctors at the Lariboisiere hospital that his brother was not a U.S. citizen.[1] Despite the most modern medical treatment he grew progressively weaker from tuberculosis and blood poisoning. In despair Vildebart demanded that he be released to a French facility, and Johnny duly arrived at the Hopital St. Antoine.

He never conceived that he was destined, in spite of his grandest designs, to breathe his last in a public-welfare institution. The youth who had hungered for excitement and wealth and purchased the first at the expense of the second: he died at the Hopital St. Antoine on 4 September 1945 at two o'clock in the morning.

His body is buried between the graves of two nieces,

[1] When the war ended and the thousands of French prisoners of the Germans were flooding back home, Vildebart began searching for his brother. Eventually the International Red Cross notified him that Johnny was in an American hospital. The French Ministry of Prisoners, Deportees and Refugees issued him Repatriation Card No. 1628080 on 26 June 1945. The card recorded the fact that his last place of internment was Ravensbrueck.

who died in infancy, in the Cemetery of Pantin in northeastern Paris.

He had cheated death by four months as a result of his escape from the Isenschnibbe barn.[2]

Twelve days after that holocaust, at 2:30 p.m. on April 25, the 102nd U.S. Infantry Division summoned the citizens of Gardelegen and the surrounding villages to the barn area for a full-dress memorial service. It was Wednesday. The sun flooded from a cloudless sky. The prayer books of a Christian, a Protestant and a Jewish chaplain fluttered in the spring breeze.

Ashes to ashes; dust to dust . . .

A bugler sounded the funeral dirge. An honour guard in olive-drab woollen shirts stood inside the white picket fence around the graveyard and fired their volleys. Flags snapped as 1,016 bodies – plus two found shot in a nearby woods – were commended to German soil with full military honours.

The division chief of staff, Col. George P. Lynch, addressed the assembled Germans: '. . . You have lost the respect of the civilized world . . .'

And as the silent soldiers trooped away and the civilians melted into the landscape, other soldiers erected a sign which read in English and German:

GARDELEGEN MILITARY CEMETERY

Here lie 1,016 prisoners of war who were murdered by their captors. They were buried by citizens of Gardelegen, who are charged with responsibility that graves are forever kept as green as the memory of these unfortunates will be kept in the hearts of freedom-loving men everywhere. Established under supervision of

---

[2]The East German government has converted what remains of the barn – a single wall – into a national monument. In front of the wall is a brownstone sculpting of slaves huddled in agony. Nearby is a tall, metal standard with a perpetual flame burning. Each April 13 the survivors of Dora and its subcamps make a pilgrimage to the spot from all over Europe. The cemetery is maintained immaculately and abounds in flowers, shrubs and poplars.

102nd Infantry Division, United States Army. Vandalism will be punished by maximum penalties under laws of military government.

Frank A. Keating
Major General, U.S.A.
Commanding

Mme. Nicolas often pondered the dream she had before Johnny was born: the strange man in her vision told her that the child in her womb was a boy and commanded her to call him Jean. That part of the dream she related joyfully to all who would listen.

But the second part she had kept locked inside because it frightened her; it nagged at her peace of mind all during his childhood. And when she stood at the Port-au-Prince dock with Jean, about to leave for the Navy, she could not exorcize it from her thoughts.

She related the second part of the dream to the authors in 1972:

'He was a very sad man, and he took me to a cemetery. Not the kind we have here in Haiti but one with many, many crosses. White crosses.

'And he told me: "When Jean goes away from here you will never see him again."

'And I said: "Why do you take me to a place like this?"

'And he said: "Just remember that you will never see him again when he goes away."'

Haitian cemeteries are very different from European cemeteries, and Madame Nicolas had never been outside the Caribbean; yet the scene she had beheld in her dream just before Johnny's birth and described fifty-four years later was uncannily the Gardelegen Military Cemetery.

How totally ironic that this talented but impatient youth, who manifested such glowing potential as a free man, would become a legend in the meaningless horror of Camp Dora and fathom the true depths of his humanity as a *Helf Arzt* in 'the hell of all concentration camps.'

360

And the dream of his mother, the grand dame of the herbs, potions and visions, had been frighteningly prophetic: Johnny had remained at the side of the sick during the horrendous journey from Rottleberode to Gardelegen, even though all his instincts had shrieked for him to save himself; something that he was not aware of had held him there. And even though his body lies in Paris, the spirit of his life is interred with his comrades beneath that regiment of Christian crosses and Jewish stars radiating symmetrically across the flat meadowland of East Germany.

Appendix

PRINCIPAL SOURCES AND REFERENCES

I FAMILY
   Lucie Dalicy Nicolas (deceased), mother; Port-au-Prince, Haiti.
   Carmen L. Nicolas, sister; Port-au-Prince, Haiti (deceased).
   Vildebart Nicolas, brother; Paris, France.

II FORMER INMATES AT CAMP DORA AND SUBCAMP
   ROTTLEBERODE
   Romuald Bak, Brampton, Ontario, Canada
   Franz Becker, Berlin, East Germany
   Jean Berger, Angers, France
   Babriel Boussinesq, Brive, France
   Dr Robert Gandar, Strasbourg, France
   Vincent Hein, Krakow, Poland
   Cecil A.F. Jay, Springe, West Germany
   Pierre Juliette, Paris, France
   Fritz de LaCour, Berlin, East Germany
   Honore Marcelle Heinaut, Belgium (deceased)
   Roger Maria, Paris, France
   Marcel Patte, Paris, France
   Thaddeus J. Patzer, Johannesburg, Republic of South Africa
   Jean Plus, Landeseuvre-les-Nancy, France
   Walter Pomaranski, Terrace, British Columbia, Canada
      (deceased)

III ACCUSED AND WITNESSES AT THE NORDHAUSEN WAR
   CRIMES TRIAL
   Accused:

   Arthur Kurt Andrae   Georg Wilhelm Koenig
   Erhard Brauny   Paul Maischein
   Otto Georg Brinkmann   Hans Moeser
   Otto Buehring   Georg Johannes Richkey
   Heinz Georg Detmers   Heinrich Schmidt
   Josef Fuchsloch   Wilhelm Simon
   Kurt Heinrich   Walter Ulbricht
   Oscar Georg Helbig   Richard Walenta
   Rudolf Jacobi   Willi Zwiener
   Josef Kilian

363

Witnesses:

Dr Juan Cespiva
Joseph Gastow Coune
Dr Karl Kahr
Ferdinand Karpik
Dr Alfred Kurzke
Valentin Kovalj

Boruch Seidel
Stanislaw Ziba
Walter Ulbright
Richard Walenta
Willi Zwiener

IV ESCAPEES EN ROUTE FROM SUBCAMP ROTTLEBERODE TO GARDELEGEN

Rene Autard, France
Pierre Ego (deceased), Lille, France
Wilhelm Fentzling, Hamburg, West Germany
Dr Robert Gandar, Strasbourg, France
Franciszek Krawczyk, Zory, Poland
Mathiew Lambert, Putten, Netherlands
Ivan Marchenko, Romni, Poland
Jacques Matarasso, Salonika, Greece
David Nahama, Salonika, Greece
Zdzisla Pnjewski, Poland
Rene Thomas, Lyons, France
Waclaw Wochowiak, Lublin, Poland
Ludwok Wrobel, Lecka, Poland

V ESCAPEES FROM INSIDE THE BARN AT GARDELEGEN

Edward Antoniak, Wielun, Poland
Romuald Bak, formerly of Brunswick, Germany; now living in Canada
Geza Bondi, formerly of Budapest, Hungary; now living in Australia
Hermann Brandien, Hamburg, Germany
Pietrow Dimitry, Stalino, USSR
Feder Dugin, Bielok Lody, USSR
Armand Dureau, Douai, France
Leonid Kaistrow, Klince, USSR
Enginy Kateba, Szlorucyjuaka, USSR
Mieczyslaw Kilodziejski, Drezewica, Poland
Ivan Matwegeo, address unknown
Borys Mawjow, Rostov, USSR
Witold Modzelewski, Warsaw, Poland
Eugeniusz Sciaiarski, Sosnowiec, Poland
Aurel Zobel, Vienna, Austria
Momochuk Wasel, Wasel, USSR

Stanislaw Woleszynski, Lublin, Poland
Woldzinierz Wozny, Poland

VI UNITED STATES GOVERNMENT AGENCIES
Central Intelligence Agency
John Bross, Deputy Director
Howard J. Osborn, director of security
Department of the Army
  Brig Gen William H. Blakefield, commander, US Army Intelligence Command
  Col Robert H. Fechtman, chief, Historical Services Division, Office of the Chief of Military History
  Lt Gen William A. Knowlton, chief of staff of the US Army European Command; former commanding officer of B Troop, 87th Cavalry Reconnaissance Squadron
  Lt Col Harvey M. Ladd, deputy chief, Magazine and Book Division, Directorate of Defense Information, Department of Defense
  Maj William D. Newbern, chief, Foreign Law Branch, International Affairs Division, Office of the Judge Advocate
  Col Maurice S. Weaver, chief, Field Operations Division, Office of the Assistant Chief of Staff for Intelligence
  Oren Womack, Disposition Branch, Memorial Division, Office of the Chief of Support Services
  John J. Slonaker, Chief of Research and Reference
  Charles J. Simpson, deputy director, Fort Detrick Historical Unit
  US Army Military History Research Collection
Department of Health, Education and Welfare
  William E. Hanna, Jr., director, Bureau of Data Processing and Accounts, Social Security Administration
Department of Justice
  Helen W. Gandy, secretary to the late J. Edgar Hoover, Federal Bureau of Investigation
  E.A. Loughran, associate commissioner, Immigration and Naturalization Service
  Andrew W. Tartaglino, assistant director for Enforcement, Bureau of Narcotics and Dangerous Drugs
Department of the Navy
  W.C. Keene, head, Records Service Section, US Marine Corps
  H.F. Ott, head, Disposal Section, Correspondence and Services Branch, Bureau of Naval Personnel
Department of the State
  John J. Baker, US Embassy, Prague, Czechoslovakia
  Arthur E. Breisky, US Embassy, The Netherlands

Mary T. Chiavarini, American Consul, US Embassy, Brussels, Belgium

Terrence Douglas, American Consul, US Embassy, Warsaw, Poland

Patrick J. Flood, American Consul, US Embassy, Hungary

Alta Fowler, American Consul, US Embassy, Belgium

William D. Heaney, US Embassy, Haiti

Andor Klay, Berlin office of US Embassy, West Germany

Francis G. Knight, director of the Passport Office

Norbert J. Krieg, US Embassy, West Germany

James W. Lamont, vice consul, US Embassy, Greece

Donald Wehmeyer, US Embassy, West Germany

Edward L. Williams, US Embassy, Peru

Department of the Treasury

Foreign Claims Settlement Commission

Dorothy Ladue, Office of Information and Publications, Bureau of Customs

Andrew T. McGuire, general counsel

National Archives and Records Service (Washington National Records Centre)

Joseph Avery

Mark G. Eckhoff

Edwin R. Flatequal, acting chief of Archives Branch

Thomas Hohmen

Harry Schwartz

Robert Wolfe

National Personnel Records Centre

M.D. Davis, Civilian Reference Branch

M.T. Vranesh, supervisor, Army Organization Records Unit

Office of Strategic Services (defunct)

William J. Casey, former deputy commander; currently director of the CIA

Thomas G. Cassady (deceased), former head of secret intelligence for France and Germany; Lake Forest, Ill.

John Howley, secretary, Veterans of the OSS: New York, NY

John M. Wigglesworth, executive secretary, Strategic Services Unit

Selective Service System

Veterans Administration

R.G. Bowman, VA liaison officer, Military Personnel Records Center

Edward P. O'Dell, chief, Contact Division, Veterans Benefits Office

VII UNITED STATES CIVILIAN SOURCES

Joan Alvarez, Physicians Information Service, American Medical Association, Chicago, Ill.

William Berman (deceased), chief prosecutor in the Nordhausen War Crimes trials; Portland, Me.

Joseph C. Breckinridge, investigator for US Army's War Crimes Branch; Lexington, Ky.

Ernest L. Chambre, historian, New York, NY.

H. Jackson Clark, B Troop, 87th Cavalry Reconnaissance Squadron; Durango, Colo.

Burton F. Ellis, 7708th War Crimes Group; Merced, Calif.

Alonzo P. Fox, assistant division commander of 102nd Infantry Division; retired lieutenant-general, Wash., D.C.

Earl Harrell, B Troop, 87th Cavalry Reconnaissance Squadron; San Antonio, Texas

M.A. Harris, president, Negro History Associates, New York, NY

Leon Jaworski (Watergate prosecutor), 7708th War Crimes Group; Houston, Tex.

Jerome Kabel, former administrative aide to U.S. Senator Philip A. Hart; Detroit, Mich.

Frank A. Keating, commander of 102nd Infantry Division; retired brigadier-general, Clearwater, Fla.

Jacob F. Kinder, 7708th War Crimes Group; Fort Lauderdale, Fla.

George P. Lynch, chief of staff of 102nd Infantry Division; retired brigadier-general, La Jolla, Calif.

David L. Matthews, 7708th War Crimes Group; South Bend, Ind.

Robert G. McCarty, War Crimes Investigation Team No. 6822; Portland, Ore.

Dr Shelby T. McCloy, Black history authority, Lexington, Ky.

A.E. Schwabacher, Jr., F Company, 405th Battalion, 102nd Infantry Division; San Francisco, Calif.

Clio Straight, commander of 7708th War Crimes Group; retired major-general, New York, N.Y.

Horace Sutton, Intelligence Detachment of 102nd Infantry Division; associate editor of Saturday Review, New York, N.Y.

Lauren L. Williams, 102nd Infantry Division; retired lieutenant-general, La Jolla, Calif.

VIII REPUBLIC OF FRANCE SOURCES

The American Hospital, Neuilly-sur-Seine

Amicale de Neuengamme et des Commandos, Paris

Amicale des Reseaux Adction, Paris

Roger Arnould, FNDIRP, Paris

Edmond Bricout, Amicale des Reseaux Action de La France Combattants, Paris

Dr R.J. Brocard, Ordre National des Medecins, Conseil National de l'Ordre, Paris

Jacques Brun, secretary general of Amicale de Dora-Ellrich, Paris

La Confederation des Syndical Medicaux, Paris

Jacques Delarue, author of 'The Gestapo' and member of the Direction de la Surete Nationale; LePecq

Pierre Dumont, Prefet de La Region du Nord, Lille

Roger Fouillette, Offwiller

Federation Nationale des Deportes et Internes Resistants et Patriotes

Nicole Girard-Reydet, vice consul of the French consulate in Detroit, Mich.

Hopital Lariboisiere, Paris

Hopital St Antoine, Paris

Rear Admiral N.M. Houot, naval attache in the Franch Embassy, Washington, DC.

M.R. Mamelet, Ministere de La Sante Publique at de La Securite Sociale, Paris

Henri Michel, secretary general of the Comite D'Histoire de le Guerre Mondiale Republique Francaise, Paris

Ministry of the Army, Paris

Ministry of Defense, Paris

Ministry of the Interior, Paris

Capt. Isaiah Olchs, US Navy (ret.), Nice

Prefecture of Police (Archives), Paris

L. Repesse, secretary general of the Union Nationale des Associations de Deportes, Internes et Familles de Disparus

Andre Sabliere, Lyon

IX REPUBLIC OF HAITI SOURCES

Fortune Bogat (deceased), secretary of the Societe Haitienne de Automobiles S.A., Port-au-Prince

Etienne Bourand School (where Jean Nicolas studied), Port-au-Prince

Dr Jacques Coicou, Port-au-Prince

Pierre Gabrielle, Port-au-Prince

Msgr Francois Wolff-Ligonde, archbishop of Port-au-Prince

Dr Hans C. Pape, Port-au-Prince

Lalier C. Phareau, reporter and columnist for *Le Nouvelliste*, Port-au-Prince

Dr Raoul Pierre-Louis, dean of the School of Medicine and Pharmacy, University of Haiti.

St Louis de Gonzague School (elementary school attended by Jean Nicolas), Port-au-Prince

Laurore St Juste, director of the Haitian National Archives

Harry Tippenhauer, principal of the high school attended by Jean Nicolas, Port-au-Prince

X   WEST GERMANY SOURCES

Bundesarztekammer, Stuttgart-Degerloch

A. de Cocatrix, deputy director of the International Tracing Service, Arolsen

Deutsche Dienstelle, Berlin

Hans Hueckel, High Court of Essen, which is investigating atrocities committed at Nordhausen during World War II

Militargeschichtliches Forschungsamt, Freiburg im Breisgau

Zentrale Stelle fuer NS Verbrechen, Ludwigsburg

XI   UNITED KINGDOM SOURCES

J.E. Blishen, Ministry of Defence, London

Thomas Cochrane, deputy director of Public Relations, Ministry of Defence, London

Maurice J. Buckmaster, former commander of French Section, Special Operations Executive

Library and Records Department, Foreign and Commonwealth Office, London

XII   MISCELLANEOUS SOURCES

Hans Aalmans, Kerkrade, The Netherlands

William J. Aalmans, investigator for the 7708th War Crimes Group; Embassy of Holland, Madrid, Spain

Institute of Documentation, Haifa, Israel

Dr Karl Kahr, Graz, Austria

Magyar Izraelitak Orszagos Kepviselete Irodaja, Budapest, Hungary

Jean Nothomb, Brussels, Belgium

Osterreichische Artztekammer, Vienna, Austria

the trade

william h. hallahan

'Puts William Hallahan up above Le Carré, Deighton and Co.'
The Bookseller

Journalist Bernie Parker didn't make a lot of sense that day. His words needed a bit of explanation. But Bernie is in no position to do that right now because he's just stopped several bullets outside a Paris metro. Bernie is dead. And no one knows what his last words mean.

The least Colin Thomas owes his late friend is a reason. As an international arms dealer scoring off the hotter edges of the cold war he has contacts. Contacts that lead him back to a ruthless and uninhibited woman and to the centre of a devastating plan to change the face of Europe – even if it means starting World War 3 – even if it means starting the countdown to doomsday . . .

ADVENTURE THRILLER   0 7221 4215 3   £1.75